STEALING THE GILA

STEALING THE GILA

The Pima Agricultural Economy and Water Deprivation, 1848-1921

David H. DeJong

The University of Arizona Press Tucson

The University of Arizona Press
www.uapress.arizona.edu

First paperback edition 2016

Printed in the United States of America
21 20 19 18 17 16 7 6 5 4 3 2

ISBN-13: 978-0-8165-2798-4 (cloth)
ISBN-13: 978-0-8165-3558-3 (paper)

Cover design by Lori Lieber Graphic Design, Inc.
Cover photograph: An irrigation canal that was part of the U.S. Indian Service's Agency Project in 1913. (Courtesy of the National Archives and Records Administration, Washington, D.C.)

Publication of this book is made possible in part by the proceeds of a permanent endowment created with the assistance of a Challenge Grant from the National Endowment for the Humanities, a federal agency.

Library of Congress Cataloging-in-Publication Data
DeJong, David H.
Stealing the Gila : the Pima agricultural economy and water deprivation, 1848–1921 / David H. DeJong.
p. cm.
Includes bibliographical references and index.
ISBN 978-0-8165-2798-4 (hard cover : alk. paper)
1. Pima Indians—Agriculture—History—19th century. 2. Pima Indians—Agriculture—History—20th century. 3. Pima Indians—Economic conditions. 4. Subsistence economy—Gila River Region (N.M. and Ariz.)—History. 5. Water-supply—Gila River Region (N.M. and Ariz.)—History. 6. Water rights—Gila River Region (N.M. and Ariz.)—History. 7. Whites—Gila River Region (N.M. and Ariz.)—History. 8. Immigrants—Gila River Region (N.M. and Ariz.)—History. 9. Gila River Region (N.M. and Ariz.)—Ethnic relations. 10. Gila River Region (N.M. and Ariz.)—Economic conditions. I. Title.
E99.P6D45 2009
979.1'7—dc22

2009020136

♾ This paper meets the requirements of ANSI/NISO Z39.48-1992 (Permanence of Paper).

Contents

Figures

Maps

Tables

Acknowledgments

I appreciate the support and encouragement of my wife Cindy and my children, Rachelle, Rebecca, Joshua, Ralissa, and RaeAnna. Each gave up precious time that I can never reclaim, but that I trust has served a larger benefit. I value the constructive feedback provided by Joseph Hiller, K. Tsianina Lomawaima, Tom Holm, Roger Nichols, and Jennie Joe, all of the University of Arizona. I personally dedicate this study to Mr. Gerald F. Brown, a Pima elder who has been a friend, coworker, and fellow laborer.

STEALING THE GILA

Introduction

A West of Jeffersonian Farmers?

IN THE MID-NINETEENTH CENTURY, a remarkable, although ephemeral, economic transformation occurred among the Pima Indians of central Arizona. Continuing their irrigated agricultural economy bequeathed to them by their Hohokam ancestors, the Pima leveraged a favorable geopolitical setting into a viable and sustainable agricultural economy that resulted in material prosperity. They sought inclusion in the emerging American economy of the Southwest and, by the 1850s, were an economic force in the middle Gila River valley.

Parlaying their economic savvy stimulated by Mexican and early American emigrants and settlers, the Pima for a brief period of several decades enjoyed economic success, producing food and fiber crops for emigrant and military expeditions alike. Moreover, crops from their fields provided food for the growing Mexican town of Tucson, as well as for the American mining districts centered near Prescott. But, as was frequently the case in the boom and bust frontier West, this economic vitality did not last. As emigrants settled above the Pima villages, they deprived the Pima of the water resources that sustained their economy. Divested of their rights and access to the waters of the Gila River and its tributaries, the Pima's agricultural economy was shattered, and by the 1890s, the Indians faced the pangs of hunger and poverty. Forced into a subsistence economy, the Pima were displaced from the market forces of the territory by the 1890s.

In the American West, water was a resource that made or ruined economies. While historically our understanding of the West was predicated on the theory that the federal government took a laissez-faire approach to settlement of the West, in reality, a strong federal presence influenced settlement. Using liberal land and resource policies, the federal government directed both the development and exploitation of the region's land and resources, a matter the new Western historians refer to as "the fact of conquest."[1] Consequently, the settlement of the West and the concomitant American Indian displacement from the land resulted from government action, with federal policies shaping social thought and action in dispossessing tribal nations of most of their resources, including water.

Federal influences stemmed from American independence from England. Almost immediately after the American Revolution, the federal government asserted a legal theory based on conquest to assume control over the lands within its geographical borders.[2] As national expansion advanced westward, the United States asserted sovereignty over the new lands it acquired, institutionalizing this legal theory in the *Johnson v. M'Intosh* (1823) U.S. Supreme Court decision.[3] While tribal nations retained usufruct rights to their land, the Supreme Court asserted federal rights to pre-emption, and while some states enacted their own preemption statutes, federal acts in 1830, 1834, 1838, and 1841 granted settlers a legal right to the land upon which they had settled.

The most far-reaching of the federal land laws was the 1862 Homestead Act, which, with its companion legislation found in the Timber Culture Act (1873) and Desert Land Act (1877), influenced how and where the West was settled. Social reformers envisioned these acts supporting a "Jeffersonian utopia of small farming."[4] The intent was to carve up the West into parcels of land, sell them for a nominal fee, and enable settlers to develop the nation's resources. In short, these laws were designed to populate the West by throwing it open for settlement.

While designed to shape American social thought and action and serve, as Frederick Jackson Turner argued more than a century ago, as a safety valve for an overpopulated East, federal land policies stimulated abuse, with fraudulent and dummy land entries leaving large blocs of public domain in the hands of land speculators. Rather than facilitating individual landownership, federal land laws frequently "promoted monopoly and corruption."[5]

As settlers quickly discovered, the real wealth of the West was water. While the Homestead Act and the Desert Land Act were part of a larger social policy of transforming the West into a series of yeoman farms, the lack of precipitation necessitated an alternative means of applying water to the land. In 1879, John Wesley Powell hinted that the development of the West could proceed only with a communal development effort.[6] Recognizing the need for irrigation in the West (and reflecting the West's increasing political power), both houses of Congress in 1889 established the Committee on Irrigation and Arid Lands. Two years later, the National Irrigation Congress was organized. When the National Irrigation Association was formed in Chicago in 1893 for the purpose of advocating federal subsidies for western reclamation projects, the Pima served as its national poster child, demonstrating for the public and politicians alike the need for federal action in utilizing scarce water resources in the arid West.

Across the West, land speculators and settlers agitated for federal involvement. Not yet willing to commit to a federally subsidized reclamation policy, in 1894 Congress enacted the Carey Act, which authorized the sale of up to one million acres of federal land in each state, with the proceeds to be used for reclamation. While beneficial to states such as Idaho, whose population doubled in the 1890s, the law had limited impact and was conspicuous in that it did not apply to territories such as Arizona.[7]

Westerners, including Nevada senator Francis Newlands, continued to advocate for federal support for reclamation projects. The U.S. Geological Survey (USGS), then surveying potential western water development, promoted "single use resources [with] many potential uses," including reclamation. The older, more-established U.S. Army Corps of Engineers, on the other hand, "placed upon private landowners" responsibility for reclamation, holding a more conservative opinion of water use and development.[8]

By the closing years of the nineteenth century, the federal government hinted at control of water independent of state law. The Corps of Engineers, for instance, asserted control over the construction of dams on all navigable rivers. In 1898, Congress asserted federal authority over all water passing through national forests if it could be used for "domestic, mining, milling or irrigation" purposes. The following year, the U.S. Supreme Court opined in *United States v. Rio Grande Dam and Irrigation Company* that if any part of a river, including its tributaries, was used for transportation, it fell under federal auspices.[9]

Just as importantly, in the Desert Land Act, Congress subjected to prior appropriation all public land titles as long as such rights did not include "surplus waters over and above such actual use."[10] States might distribute water, but all federal rights were retained.[11] By the turn of the twentieth century, Congress was primed for a national reclamation policy that facilitated land development. With the ascendancy of Theodore Roosevelt to the presidency, a progressive leader occupied the White House. Despite tepid eastern support, backing for reclamation was assured, and on June 30, 1902, Congress enacted into law the National Reclamation Act.

The National Reclamation Act was one of the most decisive laws in the history of the American West, initiating an era of federally subsidized reclamation projects. While intending to complement land laws and foster yeoman settlement of the West, powerful and politically well-heeled speculators, government bureaucrats, and congressional allies asserted control over the region's water resources and manipulated the act to their benefit. In the initial years of the twentieth century, western water advocates strengthened their position by forming political alliances to further determine and manipulate water policy in the West.[12] This alliance consisted of key congressional committees and legislators, executive agencies (i.e., the U.S. Reclamation Service and the U.S. Army Corps of Engineers), and special interest groups (water users in the West). This "iron triangle" influenced public policy to its own advantage and, rather than benefiting yeoman farmers, the National Reclamation Act became part of an overall "incongruous land system" that encouraged speculation.[13] While affecting the economy of the West, the act did not fulfill its purpose of fostering yeoman farming.[14] For American Indian farmers, the federal goal of yeoman agriculture was rhetorical, as tribal nations with agricultural economies, such as the Pima, were deprived of the water needed to sustain them.

While iron triangles influenced the development of western land and resource policies, Congress had greater control over tribal nations via its constitutional authority to direct federal Indian affairs.[15] In 1790, President George Washington encouraged Congress to enact legislation authorizing the United States to lawfully interact with tribal nations. Congress followed Washington's lead with the first in a series of trade and intercourse acts, by which the United States asserted the authority to regulate Indian trade. With the territorial expansion of the United States, the Indian Trade and Intercourse Act was amended to reflect the geographical growth of the nation.[16] In 1851 and, again, in 1856 an amended act extended federal authority over the Pima villages.

As the commercial interests of the United States expanded west via the Santa Fe, Southern, and Oregon trails, trade increased, with tens of thousands of emigrants crossing the territory of the western tribes. Protection of U.S. citizens traveling on, or engaging in commerce along, the trails became paramount, leading to a series of treaties with the western tribes beginning in 1846. With thousands of emigrants arriving in the California goldfields in 1849, local tribes were subjected to policies of extermination.[17] Further hostilities erupted on the plains and interior deserts, with local calls for extermination forcing Congress to establish the reservation system in 1851. The new policy was to reduce Indian land holdings by transforming the Indians into passive yeoman agriculturalists.[18]

After the Civil War, Congress initiated an intensive effort to assimilate American Indians. President Ulysses S. Grant appointed a group of eastern philanthropists to the Board of Indian Commissioners and charged them with guiding and advising the president on federal Indian relations. The board advocated bringing about the "humanization, civilization and Christianization of the Indians." This era of land severalty and assimilation represented an extraordinary attack on tribal nations, with the federal courts supporting such policies. In *Lone Wolf v. Hitchcock* (1903), the Supreme Court upheld federal authority to act without tribal consent.[19] Nonetheless, the Supreme Court recognized tribal resource rights in *United States v. Winans* (1905) and *Winters v. United States* (1908), the latter of which upheld tribal rights to water resources.[20]

Federal land and resource policies created an incongruous set of federal codes that were a patchwork of laws that conflicted and undermined each other. These policies became more extraneous with the passage of a western water policy and had significant impacts on American Indians, as great demands were placed on tribal lands and resources. Under intense pressure by land-hungry settlers and government agents to part with their land and resources, tribal nations faced a juggernaut of continental imperialism. Among the impacts were water deprivation, cultural loss, and economic privation, socioeconomic factors that reverberated into the twentieth and twenty-first centuries.[21]

When combined with federal Indian policies designed to displace American Indians from their remaining lands and assimilate them into

American society, federal land and resource policies were especially deleterious. As reservations were allotted, most were thrown open to non-Indian settlement, resulting in the loss of more than eighty-six million tribal acres between 1887 and 1934.[22] While allotted in 1921, the Pima were among the fortunate few in that no surplus lands were opened to settlement. Nonetheless, as with other tribal nations, federal action despoiled the Pima agricultural economy and pushed the Indians to the periphery of the national economy.[23] Federal policymakers, having "little real interest in the welfare of Native Americans," manipulated a dynamic federal resource policy for the purpose of controlling and directing the land and its resources for their own or their constituents' benefit.[24] Rather than promote agriculture in the West, federal land and resource and federal Indian policies diminished Indian agriculture. Economic and social policies designed to foster the yeoman farm instead fractionated the land and isolated American Indians on scattered lands across the West, making economic enhancement of tribal lands difficult. Consequently, while federal activity facilitated the settlement of the West and the development of its resources, it came at the social and economic expense of displacing American Indians and reducing them to poverty. This transformative process was complete when these ideals were institutionalized at the 1915 Panama-Pacific International Exposition in San Francisco, where James Earle Fraser's "The End of the Trail" served as a not-so-subtle metaphorical representation of American Indians.[25]

The story told here examines the efforts of the Pima Indians to participate in the national economy between the years of 1848 and 1921, a period of time that corresponds with the advent of U.S. economic impacts and federal protection of Pima water resources. In 1848, tens of thousands of emigrants traversed Pima Country en route to California, stimulating the Pima agricultural economy and rousing the Pima desire for technology. By 1921, the federal government stood poised to initiate federal legislation (San Carlos Irrigation Project Act) and litigation (*United States v. Gila Valley Irrigation District*) on behalf of the Pima to protect their rights to the water. The era between 1848 and 1921, therefore, represents the bookends of unmitigated federal action on Pima resources and economy.

In the end, this story chronicles the dynamic inter-relationship between Pima farmers, the national economy, and liberal land and resource policies and concludes that had Pima farmers not been deprived of their access to the waters of the Gila River and its tributaries, they may well have continued their highly successful adaptation to a market economy and might have gained parity with local farmers and remained part of the national economy. Handicapped by federal land and resource policies, the once-prosperous Pima descended into poverty, and their overall irrigated acreage declined precipitously (table I.1). Convenient scholarly assumptions that American Indians were inherently unfit for, or overwhelmed by, unfamiliar western economies, however, are specious. In the case of the Pima, it was not a matter of the triumph of western civilization that displaced their economy as much as it was federal and territorial laws that prevented them from building on their economic success.

TABLE I.1. Estimated Pima Irrigated Acreage, Select Years, 1850–1921

Year	Acres
1850	12,500
1859	15,000
1860	14,582[a]
1876	7,000–8,000
1893	less than 5,000
1896	less than 4,000
1900	less than 3,600
1911	4,500
1914	12,069[b]
1921	7,693

[a] Double cropping
[b] Eligible for water

CHAPTER 1

The Prelude

BETWEEN 1694 AND 1848, a medley of ecclesiastical and military chroniclers described an emerging and dynamic cultural adaptation occurring among the Pima, or the Gileños as the Spaniards called them. While Pima culture was not static prior to 1694, it was less so after, as they adapted to new crops and growing patterns. While the hydraulic regime of the Gila River has historically been erratic in flow, with long cycles of drought followed by devastating floods, a moist eighteenth and first six decades of the nineteenth centuries benefited the Pima. Villages clustered together more frequently than before, and other Piman groups, including some of those in the San Pedro Valley (Sobaipuri) and in the Santa Cruz Valley (Koahadk), moved to join the Pima (see map 1.1). Core cultural values such as industriousness, virtue, and an agrarian economy guided the Pima.[1]

The Gila River, variously labeled the Rio Grande, Rio de hila, Rio Grande de hila, Rio Azul, Rio de los Santos Apostoles, Rio del Nombre de Jesus, the River of Hila, the Jila, Hee-la, Helay, Xila, and Jee-la, was simply called Keli Akimel ("Old Man River") by the Pima.[2] The river was the socioeconomic lifeline of the Pima, with its waters embodying the very essence of their existence. With its waters, the Pima cultivated a variety of crops to sustain a salubrious diet and economy in the midst of an otherwise inhospitable desert.

Written accounts of the agricultural economy of the Pima abound, beginning in 1694 when Jesuit priest Eusebio Francisco Kino recorded the first observations of the Indians. These accounts, like those of eighteenth-century Franciscan priest Pedro Font, concluded that the industriousness of the Pima was multiplied by the river and was responsible for their hospitality, enabling them to provide for their own needs and trade with their neighbors.[3] Cultivating food and fiber crops, the Pima developed

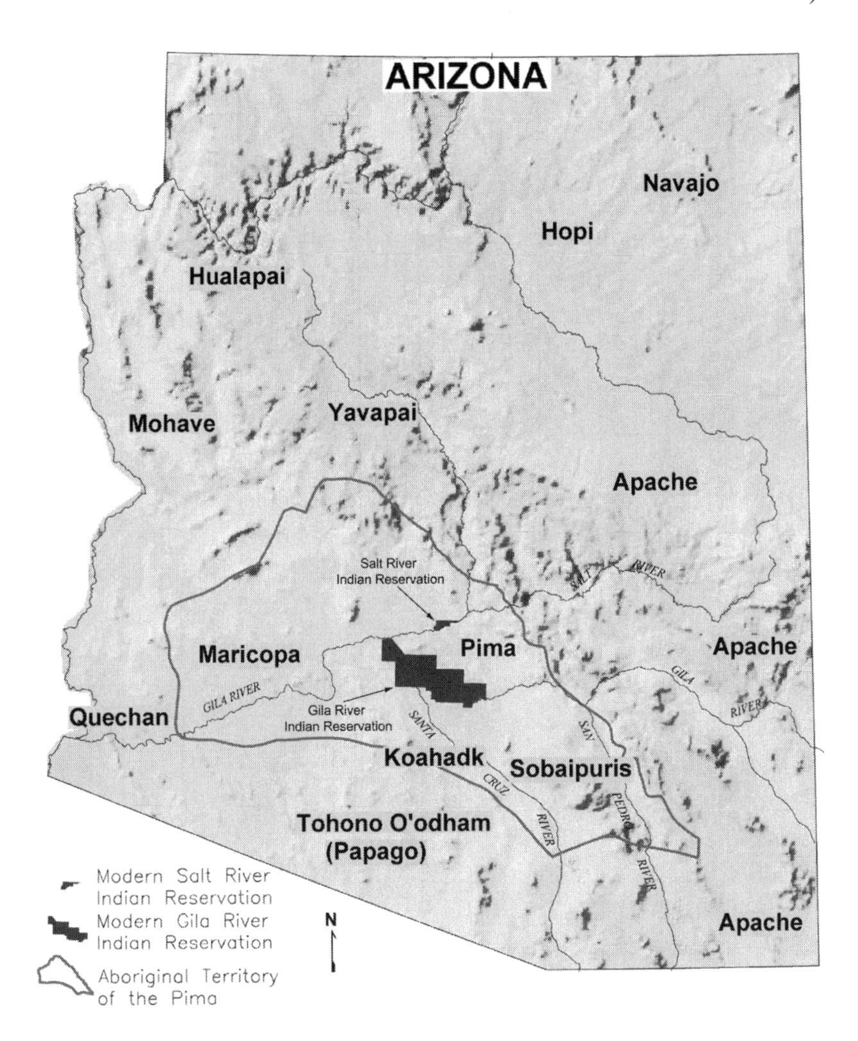

MAP 1.1. Eighteenth-century location of tribal nations. (Courtesy of Indian Claims Commission)

and sustained a stable economy that endeared them to Spaniards, Mexicans, and Americans.

The Keli Akimel defined the Pima and shaped the ways in which they perceived those around them. It allowed the Pima to grow two crops annually: summer cotton, corn, melons, beans, and squashes, as well as winter wheat. The latter, introduced by the Spaniards, became a mainstay of their autochthonous cropping patterns.[4] Their relatives to the south, called Papago by the Spaniards, are the Tohono O'odham or "Desert People." Absent a perennial source of irrigation water, the Papago response to their environment differed from the Pima in that they subsisted by annually migrating from summer, floodwater-farming (or *ak chin*) villages in the desert to winter, hunting settlements in the mountains.[5] After the eighteenth century, the Pima, while acknowledging their kinship with the Papago, recognized the Gila River gave them a level of affluence not enjoyed by their relatives or any other tribe in the region. They understood that Akimel O'otham not only meant "River People" but also implied they were "the resource-rich elite."[6] Lacking the resources of their kin, the Papago annually trekked to the Pima villages to work in the harvest and trade Spanish goods and items lacking among the Pima, such as salt, for agricultural goods. While many families were related through the economic reciprocity of the tribes, the Pima exerted a level of authority over their relatives through trade.[7]

Beginning in the late seventeenth century and continuing into the nineteenth, the Pima exhibited a pattern of continual ecologic and economic adaptation. Combined with an affinity for improving their standard of living, the Pima demonstrated propitious agricultural production. An agriculture-based economy ensured a dependable food supply, manifesting itself in a confident, affable outlook. Such was the entrepreneurial spirit of the Pima that they maintained a thriving trade with Indian, Spanish, Mexican, and, later, American communities. Astute traders who possessed an extensive and fertile tract of land along the middle Gila River, the Pima adapted to new means of economic activity in the eighteenth and nineteenth centuries and in the process became a materially "wealthy" people.[8]

When Kino first visited the Pima villages, he was quick to note the quantity and quality of cultivated and natural Pima food stores. The Pima grew a variety of food crops and enjoyed a supply of fish from the river. Kino observed the Maricopa (who in the 1790s began migrating into Pima territory and by the 1820s confederated with them) living downstream of the Pima below the Gila bend fishing with "nets and other tackle." They provided him with "so much and so very good fish" that he issued it as rations to the troops accompanying him "just as beef is given where it is plentiful."[9] The Pima likewise engaged in fishing as a source of food.

The Pima's propitious environment is evident in that neither the Spaniards nor the Mexicans reported any instance of famine in the middle Gila River valley in the eighteenth century. While there was episodic drought and the river periodically went subterranean along the middle Pima villages during the dry summer months, crops, cultivated or natural, never completely failed. Other Piman groups to the south, including one living north of Tucson on the Santa Cruz River, occasionally experienced famine and depended on their Gila River relatives for food. Juan Bautista de Anza Jr. noted in 1774 that many of the Piman people near Tucson moved north to join the Pima "on account of the great drought and the still greater famine" which gripped the upper Santa Cruz Valley.[10]

Agriculture dominated the Pima economy, and corn, tepary beans, cotton, and a variety of squashes served as staple food and fiber crops. Grown in sixty days, small-eared Pima corn required minimal amounts of water beyond its pre-planting irrigation and could be planted, cultivated, and harvested three times a year. Its yield, while not extravagant, was ten to twelve bushels per acre.[11] By 1680, Pima corn was traded as far as the New Mexico settlements near Santa Fe, as well as with tribal nations in the region.

While engaged in trade, the Pima did not grow food as a commercial crop, instead growing sufficient crops for subsistence, limited trading, and seed for the following season's crop. Their incorporation of Spanish wheat altered this pattern and served as the basis for Pima prosperity in the eighteenth and nineteenth centuries. Planted in the fall and harvested in late spring when winter stores were at their lowest, wheat was a complementary crop planted off-season from the traditional crops of corn, beans, and squash. Since it could be stored for long periods, wheat provided the people with a balanced food supply and ensured a stable economy. While it did not immediately modify their economy, within decades it joined corn as the principal Pima crop. By 1744, Jesuit priest Jacobo Sedelmayr observed the cultivation of wheat at Sutaquison, the largest Pima village.[12]

Wheat influenced the Pima economy in a variety of ways, including the expansion of the Pima irrigation system. Kino, observing abandoned Hohokam canals at Casa Grande and chronicling Pima agricultural production, never specifically mentioned irrigation farming on the Gila

River, although this does not mean the Pima were ignorant of irrigation canals or did not use them. As descendants of the Hohokam, it is highly likely they were engaged in some level of irrigated agriculture. Captain Juan Mateo Manje, accompanying Kino to the villages in 1699, noted irrigation canals in use among the Sobaipuri along the San Pedro River just weeks before arriving among the Pima. Manje opined that if Spain were to establish missions near the Gila River, irrigation farming was possible, suggesting irrigation canals could be (or perhaps already were) extended away from the river. While the Pima utilized irrigation prior to the introduction of wheat, there may have been little economic incentive for them to irrigate away from the river since the fields planted in the floodplains and on the islands within the Gila sufficiently provided for their needs.[13]

By the 1740s, the Pima were growing a surplus of cultivated foods. So extensive were these crops that the Papago began assisting them with the harvest in return for a share of the crop. While there was a limited supply of food crops to trade, grain was bartered by the Pima in Tucson in time of famine on the upper reaches of the Santa Cruz River. Pima wheat was cultivated and irrigated "on either bank of the river and on the islands." They grew large quantities of crops by means of irrigation canals, and by the mid-eighteenth century, their lands were "fruitful and suitable for wheat, Indian corn, etc." Such was their cotton production that their Sonoran neighbors coveted their excess.[14]

Adoption of wheat shifted the economic focus of the Pima. Once bartering simple manufactured goods, such as cotton blankets, woven baskets, and pottery, by the latter eighteenth century the Pima were exporting agricultural commodities and moving towards a commercial economy. While they made their own woven and cotton blankets, trade with Spanish settlements or Indian middlemen allowed access to both *bayeta* (flannel) and *sayal* (woolen) cloth. The integration of wheat into their economy enabled the Pima to improve their standard of living and acquire new technology, such as metal tools. Having used the river to their advantage for centuries, the Pima now combined their agricultural expertise and the Gila River with a new crop, wheat, to expand trade networks. Fray Juan Diaz noted the Pima were well dressed and gave as the reason their agricultural production and trade networks with Spanish and Indian communities to the south.[15]

By the waning years of the eighteenth century, the Pima were well on the road to economic prosperity. Passing through the villages in the spring of 1774, de Anza described "fields of wheat . . . so large that, standing in the middle of them, one cannot see the ends, because of their length. They are very wide, too, embracing the whole width of the valley on both sides [of the river]." Pima cornfields were "of similar proportions." A day earlier, de Anza traveled through the village of Sutaquison and described fields planted with "sixty to eighty *fanegas* of wheat, marvelously fine and about ready to harvest." This particular field was "the smallest one they have." Even Diaz admired how each village planted large fields of wheat, corn, and other crops, despite the drought and famine plaguing other Piman tribes.[16]

The Pima villages were not immune to the periodic drought that could grip the Sonoran Desert. Franciscan priest Pedro Font, traveling with de Anza in the fall of 1775, observed that the lack of rain affected the Pima as well. While they were not without food, Font noted that "only in the time of floods is [the river] useful for the grain fields and corn fields of the Indians." Pima crops required "much water" to ensure a bountiful harvest. Fray Francisco Garcés, traveling with Anza and Font, noted that in spite of drought conditions, the Pima still "raise large crops of wheat, some of corn, cotton, calabashes, etc." To raise such crops, the Pima "constructed good irrigating canals, surrounding the fields in one circuit common and divided [are] those of different owners by particular circuits."[17]

The Pima also modified their mode of agriculture in the latter eighteenth century. Irrigation canals were extended to lands on the south bank of the river, and log and brush dams were increased in size and used to elevate the water and ensure a sufficient head to reach fields farther from the river. The people of Uturituc, for instance, fastened together "many logs in the middle of the river" and then used brush to raise the water into canals that watered individual fields. Intensive agriculture meant fields were flooded before planting, with the entire flow of the river "drained off." Tail waters were returned to the river to be used by the next village downstream. Increased and widespread flood irrigation flushed salts out of the soil and kept the land productive.[18]

In areas south of the Gila, and where the Gila flowed beneath the surface, the Pima dug wells. Garcés noted a large well south of the Pima village of Pitac and, thirty miles farther south, found several more at the

Papago village of Pozos Salados. Pima farmers also constructed fences around their irrigated lands. Font described farms that were "fenced in with poles and laid off in divisions." Garcés reported fence building as a communal event, noting individual farmers had "their lands within divided" into rectangles about two hundred by three hundred feet for "convenience of irrigating."[19]

Year-round crops, intensive cultivation, and trade supported Pima affluence in well-built villages. Sutaquison, the principal Pima village and seat of government, occupied "a pleasant, abundantly tree-covered country fourteen miles long and irrigated by aqueducts." The Pima employed all the agricultural "advantages offered them by the Gila River" and hosted annual trade fairs with residents of Tucson, Tubac, and other villages along the Santa Cruz River.[20]

Their agricultural skill and a natural enmity with the nomadic and raiding Apache to the east made the Pima of geopolitical importance to Spain. If Spain were to maintain its California settlements, then connected to New Spain via maritime communication lines, they had to be tethered to the towns of Sonora and New Mexico. A desired land route to California put the Pima villages in the middle of Spain's route to the west. If Russian, English, and French influences were to be contained, the Gila River had to be under the tacit, if not outright, control of Spain. This could be accomplished only through Pima fidelity to the Crown.

The Pima were not passive as Spain made its inroads into the Pimería Alta. They clearly perceived Spain as an ally against their traditional enemy, the Apache. From Spain the Pima could acquire new technology such as horses, metal tools, guns, and new crops that might give them an edge in expanding their own sphere of influence. An alliance would ensure preferential treatment and a continual supply of new ideas and technologies. In this respect, Spain served as both a social resource and a military ally. A reciprocal relationship would aid Spain in establishing political hegemony over other colonial nations and allow the Pima to exercise a level of economic supremacy over neighboring tribes.

In the process of extending and protecting its northern frontier, Spain indirectly encouraged the Pima to concentrate their villages along the middle Gila River. Pima *rancherías* were thinly dispersed along the river and moved periodically. A moist eighteenth century and increasing trade demands inspired the Pima to increase their production of crops and extend their politically autonomous villages along the middle Gila.[21]

While agricultural lands were more compact along the river and adjacent to the villages, the Pima utilized the lowlands of the Gila, Salt, and Santa Cruz rivers. West of El Picacho, Koahadk villages engaged in ak chin farming. The Sobaipuri farmed the San Pedro River valley and bartered corn for "hatchets, cloth, sackcloth, blankets, chomite, knives, etc.," from colonists in New Mexico. Cultural adaptations, encouraged by the introduction of wheat and the horse, and continued Apache raids fostered the concentration of villages throughout the eighteenth century.[22]

While the Pima population increased over the latter part of the eighteenth century, it benefited from the depopulation of other Piman tribes to the south and their settlement along the Gila.[23] The Sobaipuri villages, for instances, had "broken up" due to Apache harassment, and when Jesuit missions in Arizona faced a crisis of survival due to Indian depredations, the Catholic Church strengthened its missions in the Santa Cruz Valley by using military force to consolidate the remaining Sobaipuri with the San Xavier Papago and other Piman tribes on the Santa Cruz River north of Tucson. Within two years, the San Pedro Valley was abandoned. The villages along the Santa Cruz River north of Tucson eventually faced a similar fate, adding to the Pima population.[24]

Pima agriculture handsomely rewarded the villages with an ample supply of food, but also attracted Apache raids, precipitating the concentration of most Pima villages in the area of Sutaquison.[25] Here, a fertile floodplain four miles wide and continually restored by the flooding of the Gila River enabled the Pima to farm the river terraces. While centered in Sutaquison, the villages, made up of related families, were concentrated in three large rancherías some thirty miles in length with political authority in the hands of village leaders.[26]

Apache raids increased in frequency as horses allowed them to quickly harry the agrarian and sedentary Pima. In April 1780, they dealt the Pima one of their most disastrous assaults. Disguised as Spanish soldiers, the Apache descended on a party of Pima, killing or capturing 120. To better protect themselves from such attacks, the Pima moved their villages to open country away from the river. As raids intensified, villages withdrew to the south bank of the Gila to higher and more strategic environs. Smaller villages and rancherías pulled closer together to create a "metropolis form of settlement."[27] Villages were now surrounded by irrigation canals and agricultural fields.[28] Apache raids encouraged concentration of the villages, although ecologic and economic adaptations to wheat and increased trade supported it. As Pima agriculture intensified, production increased. Rising production enlarged trade networks and modified settlement patterns. By the nineteenth century, the Gila River was used by the Pima to sustain a thriving agriculture-intensive economy.

While the stated goal of its intercourse with the Pima was "the progress of our holy Faith and the spiritual benefits" of Christianity, the driving force of Spain's activity was economics. Since Marcos de Niza's tales of the cities of gold, Spain hungered for the mineral wealth of the frontier. Nomadic and militarily powerful, the Apache controlled the exploration and development of these mountain resources. To accomplish its objective of mineral exploitation, Spain needed an ally to extend its frontier; the Pima, desirous of maintaining preferential treatment from Spain, also needed an ally. Such an alliance for Spain might extend the rim of Christendom and open up more of the wealth of the northern and northeastern mountains. The concurrence of the Pima "as a means . . . of securing the conversion of the other tribes" was essential, since the Pima administered the gateway to the north.[29]

Conversion of the Pima to Christianity would extend the Spanish frontier to the Gila River, giving Spain "an advantage over European nations" in maintaining its claims to the interior West. Kino saw Spanish influence over the Pima as a means of opening "communications with New France" as it made its own "apostolic journeys from east to west." Sedelmayr, aware of growing French influence in the Mississippi River valley, eyed the Gila and Colorado rivers frontiers as one means of stemming French hegemony in the Mountain West.[30]

Bringing the Pima villages under the influence of the Church would aid Spain in its immediate objective of establishing a presidio on the upper Gila River. Combined with presidios in Terrenate (on the San Pedro River), Janos (Chihuahua), El Paso (on the Rio Grande), and in New Mexico, Spain assumed the Apache would have little choice but to confine their attacks on "the heathen [tribes] of the north," rather than on the Spanish and Indian settlements to the south. This in turn would open up new "districts, ranches, haciendas, and mines of good quality" to Spanish settlement. Should the country be settled, Sedelmayr opined, "God would reward the royal largess for all disbursement with this additional allurement of mines of gold and silver."[31]

During the final years of Spanish administration, there was limited commerce between Spain and the Pima. Diego Bringas, traveling north from Sonora to resolve internal disputes among the Franciscan priests laboring in the Pimería, visited the Pima villages in 1796–1797, unsuccessfully seeking to persuade the Crown to authorize missions on the Gila. Reminding the Crown that providence had placed the Pima "at the doors of a large gentile population so that, blessed by religion and the rule of His Majesty, they might give to those barbarous peoples proofs which are unmistakable that they, too, may share in this happiness [Christianity] by following their example," Bringas boasted a road from Tucson to the villages could easily be constructed to tie the missions with those to the south. "If you wish to consider [crops] which can be grown there," the Franciscan explained, "every species of grain, tree, and legume would do well because of the mild climate and even temperature."[32]

A deepening political crisis on the Spanish home front and on its colonial northern frontier interrupted both the ecclesiastical and economic objectives of the Crown. In the closing decades of the eighteenth century, disputes over the limited water supplies in the Santa Cruz Valley north of Tucson surfaced. By the beginning of the nineteenth century, political dissension between the Church and military added to the growing crisis and ended all prospects for establishing a mission in the Pima villages.[33] Political infighting and Napoleonic events in Europe turned the Crown's attention to more pressing matters. The drive for Mexican independence mounted and by 1821 was complete.

Mexican independence had little impact on the Pima. While Spain never conferred citizenship on the Indians, Mexico did, no longer recognizing colonial social distinctions. This meant the legal status of "Indian" was no longer recognized. Distant from the center of Mexican administration, both in the Federal District of Mexico City and in the provincial capital of Hermosillo, the Pima were not affected by the social experiment. The arrival of Americans, however, did affect them. While Americans were prohibited from entering the country under Spanish rule, Mexican law was relaxed, and hundreds of American mountain men descended on the Gila River and its tributaries.

The arrival of James Ohio Pattie in the winter of 1826–1827 initiated a stampede of beaver trappers to the region, including Old Bill Williams, Pauline Weaver, Kit Carson, and Ceran St. Vrain. The arrival of the fur trappers did not go unnoticed by the Pima or the Mexicans. To combat the number of illicit trappers in Mexico, all frontier presidios, including Tucson, were ordered to provide detailed reports on the activities of foreigners. When Williams and St. Vrain passed through the Pima villages in October 1826, head Pima chief Antonio Culo Azul requested the men show proper identification or proceed to Tucson to report their activities. Finding the Americans friendly and open to trade, the Pima initiated a brisk business of commerce. Passing through the Maricopa villages several days later, the trappers reveled in four days of gift exchange and trade with the Maricopa.[34]

While trading with Mexican towns to the south (and through the annual trade fair on the Gila River), the Pima recognized the benefits afforded them by trade opportunities with Americans. While there is little record of trapping on the Gila River after 1827, trappers and explorers continued to follow the river west to California. Trade with villages to the south continued, although by 1840, the Pima were seldom visited by anyone except those who "in distress" visited the villages, where they were "generously furnished horses and food." Apache raids at San Xavier resulted in Pima food crops becoming increasingly more important to Mexican and Papago settlements in the Santa Cruz Valley south of Tucson.[35]

The advent of the Mexican War in 1846 ended Pima isolation. That fall, two U.S. military detachments descended upon the Pima villages. In November, General Stephen Watts Kearny led U.S. troops down the Gila and through the Pima villages en route to San Diego. Henry Smith Turner, one of 120 dragoons forming the column, welcomed the "hospitality and friendship" of the Pima. They were, Turner concluded, "more industrious than I have ever found Indians—they have all the necessaries of life in sufficient abundance, & all produced by their own industry."[36]

The Army of the West camped eight or nine miles above the Pima villages on November 10, where it was met by a Maricopa man searching for his cattle. The man approached the troops in a "frank, confident manner," topographical engineer Lieutenant William H. Emory observed, a "strange contrast with that of the suspicious Apache." Soon a half dozen or more Pima approached the camp, ascertaining the purpose of the visit. After the Indians dispatched word to the villages regarding the friendly nature of the visit, it was only a matter of hours before the camp was filled "with Pimos loaded with corn, beans, honey and *zandias* (watermelons)" to trade. While a "brisk trade was at once opened," when Army scout Kit Carson asked to purchase bread to sustain the dragoons, he was informed, "Bread is to eat, not to sell; take what you want."[37]

The Pima knew the value of trade. When Kearny informed Azul that he had heard many good reports on the Pima and knew them to be an honest people, the chief invited the general to pass the day in trade "for such articles as [you] might require." Turner noted the Pima "furnished supplies for [all] parties of strangers who may pass this way." The ease and confidence by which they approached the military camp struck many of the troops as unusual. Quartermaster Major Thomas Swords erected an awning "under which to conduct the business" of trade, an event Emory described as a "perfect menagerie" of "Pimos, Maricopas, Mexicans, French, Dutch, English and Americans."[38]

The troops, some of whom had prior knowledge of the Pima, were struck by the nature of agriculture in the villages, including the draining of the water from the land. "We were at once impressed with the beauty, order and disposition of the arrangements for irrigating and draining the land," Emory noted. "All the crops have been gathered in, and the stubbles show they have been luxuriant." Large fields were divided by earthen borders into smaller fields for convenience of irrigating. Fifteen miles downstream, the troops passed over a luxuriantly rich, cultivated land. "The plain," Emory estimated, extended "in every direction 15 or 20 miles." The farmers drew off the "whole water" of the Gila for irrigation, taking care to return the unused water to the river "with little apparent diminution in its volume."[39]

As the troops pushed west on November 12, they came to the downstream Maricopa villages, finding a "great deal of land" cultivated. "[A]ll that has been said of the Pimas," Emory explained, "is applicable to them." Maricopa men and women "came into camp at full speed, unarmed and in the most confident manner, bringing water melons, meal, pinole and salt for trade." On the following day, a Maricopa chief met with Kearny and told him it was good to trade, but if the Americans had arrived hungry and in need "it would have been his pleasure to give us all we wanted without compensation." Before the troops moved on, head Maricopa chief Don Jose Messio offered Kearny many "expressions of peace and friendship."[40]

The Pima were all that the Americans had heard and read about. They were honest, industrious, confident, and "perhaps better than some others we had seen." They "surpass[ed] many of the Christian nations in agriculture," Emory concluded, and were "little behind them in the useful arts, and immeasurably before them in honesty and virtue." Their "high regard for morality" was evident in that no soldier reported any items stolen during his visit with the Indians. While initially suspicious of their motives, Emory soon "got an indifferent set of observations," discovering "theft is seemingly unknown among them."[41] Aware of the long history of Pima fidelity and honesty, Kearny left ten or eleven travel-weary mules and sundry supplies in the villages to be picked up by Colonel Philip St. George Cooke, trailing the Army of the West by six weeks. While difficult to acquire, Kearny managed to secure half a dozen oxen from the Pima. Before departing, the colonel gave Azul a letter "directing all troops that might pass, to respect his excellency, his people, and their property."[42]

On the twenty-first of December, 340 tired Mormon troops arrived in the villages from the south, having spent twenty-six of the previous thirty-six hours on a forced march from Tucson. Hot, thirsty, and hungry, the troops were met by a cadre of mounted Pima eight miles from the villages. They came with "sacks of corn, flour, beans, etc.," soldier Henry Standage recalled. They were "glad to see us, running and taking us by the hand." Upon meeting the "singularly innocent and cheerful people," Cooke was given the letter Kearny left behind listing the "broken down mules and two bales of Indian goods." He then traded "every spare article for corn," mustering twelve quarts per animal for the trip to California. The "wonderfully honest and friendly" Pima eagerly traded and sold food crops "for bleached domestics, summer clothing of all sorts, showy handkerchiefs, and white beads." So industrious were the people, Sergeant Daniel Tyler opined, "our American and European cities would do well to take lessons in virtue and morality from these native tribes."[43]

When the troops left the Pima villages, they were met by "groups of men, women and children" wanting to trade all sorts of "eatables, including watermelons," and wanting only "clothing or cotton cloth and beads" in exchange. The menagerie described by Emory reminded Cooke of a crowded New Orleans market, with more than two thousand Indians in camp, "all enjoying themselves very much." Before departing, Cooke told Azul the Pima were "the happiest and most prosperous" Indians he had ever seen. If they continued to hold to the "principles of industry, honesty, peace and cheerful content," they would remain so. The colonel then presented the chief with a gift of three ewes with young. From the Maricopa, Cooke picked up Kearny's abandoned mules. Impressed with the nature of farming in the desert, Cooke prophetically suggested to his officers "this vicinity would be a good place for exiled saints [Mormons] to locate."[44]

The Mexican War ended with the signing of the Treaty of Guadalupe Hidalgo in 1848, with all land north of the Gila River under American administration. While the Pima villages on the south bank remained under Mexican rule, they had little contact with the Mexican government to the south after the war. Their intercourse with the American emigrants traversing their land en route to California increased. These travelers looked forward to visiting and trading with the Pima, aware of their friendly and hospitable disposition from the many reports left by Spanish, Mexican, and American explorers.

By the early nineteenth century, the Pima economy shifted in important ways. First, the Pima increased the amount of land over which they engaged in irrigated agriculture, a venture that resulted in increased raids from the Apache. Second, as Apache raids intensified, the Pima villages shifted to the south, where they were established in the open away from the Gila River. Canals and ditches surrounded their villages, and since fields were enclosed, fences encased villages as well. Third, as villages consolidated and agricultural production increased, Pima military authority concentrated in the hands of a central tribal leader. While the villages remained autonomous in civil matters, they were united under the authority of a single military leader. Such protection enhanced agricultural production and trade, making the Pima the most economically powerful tribe in the region.

In the century leading up to the American era in 1848, the Pima enjoyed relatively moist years, aiding their agricultural endeavors. They established new trading partners with Spanish and Mexican towns and American emigrants, all of which further encouraged the Pima agricultural economy. By the middle of the nineteenth century, the Pima stood poised to reap material benefits from the increased American emigrant traffic through their territory.

CHAPTER 2

The Pima Villages and California Emigrants

THE DISCOVERY OF GOLD near Sutter's Mill, California, in 1848, spawned a torrent of migration across northern Sonora, Mexico (modern southern Arizona), with forty thousand emigrants traveling over the four southern trails that converged at the Pima villages. Some eight thousand, mostly Mexican, emigrants journeyed across the Sonoran Desert between April 1848 and January 1849, with twenty thousand emigrants taking one of the southern routes in 1849. These travelers were aware the Pima villages were respites where stock could be recruited, rest assured, food and forage obtained, and protection from marauding tribes secured. Emigrant Robert Green spoke for many when he wrote, "We are all talking strongly of being compelled to eat mule beef on the road as we wont [*sic*] be able to get any provision until we get among the Peima Indians." Louisiana Strentzel, one of the few women on the trail, credited the Pima with the success of her party. "Had it not been for this water, the muskite [mesquite] beans, and the corn at the Pimose village, not one wagon could have come through."[1]

Personal recollections of the forty-niners visiting the Pima villages reveal much more than accounts of half-starved, thirst-craved emigrants in need of food, water, and hospitality. While the journals describe the villages as the last opportunities emigrants had to purchase fresh food and find good forage for their animals before arriving in California, they also provide a window into the economic output of the Pima. While the emigrants contemplated their visit to the villages, the Pima, with little foreknowledge of the torrent of emigrants heading their way, supplied the requisite food for the travelers, a testimony of their agricultural ability.[2]

Using as guidebooks the journals of topographical engineer Lieutenant William H. Emory and Colonel Philip St. George Cooke, tens of thousands of emigrants anticipated their visit to the Pima villages. Here they could acquire food and receive a friendly reception, something they would not have enjoyed since leaving Mexican towns and villages along the Rio Grande and in the upper Santa Cruz River valley. For these travelers, the Pima villages represented an oasis where weary souls could be restored.[3]

Two main southern trails converged at the Pima villages. The more difficult was the Gila Trail, which entered the villages from the east. The more frequently traveled route was the Southern Trail, which left El Camino Real near Doña Ana, New Mexico, and followed a southwesterly direction to the Santa Cruz River valley, whence it turned north into Tucson and then northwest to the Pima villages (see map 2.1). East of the villages, the Southern Trail converged with the Gila Trail and continued down the Gila River to the confluence with the Colorado River near Yuma Crossing.[4]

One of the most difficult parts of the journey for emigrants on the Southern Trail was the *jornada* between Tucson and the Pima villages. It was regarding this portion of the trail that a group of Missouri emigrants "heard awful tales of the route ahead of us, dead animals strewing the road, wagons forsaken, human skeletons, who had famished for want of water."[5] Understanding these difficulties places into perspective the feelings of exhilaration and relief travelers experienced upon reaching the Pima villages. The ninety miles of dry, barren desert represented a challenging test for emigrants en route to California.[6]

An ambitious emigrant party traveling under ideal circumstances could complete the trip from Tucson to the Pima villages in thirty-six hours, although most took between two and six days. While scores of travelers suffered from thirst and dust, there was reason for optimism if emigrants could get within fifty miles of the villages. As the stream of travelers grew to a torrent, and as more suffered from thirst and heat, young Pima men patrolling the desert south and east of the Pima villages began searching for travelers in distress. Seizing an opportunity to improve their economic well-being by providing water to thirsty travelers earned the Pima the reputation as "Good Samaritans of the desert." Carrying "gourds of water, roasted pumpkins, and green corn," Pima men and women encouraged emigrants and advertised their products to travelers in distress.[7]

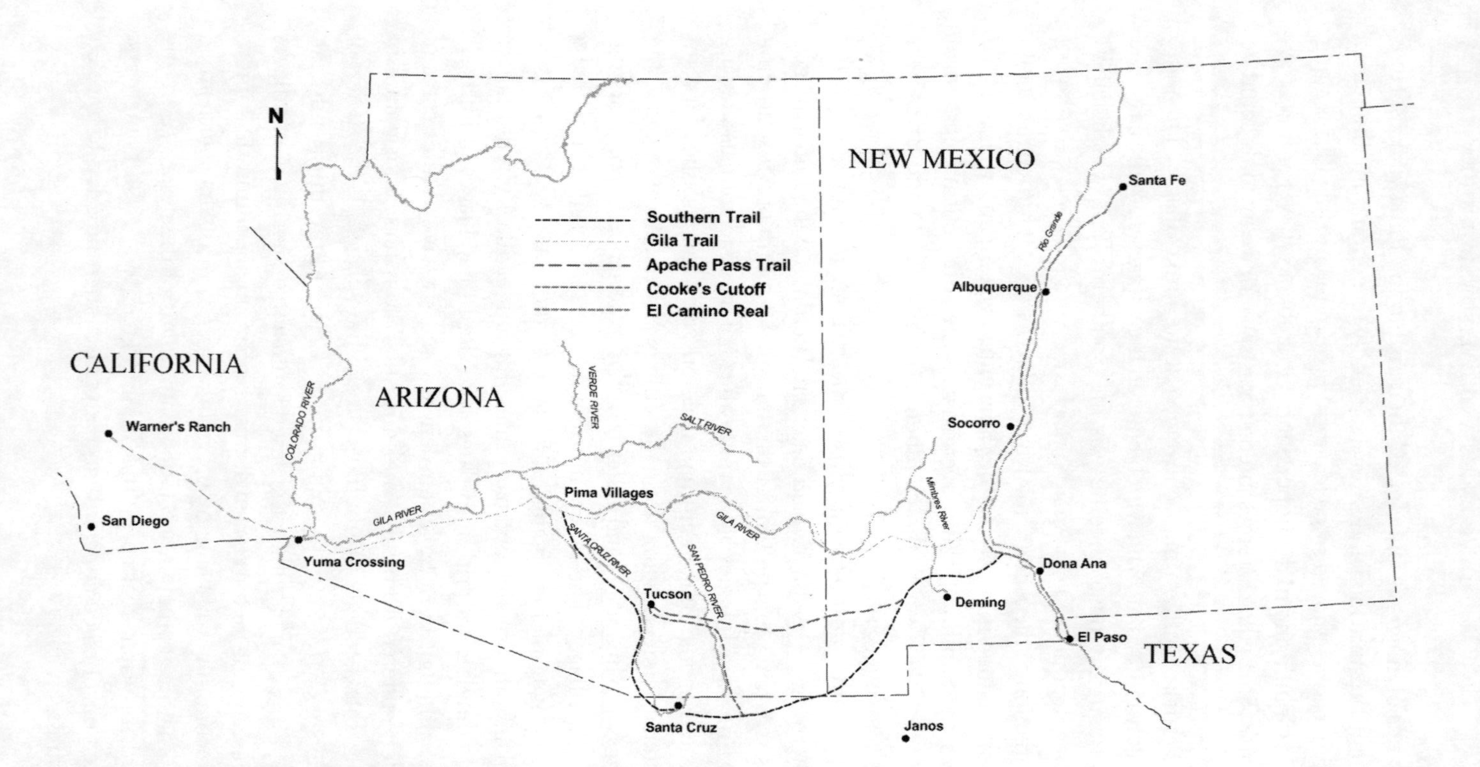

MAP 2.1. Southern gold trails through the Pima villages, 1849–1852.

The Gila River represented more than just water for parched and famished emigrants. The Pima welcomed the travelers to their riverine villages, "shaking hands as old friends when meeting [as if] being separated for years."[8] The agrarian villages also meant food and forage could be acquired and, consequently, symbolized a sustaining force for man and beast. Plenty of good-tasting water was available and could be packed for the journey across the challenging "Forty-Mile Desert," as the cutoff between the Pima villages and the Gila bend was referred to.[9]

The Gila River, and the Pima villages twelve miles downstream from where the main emigrant road obliquely struck the river, was easily identified due to the gallery of cottonwood, willow, and mesquite that graced its banks. It was "really a beautiful stream, flowing clear & rapidly," Green wrote, allowing us to "quench our rageing thirst."[10] Robert Eccleston, traveling to the villages via Tucson, observed: "It was not long before the road came close to the long-looked-for [Little] Gila. I rode in to see it,

FIGURE 2.1. The Gila River represented rest and recruitment for emigrants. (Photograph by author, 2003)

as the cottonwood, willow, &., obstruct[ed] the view, and found a swift stream about 40 ft. wide, not as clear as I expected to see it, but perhaps this may have been caused by the late rain." One emigrant noted his party paid a Pima guide $10 "to conduct us to the river Gila."[11]

The middle Gila through the heart of the villages was an oasis in the desert and dotted with a series of springs and marshes. John James Audubon noted "a great many lagoons" and an abundance of water and trees along the river, with the cienegas sustaining colonies of birds, ducks, geese, swans, cranes, and quail.[12] Some cienegas were fed by springs and were used by the Pima to irrigate farmland. At least three natural springs, including Blackwater slough east of the villages, were fed by underground water sources. Springs near Maricopa Wells supplied water for crops in addition to providing wildlife habitat.[13]

FIGURE 2.2. A view of the Pima villages and fields in the 1850s, looking north. (John Russell Bartlett print, 1852; Bartlett, *Personal Narrative*, 1854, 2:14)

Cave Couts, traversing through the villages in November 1848, described the bottomlands along the river as "far surpass[ing] anything we have ever witnessed for fertility" and hosting "a series of the finest fields" he had ever seen.[14] Emigrant Asa Clarke estimated fields extending along the river for at least five miles, being "laid out in little squares, with sluices in between, to admit the water."[15] One emigrant described "nearly a thousand separate [fields]."[16]

Free to adopt those forms of technology they believed would enhance their economy, the Pima accepted select foreign ideas and tools that correlated with their agricultural values. Economic ventures such as mineral exploitation and sheep raising (Spanish ventures) were rejected. Adoption of Spanish and American tools that facilitated agriculture, however, was coveted. This, in turn, increased agricultural output, fostering a Pima strategy of military preparedness, which enabled them to increase their productivity and position themselves as market players on the Gila and Southern trails.

The Pima used a sophisticated water distribution system and strict social controls to irrigate their lands and ensure the continuation of their economy. Emigrant Benjamin Hayes observed individual Indians "have regular days of work to which they were assigned," with each village under a captain.[17] Committees were set up in three zones along the river to manage the irrigation system, and "there were certain people in each village who decided how each ditch was to be handled," as well as to determine who was to get water. Brush dams diverted water at various points along the river into a series of acequias centered in the Vah ki (Casa Blanca) area.[18] The cooperative distribution of water enabled acequias to serve a "half a dozen fields, giving off branches to each."[19] The Pima drained their fields of excess water, a measure vital to prevent waterlogging and ensure the leaching of salts from the soil. Such processes also deposited fertilizing silt over the land, helping maintain its productivity.[20]

Because of a good supply of water, a high water table, and a fertile soil, the Pima initially did not use ploughs in cultivating their fields, using handmade wooden axes, hoes, and harrows on the "rich and easily worked" soil. Sergeant Daniel Tyler observed the Pima used "only forked sticks . . . to loosen the soil, as it was loose, rich and easily worked."[21] Other emigrants agreed agricultural implements were unnecessary as the "soil is so easily pulverized that ploughs are not needed." Simple tools such as "a stick of wood for a plow, brush for a harrow, and a stone Muller for a Mill" served the Pima well. While utilizing simple technology, Pima fields were systematically prepared before they were planted and irrigated. Nonetheless, having seen the Americans and Mexicans use modern equipment, the Pima desired to acquire such implements so they could culivate their land more efficiently and effectively and expand production, especially seeking tools from military officials who might have the authority to fill such requests. When Major Lawrence P. Graham passed through the villages from the west in 1848, the Pima asked for "a thousand or two spades, so they might have a great deal of corn for the next time white men came along."[22]

By 1850, change was afoot in the Pima mode of farming. Having learned of them from the Mexicans, the Pima used wooden ploughs, although they lacked a sufficient number of draught animals with which to utilize such implements. While the Pima had good horses, mules and oxen were in short supply. And while a horse might be purchased from the Pima at a high price, mules and oxen were rarely sold, demonstrating the Pima needed these animals in their expanding agricultural endeavors. "Being an agricultural people," emigrant William Chamberlin wrote, "they require what few animals they have for that purpose."[23] In December 1849, Benjamin Hayes noted the Pima had "no good animals to trade," and John Russell Bartlett, entering the villages as part of the U.S.-Mexico boundary survey in 1852, wrote it was "impossible to procure a single mule."[24] William Hunter, however, noted Pima Chief Antonio Culo Azul told him he "could procure from his people whatever we stood in need of," going so far as to indicate the Pima had "plenty of horses, mules and oxen," which it turned out they did not have.[25] What few draught animals the Pima had were carefully guarded because of their desire to increase their economic output.

The Pima occasionally made use of Mexican ploughs. One emigrant noted oxen were used to pull "a long hooked-shaped stick used as a plough."[26] Metal axes and hoes were used more frequently, being acquired via trade for food and forage. According to emigrant William Goulding, the Pima were using oxen to plough their land. Hayes also noted the "Pimos ploughing their lands." Bartlett noted not all land was yet ploughed by draught animals, implying the Pima used ox-driven ploughs to break new land for cultivation of additional crops to market to emigrants on the western trails.[27] Nonetheless, the Pima did not yet have access to the art of blacksmithing, a skill central to keeping American ploughs and iron tools in good repair.[28]

Emigrants, especially if they carried Robert Creuzbaur's 1849 guide to California or were familiar with Emory's and Cooke's journals, were quick to note the Pima were "all that Colonel Emory has described them—peaceable, quiet, and honest Indians, and possessing considerable intelligence."[29] Benjamin Butler Harris was so struck by their integrity that he opined Americans could learn a lesson from them. "Finding a heathen people so kind, good, sympathetic, simple, honest and hospitable," Harris chronicled, "was indeed a surprise well worth all the toil and privation of the trip, and calculated to make Christianity blush for its meager attainments." In an April 15, 1850, letter to his sister, W. Wilberforce Alexander Ramsey observed the Pima "have the character of being the most honest and virtuous tribe in the West. . . . They are peaceful and never disturb the emigrant."[30] Anxious to exchange food for cloth, tools, and coin, the "Pimos came out to the road to see us," one emigrant chronicled. Another noted the Pima greeted the emigrants by "bringing flour[,] corn meal[,] watermellons [*sic*] &c." to trade.[31]

Since the Gila and Southern trails entered the Pima villages above the Maricopa settlements, the Pima had an advantage over the Maricopa. As thirsty emigrants came down the Southern Trail from Tucson, many were disoriented, were suffering from heatstroke, or were separated from their company. While the Pima assisted emigrants back to their villages to convalesce, they also rounded up stray animals, restored their health, and sold them back to the emigrants. One emigrant noted he met two Pima men in the desert searching for "horses and mules to exchange with the American emigrants."[32] Another observed the Pima rounding up "broken down or abandoned stock" and bringing them to the villages.[33] When one traveler lost a horse in the desert, a young Pima man rode twenty-five miles south searching for it, returning two days later with the horse.[34]

Hospitality was demonstrated by permitting emigrants to recruit their stock on the limited grasslands near the villages. One emigrant explained how his party remained among the Pima "several days for the purpose of recruiting our stock." A party of Texas Argonauts spent thirteen days at the Pima villages, with one group of weary Texans remaining in the villages for five weeks.[35] When emigrant parties arrived, they were encouraged by the Pima to "dispense with the custody of [their] horses" to be "grazed and herded at good pasture at a distance of two or three miles" from the villages. While there was little forage available en route to the villages and a limited supply near the villages along the river, grasslands did exist in several locations away from the main road along ephemeral water channels. These grasslands restored many an animal.[36]

As head Pima chief, Antonio Culo Azul was justly proud of his people's reputation among the emigrants, as shown by his display of their letters of commendation. Although none of these letters are known to have survived, a number of them are referenced in emigrant journals. Cave Couts records Azul showed "passports," or letters of commendation, from a host of emigrants, including Stephen Watts Kearny. Hayes wrote Azul showed him "an imposing array of certificates of good behavior from emigrants." The New York Free Mill Party commended the chief for "the Pimos being very friendly & accommodating." A traveler from Tennessee applauded the Pima's "kindness and courtesy." The Fremont Association of New York left a letter extolling the kind treatment received from the Pima. John Audubon wrote that Azul, as was his custom, came out to meet the emigrants and presented them with an array of letters "recommending him as honest, kind and solicitous for the welfare of Americans."[37]

Inclined to generosity, the Pima expected the emigrants to engage in gift exchange or "they would think hard of it." But the Pima also knew they were highly venerated. As a result, the 6'4" Azul expected a certain level of homage. Without the requisite regards, emigrants might experience price hikes, increased charges for services, such as rounding up stray stock, or even loss of personal possessions. Powell wrote how Azul, dressed in full military regalia, came out to meet the emigrant train as the emigrants approached. The train leader, however, offended the aged chief by failing to exchange pleasantries and gifts. Such "cavalier treatment" bore just results. When the emigrants later sought to purchase food from the Indians, they found the Pima "difficult to trade with." The situation soon worsened when the Indians "stole a great quantity of things from us," including axes, hatchets, pistols, blankets, and coats. Powell attributed such theft to the train's poor treatment of Azul and inattention to protocol. If the party leader had "made the old chief some presents," Powell penned in his journal, "and paid his compliments to him in a proper way it would not have happened."[38]

To those in need the Pima did not disappoint. While trade with the Pima commenced only with the permission of Azul, many hundreds, and at times thousands, of Indians entered the fray. Eccleston wrote his party found itself in the midst of a village where Pima men and women wishing to trade bundles of cornstalks used for animal forage soon surrounded them. None would sell, however, "till permission was obtained from the chief. When this was got there was great buying and trading."[39] Another emigrant spent four days in the villages where his train was "bountifully" equipped with enough food to "supply the commissariat of an army."[40]

Already accomplished traders, the Pima welcomed the opportunity to trade with the Americans, and Azul saw it as a means to increase the overall wealth and well-being of his people. The chief, for instance, greeted Kearny while still several miles from the main Pima village, inviting the general "to pass a day in his village to give ourselves an opportunity of trading with his people."[41] John Griffin, assistant surgeon with the Army of the West, observed the Pima "were most eager to trade" and did so

FIGURE 2.3. The Pima stored thousands of pounds of food to sell and trade with emigrants in granaries. (John Russell Bartlett print, 1852; Bartlett, *Personal Narrative*, 1854, 2:236)

with "the greatest confidence, showing not the slightest fear."[42] Audubon wrote many of the Pima "who came to trade had already made up their minds only to do so for some particular article, and in those cases it was not of the least avail to offer anything else."[43]

A desire and willingness to trade and sell emerged from the surplus of food grown by the Pima. To store surplus food required efficient and effective storage capabilities. To trade and sell such quantities of food as demanded by the emigrant market further required the ability to store large quantities of crops. Such care was demonstrated by the fine Pima subterranean and woven granaries kept "full of pumpkins, mellons [*sic*], corn &c." Emory noted corn, beans, and wheat stored in "large baskets," with corn in some places stored "in baskets covered with earth, and placed on the tops of (their homes)."[44] By midcentury every Pima family had "a granary, or store house, which is much larger and better constructed than their huts."[45]

By 1849, the Pima preferred American trade goods and access to American technology, aware they could not get the supplies and trade goods they wanted from the Sonoran towns, including Tucson.[46] As emigrant traffic increased, the Pima shifted almost exclusively to the trading and selling of their products, both of which increased their material prosperity.[47] Considered "a shrewd" and "keen" people who were "willing to trade for anything that will better their present appearance," the Pima initially traded to acquire white domestics, colorful cloth, pants, vests, shoes, stone beads, and red flannel. What emigrants needed most from the Indians were food and forage. Pima corn and wheat, along with beans, pumpkins, and melons, were in demand by emigrants. While there were periodic attempts by emigrants to purchase or effect an exchange for the limited number of Pima mules and oxen, the Pima declined, as these beasts of burden were essential to their economy. Corn sold for fifty cents a basket that contained six to eight pints, and a small bundle of corn stalks to feed livestock sold for a quarter. While emigrants purchased as much food and forage as prudent, the largest single recorded purchase by an individual, outside of the military, was Strentzel's twelve bushels of corn and wheat for the journey down the Gila River.[48]

While corn and wheat were the main trade items, they were not the only items acquired by emigrants. Kearny purchased a cow from the Pima at a cost of $10, and other emigrants did likewise, although at a greater cost—Hayes reported one purchased for $32. Smaller quantities of food, such as dried corn, green corn, beans, peas, pinole, melons, pumpkins, potatoes, yams, tomatoes, corn meal, wheat flour, tortillas, molasses, and salt all sold well. Pima blankets manufactured from indigenous short staple cotton also sold, as did gourds filled with water for use across the Forty-Mile Desert. One traveler noted the Pima had plenty of food and carried "large quantities of corn and corn meal, wheat and flour, also beans [and] squashes to trade for old shirts, old shoes, pants, vests, beads and buttons."[49]

As more emigrants traversed the villages, and as the demand for shirts, cloth, and other trade items abated, the Pima shifted to selling food for cash. An emigrant passing through the villages in the spring of 1849, for instance, observed the Pima "did not appear to know the value of money," with another stating, "Money is well nigh useless to them." This was consistent with Cooke's comment of 1846 that the Pima "know nothing of the value of money or weights and measures." Even when they began accepting coin, the Pima "would not take money for anything near its value . . . prefer[ring] beads, shirts, especially red flannel, pieces of old clothe, etc." Other emigrants wrote that brass buttons, paints, looking glasses, and similar novelties remained in demand among the Indians. One emigrant found the demand for cloth so high he tore red flannel into long strips to extend his trade value. Jewelry and fancy beads were of little value, although the Pima eagerly sought stone beads when they were available. Pima women especially coveted red flannel shirts, with one emigrant noting they "would give anything to get" them.[50]

By 1850 emigrants rarely saw "one of these Indians who had not on a Shirt, Coat or pair of pants."[51] As late as October 1850, the Pima, while more often than not demanding coin, relied on trade. William Miles, in the villages that fall, wrote his party asked for water and, upon receiving it, was told to "pay for it in the way of clothes, red flannel, of which they were excessively fond, and muslin shirts." American gold coins were "indignantly refused." When the emigrants tried to purchase melons using money, the Pima laughed at them, "treating us as though they were independently wealthy, or that our cash was of no value."[52]

Cognizant they had a monopoly on the market, the Pima demanded increasingly higher prices for their commodities, especially when the multitude of emigrants increased. Hunter noted eight hundred Americans at the villages when he camped outside the main Pima village in the fall of 1849.[53] Eccleston noted the Pima "asked a large price" for everything. John Durivage noted "prices were enormously high, [with] a shirt being demanded for a very small quantity of any of the articles mentioned."[54] While the Pima did not have a set rate for their goods, allowing the market to fluctuate with demand, they were generally "reasonable in their charges." Although white domestics were the medium of exchange in November 1846, red flannel and other brightly colored cloth brought the most trade value by the fall of 1849, and in some instances was the only cloth accepted.[55]

As the Pima economy metamorphosed into more of a market-oriented economy, barter and trade lost its appeal, and the Pima demanded Mexican silver and American gold coins. Mexican silver had more of an immediate utility since Tucson was a Mexican military town that used silver coins as its medium of exchange. Since an array of manufactured items could be purchased in Tucson, it was natural for silver to be accepted in exchange for Pima food supplies. While accepting a limited number of gold coins, the Pima tried to exchange them with other American emigrants as quickly as possible. Hayes, for instance, explained Azul "was anxious to get silver for a ten dollar gold piece we gave him." He also added he met eight Pima men en route to Tucson "to buy cattle." Eccleston noted his train met five or six Pima men en route to Tucson. The men stayed with the emigrants, camped more than a day's ride from the Gila. The Pima were well armed and well mounted, and it is probable they were on the way to Tucson to use the coin acquired from the emigrants to purchase supplies they did not already enjoy. This included agricultural tools and other farming necessities.[56]

To ensure a favorable rate of exchange and perhaps to inflate prices, the Pima brought only "small quantities" of food to exchange with emigrants. They recognized and understood a basic principle of economics: limited supplies artificially inflate prices on the open market. Such economic savvy added to the level of prosperity enjoyed by the Pima. Another ploy in gaining the price they sought was to make emigrants linger before the trading began. Hayes noted the Pima kept his party "waiting half an hour" before opening the market.[57]

With tens of thousands of emigrants passing through their villages, the Pima were cognizant of the economic opportunity facing them.

FIGURE 2.4. A Pima village. (J. R. Browne print, 1864)

Emigrant journals support the theory that the Pima increased their agricultural output to accommodate the demands placed on them, perhaps cultivating as many as 12,450 acres of land by 1850.[58] This is seen in Azul's invitation to emigrants to forgo the California adventure and prospect locally for gold. Such an invitation was not lightly given, but proffered with a specific end in mind. "The Pima chief ineffectually solicited us to stop and mine a day or two's journey up the Gila," Harris wrote in the summer of 1849, "promising to furnish us a guard of fifty of his warriors with provisions, representing that gold could be dug there in paying qualities and adding that his object was to have introduced among his people trade and agricultural implements and methods from the United States."[59] Azul recognized from the technology carried by the emigrants that they had the tools and innovation his people needed to engage more efficiently in agricultural production. The Pima heard from the emigrants stories of American know-how, and Azul was mindful this would benefit his people. In 1848, for instance, Couts explained Azul was "exceedingly anxious to see the white man come and live amongst them, to teach them how to make corn, big horses [houses?], and everything they did."[60] While none of the emigrants permanently remained in the villages at this time, Azul's invitation is intriguing as it provides a glimpse into the mind of the chief as he contemplated the future economy of his people.

As their perceived level of importance increased and their recognition of the value of money heightened, the Pima's demand for coin as the medium of exchange increased. An emigrant visiting the villages in the latter part of 1849 noted the Pima knew "the value of money," while another remarked they "asked high prices in *money*" (emphasis in original).[61] The Pima were well supplied with clothing and wore only "the most flashy colors," suggesting their demand for trade goods may have been, or was nearly, saturated. When he attempted to buy some ponies, Eccleston was told the Pima would accept cash only, no trade. When he bought corn from the Maricopa a few days later, he paid "a big price" in money.[62]

While there was never a set rate for the buying and selling of Pima commodities, American extravagance contributed to its artificially inflated costs. Audubon complained American improvidence "made it difficult for anyone to make reasonable bargains with either the Pimos or Maricopas."[63] Extravagance may have been a relative concept that might not have matched the true nature of the emigrants, who dumped goods along the trail to lighten the burden on their worn and weary animals. To the Pima mind, the emigrants had a dazzling array of technology, such as metal tools and better-quality and more-colorful cloth. These goods far surpassed the available supply of goods from poverty-stricken soldiers and settlers in Sonora, including those in Tucson. Because the emigrants carried with them the products of industrial America, the Pima concluded that the Americans were a wealthy people. As a literate people, with many keeping or reading journals and making drawings, the emigrants impressed the Pima, who were intrigued with the written word and hand-drawn pictures. When the perceived waste of the emigrants is factored in—the emigrants (especially Graham's column in 1848) discarded wagons; left behind scores of dead or stray animals; littered the trail with a variety of manufactured items, such as wheels, crowbars, blacksmith bellows, carpenter's tools, stoves, chairs, tents, washing machines, guns, powder, chains, saddles, harnesses, trunks of clothing, cooking utensils, and a vast assortment of tools—the Pima concluded the Americans were wealthy and wasteful. "You can name nothing that was not lost on this road," one emigrant wrote.[64]

Another part of the perceived emigrant extravagance is attributed to "a want of small change" that compelled emigrants to "frequently pay more for an article than we would if we could make the change."[65] Part can also be attributed to the conscious decision of the emigrants to give more in trade than the purchased foods were worth. While some emigrants burned or dumped into the river everything they left behind, others traded it away, giving far more in trade value, knowing it would otherwise be lost and of no value or profit. J. G. Candee noted his train traded extravagantly with the Pima because "we must dispose of it at any rate." As a result, emigrants traded "a good garment for a water melon" that under different circumstances they would not have exchanged.[66] Whatever the reason, by the time Bartlett came through the villages in 1852, most goods were sold for coin.[67]

As the Pima recognized the value of American gold coins and their relative value to Mexican silver, they shifted their economy to one largely based on the gold standard. Concurrently, the Pima (and Maricopa), frustrated by their inability to acquire the requisite new tools from the emigrants to cultivate new fields, grew desirous of American technology, particularly metal tools. Furthermore, mules and oxen were in demand, suggesting a shift from an economy based on manpower to one based on horsepower. Powell recorded the Pima "did not like to part with their horses," although they offered "to give a horse for a yoke of oxen."[68]

Throughout the first year of emigrant traffic, journals bespeak of the honesty and integrity of the Pima, although there were isolated instances of pilferage. When Harvey Wood passed through the Pima villages, a member of his company lost a buffalo robe to theft, although Azul managed to secure its return after admonishing his people to respect the property of the emigrants. Wood was impressed with the effect. "Had the thief been a white man," the emigrant opined, "talking would hardly have restored it."[69] Harris noted Azul specifically informed the emigrants they "need fear no pilfering, as the 'Pimas do not steal.'" Chamberlin adds that Azul "took dinner with us" and inquired regarding how the

Pima "behaved towards us." If his people were caught stealing or misbehaving, the chief explained, the emigrants were to inform him and he "would punish [the Indians] accordingly."[70]

By 1850, Azul informed emigrants "his men are not all honest[.] [T]hey will steal [having] learned to do so by the Appachees [*sic*]." Consequently, an emigrant opined: "From the account given of these injuns they must have improved very much since Mr Emory was through the country for he represents them as having all the virtues of the whites without any of the vices. The only virtue I saw among them was raising corn & wheat to sell to the emigrants at high prices." Regarding the Maricopa, opinions were less kind. "Why Mr Emory has given them so good a character I cant tell unless he was very hungry & Esau like sold his words for a mess of pottage."[71]

New stresses and demands placed on the Pima resulted from market forces, which were more pronounced as the Pima economy shifted. These stresses are demonstrated partially in increased larcenous behavior. The fact that emigrants were neither soldiers under restrictive military authority nor missionaries under strict religious influence points to the beginnings of destabilizing influences in the villages. When stymied in their attempts to acquire goods, and the education that would enable them to efficiently utilize this technology, and when continuing to witness the jettisoning of a wide variety of goods, the Pima's view of integrity was modified and pilfering increased. This is observed in the loss of authority that Azul exhibited over his people. While once able to admonish his people to respect the property of the emigrants, and even able to secure the return of stolen goods through persuasion, Azul could no longer do this by 1850.

Emigrant iron tools and beasts of burden were never sufficient to meet the Pima demand, with the first signs of antisocial behavior among the Indians appearing as their level of frustration over their inability to acquire these tools and animals rose. The Pima recognized the value of American technology and that it could benefit their economy without significantly altering their cultural values. While they might reject a mining economy, they saw American agricultural technology as compatible with their long-entrenched agrarian culture and economy.

The fact that the first complaints of larcenous behavior were leveled against the Maricopa is explained by their geographically disadvantaged location. Emigrants entered the Indian villages from the east, meaning they reached the Pima villages first. The Maricopa had secondary access to the emigrant market and, as a result, received a lower quantity, and perhaps quality, of goods in trade. Durivage, for instance, wrote his company found the "Pima all that Colonel Emory had described them," yet five days later when leaving the Maricopa villages, he noted "a number of horses and mules were stolen."[72] Other emigrants were "much annoyed" [*sic*] by the Maricopa who "required much watching." Hunter went so far as to note the Pima even condemned their western neighbors and allies for ignoring "the precept 'thou shalt not steal.'"[73]

Emigrants increasingly noted they had to watch the Pima carefully. "You have to keep a sharp look out upon their movements, and your utmost vigilance will probably be insufficient to prevent their depredations," Lorenzo Aldrich observed.[74] Quaker Charles Pancoast was no kinder. "We had barely unyoked our Teams before a hundred or more Indians gathered around us, and a number of our tools (which we carried in straps outside of the wagon) were stolen so adroitly that in not a single instance could we detect the Thief. We lost so many tools we became alarmed." When a yoke of oxen was stolen Wednesday morning, three emigrants, including Pancoast, paid Azul a visit to demand its return. The chief assured the emigrants "he would get them for us" and in the meantime urged the travelers to move their camp five or six miles away from the village "where his People would not be tempted so much to steal from us." Three days later, after the chief intervened, three Pima returned the missing yoke of oxen, having found it well south of the camp.[75] As these larcenous behaviors indicate, the Pima stole that which they could not secure via trade or purchase. The fact that tools and oxen were among the most-often-reported items stolen suggests that these forms of technology were essential to the expanding Pima economy.

More than forty thousand soldiers and emigrants traveled through the villages between 1846 and 1852, finding food, water, and friendship from four thousand Pima. The Pima response to this mass migration was tempered by several factors. Much like earlier Spanish missionaries and American mountain men who simply passed through the villages buying and trading for such items as they needed, the forty-niners were transients. As a result, the Pima, desiring access to new technology and innovation, saw agricultural trade and sale as the means of market enhancement.

Furthermore, since the emigrants sought protection from the Apaches to the south and east of the villages and the Quechan, Yavapai, and Mohave west of the villages, the Pima increased in stature. The Pima found it to their advantage to provide such protection, with their villages serving not only as centers of trade and respite but also as policing centers. Since the villages were the only places between Tucson and Warner's Ranch (California) where good food and forage could be purchased and water was available, they served a vital life-sustaining function.

In the years during and after the Mexican War, the Pima took full advantage of an unprecedented access to markets to cash in on an economic bonanza. They understood they were the center of activity and their crops were in demand. As a result, the Pima leveraged their position by upgrading technology to better provide for the emigrant market. Unfortunately, this economic boom was short-lived. Within twenty years it declined, and within thirty years it was gone, but not before the Indians capitalized on their newfound wealth by expanding their market presence.

CHAPTER 3

Establishment of the Pima Reservation

DESPITE BEING LOCATED ON THE Mexican side of the Gila River, the Pima had strong economic ties to the United States. They incorporated wheat as a staple crop and adopted the Mexican technique of farming with check beds, or border irrigation.[1] By the 1850s, the Pima were poised to enter a market economy.[2] Pima lands were "better irrigated, their crops [were] larger, and the flour which they [made] from their wheat and maize" surpassed all regional growers.[3] Despite assurances from federal officials, the Pima remained concerned about their land and resources. Since the arrival of the U.S. Army in 1846, the Pima had a diplomatic protocol with the United States. The health of Antonio Culo Azul, head Pima chief since the 1820s, was failing, and U.S. Boundary Commissioner John Russell Bartlett was the last American to see Azul, as he died in the winter of 1855. By the time William H. Emory surveyed the Gadsden Purchase boundary later that year, Azul's son, Antonio, had assumed the role of head Pima chief. Antonio Azul's first official protocol ensued after the Pima villages were brought under American administration in the summer of 1855.[4] In June, Azul led a delegation of six Pima, Maricopa, and Papago chiefs to Emory's camp at Los Nogales, 150 miles south of the Pima villages, where they asserted sovereignty over their land and resources.

Meeting on June 29, Emory informed the chiefs that all rights they enjoyed under Mexican administration were guaranteed by the United States. Azul and the other chiefs expressed concern about their land and resources, "manifest[ing] much anxiety to know if the transfer of Territory would affect the grants of lands ceded them by Mexico, which they now cultivate with so much success."[5] Emory assured the men that all titles recognized by the Mexican government would be validated by the United States and issued a public call for American citizens to respect the authority of Azul and the sovereignty of the Pima.[6]

Emory informed the secretary of war that the Pima had "a just claim to their lands" and that if they were dispossessed, they would "make war on the frontier of a very serious character."[7] Emory, along with Lieutenant Nathaniel Michler and Azul, had much with which to be concerned. With Pima wheat ripening at the time of Michler's visit to the villages in May, the men recognized the potential threat American settlement posed to Pima interests, including their blossoming economy.[8]

The conference at Los Nogales underscored the rapidly growing American presence. While the first railroad survey was well to the north of the Pima villages, a second survey passed directly through the villages. Led by engineer John G. Parke, the expedition focused on potential grades between the Pima villages and El Paso, Texas.[9] Descending into Maricopa Wells, geologist Thomas Antisell described an oasis well endowed with grass and water. More pertinent to Pima concerns was the message Parke sent back east: the middle Gila River valley was "susceptible of being made productive." When the Texas Western Railroad Company hired Andrew B. Gray to survey yet another grade, Pima anxiety increased.[10]

Pima concerns over their land titles and water rights were further heightened when Congress authorized the exploration and survey of overland transportation routes for the express purpose of enticing "agriculturalists and laboring men" to the West.[11] A southern route left El Paso and stretched to San Diego, with the Pima villages included in potential routes due to the availability of "fine wheat and corn" there. With a national road and a supply of food, emigrants would "feel some assurance" in settling in the valley, an area foreseen as "one of the most productive" in the country.[12] On October 1, 1858, J. B. Leach's national wagon road opened to the public.

In June 1857, the U.S. Post Office awarded the California Stage Company a four-year contract to deliver mail between San Antonio and San Diego. To facilitate travel, the San Antonio and San Diego Mail Line constructed eighty-seven stations between its termini, with the largest and most important at Maricopa Wells, just west of the Pima villages. While most stage stops were mere camping grounds, Maricopa Wells supported an adobe building complete with stock corrals, and it was provisioned with food and forage from the Pima villages. In time, Maricopa Wells offered amenities not found in Arizona outside of Tucson.[13]

Better known and more of a concern to the Pima was the Butterfield Overland Mail Company, which began service on September 16, 1858. This mail line followed the Southern Trail through the Pima villages and provided semi-weekly mail service between its eastern terminals in St. Louis, Missouri, and Memphis, Tennessee, and its western terminus in San Francisco (see map 3.1). The Overland Mail road intersected with Leach's wagon road three miles east of Capron's Ranch (modern Sacaton), where it paralleled the south bank of the Little Gila River before veering west to the Casa Blanca Station. Continuing another five miles west, the trail bifurcated around either side of Pima Butte before descending into Maricopa Wells, where the Butterfield Overland Mail Company constructed "a substantial group of adobe buildings and a large corral."[14]

The organization of the overland mail lines and their selection of the Pima villages as a central stage and mail stop was no accident, as Special Agent Silas St. John was "to superintend the purchase of all the grain raised by these Indians."[15] Both companies were keenly aware of the services the Pima (and Maricopa) could provide, in terms of food production and protection of the overland roads. The Pima asserted sovereignty over all of their land and resources, a proposition Isaiah C. Woods, general superintendent of the San Antonio and San Diego Mail Line, quickly discovered. Woods met in conference with the chiefs and headmen of the Pima on November 15, 1858, being informed that the land, grass, wood, and water utilized by the stage line belonged to the Indians. In addition, Woods was told that he would have to pay for the protection the Indians provided the travelers and for the grass and water the mules and horses consumed at Maricopa Wells.[16] While the arrival of the mail lines was an economic boon to the Pima, they refused to relinquish their sovereignty.[17]

John Walker, assigned as the first permanent Indian agent to the "Gadsden Purchase Indians" in 1857, informed Commissioner of Indian Affairs James W. Denver the following January that the Pima were doing well and that the "mail party has made a station at the Maricopa Wells which encourages the [Pima] to farm more largely as they can find a good market for a great portion of their grains."[18] The Pima reminded Walker of the implements and tools they had requested at an earlier meeting at Fort Buchanan. In the spring, they again informed Walker

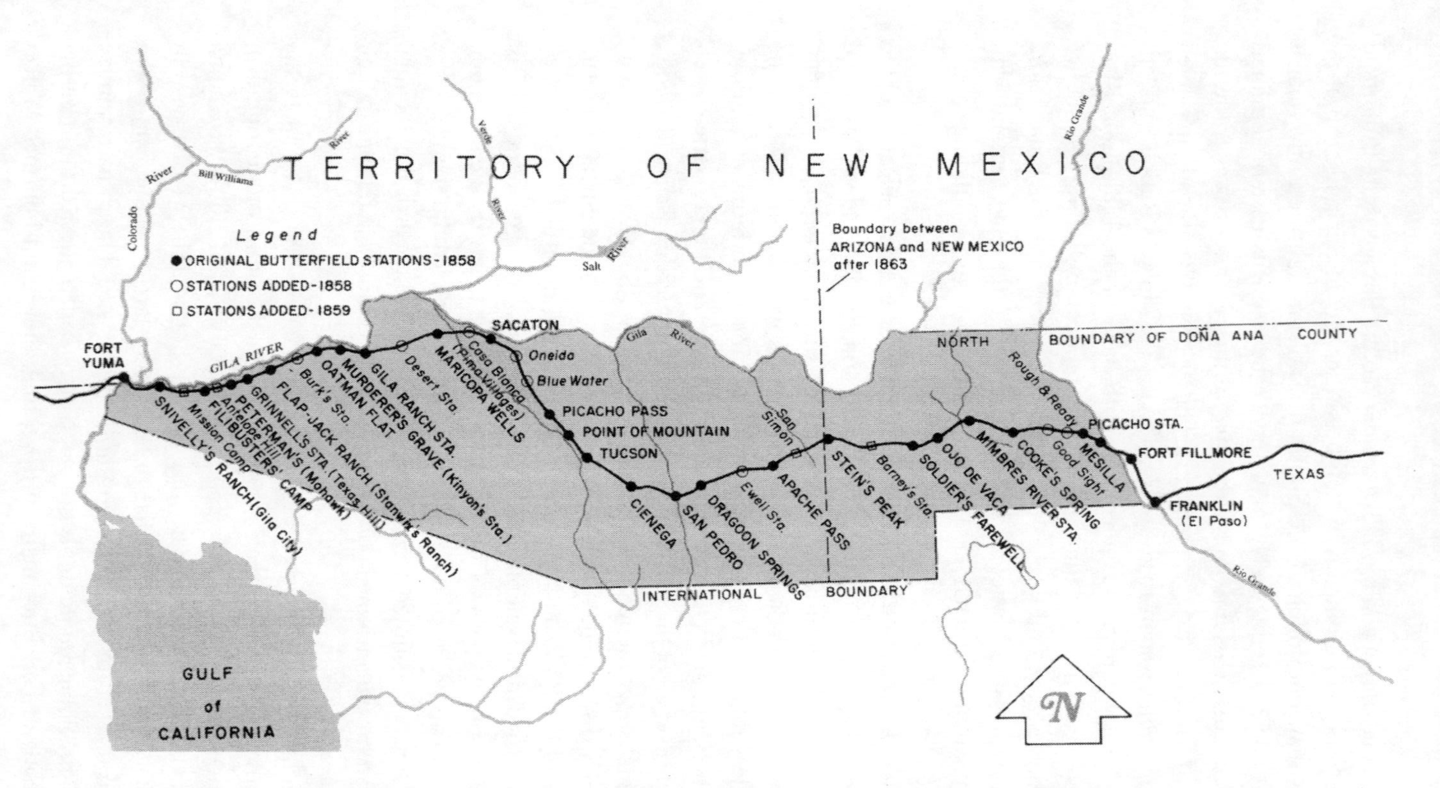

MAP 3.1. The Butterfield Overland Mail route across Arizona, 1858–1861. (Wagoner, *Early Arizona*, 1975, 352)

they needed ploughs, hoes, axes, shovels, and spades in order to expand their agricultural production.[19]

That same spring Walker informed New Mexico Superintendent of Indian Affairs James L. Collins that the Pima were restless because the agricultural tools they had requested were not yet in hand. So desirous of implements were the Pima that Walker observed them selling captive Apache children at Fort Buchanan and using the proceeds to purchase "such implements as they need for their farming operations." Collins informed Walker the requested implements had been purchased and would be forwarded to the villages as soon as practical.[20]

Delays in fulfilling the government promise strained relations with the Indians. When Lieutenant A. B. Chapman and a detachment of U.S. soldiers passed through the villages in late summer 1858, Maricopa village captain Juan Jose became incensed when Chapman refused his offer of five dollars apiece in gold for shovels and axes. Jose told the lieutenant, "I believe your people are a nation of liars. . . . I trust you no more." Even Antonio Azul was upset, scolding Special Indian Agent Sylvester Mowry that he and his people were "sick of promises made by every white man."[21] Walker found himself in a quandary, caught between the Pima and government bureaucracy. In November, he dispatched another letter to Collins reminding him that the Pima planted two crops each year and that winter crops would soon be sown. The Indians "annoy me very much," Walker wrote, and demanded the implements needed to farm land to which the Pima had constructed a new canal four miles upstream.[22]

The perennial flow of the Gila River was not fixed, although the Pima adapted their cultivation of crops to the river's natural flow. During the winter months, when the natural flow was low, the Pima planted winter wheat and legumes. As winter snow melted in the higher elevation upstream of the villages, the river's flow increased and enabled the Indian farmers to both pre-irrigate and then irrigate their summer crops of corn, beans, teparies, cotton, and various melons. While the river flow reached its nadir in late spring or early summer, by midsummer the rainy season increased the flow and provided an adequate water supply for summer crops.

The Pima reconciled their cropping patterns to this natural cycle of the river over multiple generations, culminating in a high degree of dependence on the river for irrigation of crops and a strong cultural and economic connection to the river. This understanding, coupled with a desire to increase production, resulted in new irrigation ditches in the latter 1850s, as the Pima sought to realize greater economic benefits from immigrant traffic by expanding their agricultural practices.

So it was that in January 1859 Walker notified Collins of the importance of the promised implements to the burgeoning Pima economy. The Butterfield Overland Mail Company now had three stage stations, Casa Blanca in addition to Maricopa Wells and Capron's Ranch, in or near the villages, and if the Pima were to increase cultivation to meet demand, they needed additional tools. This was critical as the Pima had men enough for constructing a new canal upstream, but if they were to sow their crops in time, they would have to abandon the construction work as they did not have tools enough to simultaneously do both jobs.[23] The Pima, Walker boasted, were "inclined to work and love[d] to make money."[24]

After more than a year of delay, the Indian Service allocated $2,000 to purchase tools and implements, with Walker distributing in March the promised ploughs, harrows, spades, axes, and blacksmithing and carpenter's tools.[25] To assist Pima farmers with a crop selection that appealed to the Butterland Overland Mail Company, Walker introduced American seed corn, the first non-native corn introduced among the Indians.[26] In addition to corn and Spanish wheat, the Pima also grew barley, a grain introduced by Walker a year earlier.[27] So desirous were the Pima of selling their grain that they oversold, finding themselves requesting a small amount of food from Walker in May to tie them over until the harvest later that month.[28]

Despite economic success, the Pima remained "anxious about the tenure of their land." When Mowry met in an official capacity with the Pima leadership, he was informed they had a recognized Spanish grant for their land, an assertion affirmed by Sonora Governor Cubillas. While no record or document existed to disprove this assertion, Mowry was convinced that justice and humanity compelled the United States to recognize and protect Pima lands.[29]

Penning a letter to officials in Washington, D.C., Mowry underscored the rationale for such action. "Their villages [will] be made of great service to the Territory by supplying large quantities of breadstuffs," Mowry asserted. Furthermore, their lands "are in all respects reservations, and have the advantage of being their homes by title of law and by preference." While concerned about non-Indian settlement, Mowry believed there was ample room for settlers above the Pima villages "without interfering with the Pimos," but only if "a man of great tact and intelligence" respected Pima sovereignty.[30]

Lieutenant Chapman echoed Mowry's sentiments and encouraged the United States to recognize Pima land rights. "These Indians have strong claims upon the consideration of the United States Government, the prompt recognition of which not only justice and humanity, but sound policy, renders a matter of prime necessity." Their agricultural economy, the lieutenant added, "present[s] an appearance of beauty and civilization that is truly pleasing." Pima fidelity and hospitality to American emigrants strengthened the cause of recognizing their rights. This latter consideration warranted the Pima receiving farm implements that would assist them in expanding their agricultural economy. "So far, they have been more blessed in giving than receiving, and have looked in vain for recognition by the government of the many kindnesses they have rendered our people." Without recognition of their land and water rights and the distribution of gifts, the Pima might be "induce[d] to throw off an alliance from which they have derived no benefit."[31]

Promised they would be compensated for their hospitality with "an abundance of agricultural implements," the patience of the Pima wore thin. When Special Agent Goddard Bailey visited the villages in the fall of 1858, he added to the chorus of concern. "It is necessary to do more than conciliate these Indians by presents. They must be secured in their possession of their lands." Without such protection, the rich soil and advantageous location of their villages "will excite the cupidity of a class of settlers not over nice in their regard for the rights of the Indians." Sound policy suggested "the necessity of preventing any cause of complaint on this score, and of doing so at once."[32]

Bailey and Mowry had ulterior reasons for cultivating a political alliance with the Pima: the traditional antipathy between the Pima and the Apache. Bailey noted the Pima (and Maricopa) were "a barrier between the Apaches and all western Arizona." As long as this alliance was secure, commerce was assured between Fort Yuma and Tucson via the Pima villages. Without it, commerce and the growth of American settlements was less certain. To this end, Bailey recommended patenting the land of the Pima to prevent emigrants from settling on it, an action prohibited by the Indian Trade and Intercourse Act. Furthermore, Bailey urged the Indian Service to assign a resident government agent to serve as the local representative of the U.S. government in its political dealings with the Pima.[33]

Two policy considerations centered on the desires of the United States in its long-term objectives for the Arizona portion of New Mexico Territory. To ensure the Pima produced an adequate food supply for the territory, Bailey favored the Indian Service distributing "a reasonable amount" of agricultural tools and seed annually. This would encourage the Pima to bolster crop production. Bailey, like Butterfield Overland Mail agent Enoch Steen before him, encouraged Acting Commissioner of Indian Affairs Charles Mix to provide the Pima with arms and ammunition. "[T]heir loyalty has been sufficiently tested that they may be safely trusted" as a "frontier militia." It was absolutely indispensable for the United States to curry the favor of the Pima, as "these are precisely the people who will least brook an invasion of their territorial rights."[34]

To maintain a policy of peace and friendship, Bailey encouraged Mix to send a diplomatic representative to visit with the Pima and "ascertain their wants and wishes." This assumed added importance when political conditions in the Pima villages grew strained when the promised agricultural implements and tools did not arrive and new traders and emigrants to the villages introduced vices, such as ardent spirits. Postmaster Cyrus Lennan encouraged Superintendent Collins to appoint a permanent agent to the villages, since the discovery of placer gold upstream brought a large number of "individuals of lawless character."[35]

When Walker called on the villages in the summer of 1859, he requested a diplomatic audience with Antonio Azul and the village chiefs, seeking to ascertain the cause of their dissatisfaction. Walker discovered that unfulfilled promises and the lack of agricultural implements were high on the list of disappointments. While receiving some implements that spring, the Pima expected more. Nonetheless, the Pima expanded their agricultural production, cultivating, according to Walker's estimate, fifteen thousand acres in 1859.[36]

In addition to selling more than 110,000 pounds of surplus wheat to the overland mail companies in 1858, the Pima sold 30,000 pounds of corn and 5,000 pounds of tepary beans.[37] In 1859, they sold an additional 250,000 pounds of surplus wheat to the Butterfield Overland Mail Company and maintained "a large trade with emigrants" and a "considerable trade" with merchants in frontier towns such as Tucson. With the subjugation and cultivation of new lands, production continued to climb. By 1860, they sold over 350,000 pounds of wheat to the mail lines. Not surprisingly, the Pima were "in a very prosperous condition, and . . . they nearly all had money, in amounts varying from fifteen to twenty-five dollars."[38]

Mowry and Bailey understood the importance of respecting Pima territorial integrity and sovereignty. Bailey encouraged Mix to confirm the Indian land titles as soon as possible.[39] Mix agreed, informing Secretary of the Interior Jacob Thompson such action would further stimulate the Pima economy. Mix stressed the propriety of distributing agricultural implements and "the means of defense" to the Pima to "confirm their friendship."[40] While this friendship was not yet threatened, Mix advanced a policy of furnishing the Pima with new agricultural technology to bolster production, implicitly acknowledging Pima rights to water.[41]

Mix's report expressed the sense of the Indian Service and, to the extent it accepted it, the views of Congress, which was in the formative stage of establishing reservations in the West. Mix opined three substantive errors impacted federal policy: removal of the tribes from their aboriginal homelands; recognition of too much Indian land; and the provision of annuities. Reciting a list of less-than-successful reservations in California, which were established after the Senate's failure to ratify eighteen treaties with the California tribes in 1851–1852, Mix faulted not the reservations per se but the "manner in which [the system] has been carried out." There were too many employees "to control, assist and work for the Indians." Mix recommended the aboriginal homelands of the Pima be recognized but, in lieu of annuities and government employees, furnishing the Pima additional agricultural tools, implements and, eventually, schools to ensure the Pima transitioned to a modern economy.[42]

Representative Alfred B. Greenwood (D-AR) and Senator William K. Sebastian (D-AR) cosponsored an amendment to the 1859 Indian Appropriation Act to recognize the Pima Reservation. Sebastian reminded his Senate colleagues that the Pima lived "right upon the great pathway of southern emigration to California." Recognizing their land and respecting their rights, the senator asserted, was important not only for ensuring provisions for travelers along the roads but also because it was a matter of "ordinary justice to secure them the homes [in] which they reside."[43]

Concerned about setting aside too much land, the House of Representatives adopted a compromise proposal to create more, although smaller, reservations, limiting the Pima Reservation to no more than one hundred square miles.[44] While Sebastian requested $15,000 to purchase suitable gifts for the Pima, the House reduced this to $10,000.[45] A joint conference committee agreed to make future additions to the reservation, provided no further expenses were incurred, and on February 28 the bill was approved.[46]

Greenwood, appointed commissioner of Indian Affairs that spring, selected Sylvester Mowry as special agent to oversee the survey of the reservation. On May 12, 1859, Greenwood informed the agent that the appropriation for the survey and gifts was at his disposal.[47] Collins, meanwhile, desired the funds and the distribution of gifts channeled through his office in Santa Fe, writing Greenwood that it was prudent to purchase agricultural implements for the Pima as it would open the door for "instruct[ing] them in the business of farming."[48]

Mowry traveled to the Pima villages where, in July, he convened a meeting with Antonio Azul, Maricopa Chief Juan Cheveria, and other village leaders to inform them of funds appropriated by Congress. Azul, distrustful of the Americans, immediately replied that he "had heard that story before" and that he did not "believe a word of it." Unlike Chapman a year earlier, Mowry scolded the chief, stating he "would tell [him] simply the truth, and that if [Azul] were silly enough to be imposed upon by every American who passed [by] their villages, it was an evidence, not of neglect or want of good faith by the government, but of [Azul's] own want of sense."[49]

Quieted in his suspicions, Azul promptly requested calico and cotton cloth for the women, and arms, ammunition, agricultural implements, cattle, and horses for the men. Informed by St. John that Walker had already distributed a number of ploughs, axes, shovels, and hoes, Mowry reduced the number of tools he planned to purchase so he could buy the cloth the women desired. Assuring the chiefs their good conduct "had not been unnoticed by the government," Mowry impressed upon them the power of the United States, reminding the leaders that although the

Pima "considered themselves a great and numerous people, their entire population would only make a small pueblo in the United States."[50]

After meeting with the headmen and soliciting their input on how to spend the $10,000, Mowry proceeded to Arizona City (Fort Yuma), where he purchased a portion of the goods, before traveling on to San Francisco to procure the remainder. When shipping arrangements were completed, the agent planned his return to the villages. While intending to purchase fifty ploughs, Mowry deemed the high costs of shipping them, $35 apiece, too costly and, since Walker and St. John had already distributed some implements, he instead purchased fifteen, along with additional shovels, spades, and axes.

On his return in September, Mowry brought together the Pima and Maricopa to distribute the gifts. With Azul translating for the Pima and Francisco (a Maricopa subchief) doing likewise for the Maricopa, Mowry remarked "that the continuation of such friendly behavior would insure for the [Pima] the favorable notice and a continuance of the bounty of the government." In other words, the Pima could expect additional tools to stimulate their economy and "make their labor more profitable." The U.S. government encouraged continued expansion of Pima agriculture, recognizing its value to territorial growth.[51]

Speaking for the Pima, Azul expressed deep gratitude for the gifts, telling Mowry in an hour-long speech to inform the president the Pima "would teach their young men to use the implements sent to them." Aware the farm implements would enable his people to expand their economy, Azul recognized the Pima would have to learn new techniques if they wanted to compete with non-Indian farmers. Currently the only growers in the region, Azul was mindful that times were changing and that emigrants passing through the villages would one day settle near his people.

Once the speech making was over, the distribution of the gifts began. If the Pima still believed the Americans were untruthful, by the fall of 1859 they felt otherwise.[52] When the remainder of the gifts and tools arrived from San Francisco, a second, larger distribution occurred on November 8. "All passed off admirably," St. John informed Mowry, "The large number of articles enabling me to give every Indian something."[53] Walker noted the distribution went by village, with goods given to over 1,100 men, beginning with the oldest and most fervent cultivators of the soil.[54] Walker estimated the Pima now had twenty-five American ploughs and sets of harnesses. Azul believed that the Pima economy, and the water and technology necessary to sustain it, was protected. In fact, he requested of Walker someone to train one of the Pima young men as a blacksmith so they could repair their own tools.[55]

Mowry did more than distribute the gifts; he also supervised the survey of the reservation (see map 3.2). When Mowry traveled to the villages to distribute the gifts, engineer Andrew B. Gray accompanied him. Gray and Mowry then met with Azul and the village leaders to discuss the survey, although they were not particularly concerned with Pima desires. Mowry explained to Greenwood the difficulty he had describing the nature and purpose of the survey. Azul repeatedly argued the Pima "claimed as their own property the entire [middle] Gila valley." To mitigate Pima concerns over the limits of the reservation, Mowry told Azul the survey was simply to protect and enclose their "villages and planting grounds" to prevent encroachment by settlers.[56]

While neither placated by, nor pleased with, these assurances, Azul and the headmen consented to survey parties commencing work. Mowry remained in the field with Gray only long enough to establish the initial points of the reservation and the general lines that would run on both sides of the Gila River to encompass the Pima villages and fields. This was critical to determining where and for what purpose the boundary line was drawn. Mowry then departed for San Francisco, with Gray returning to Tubac.[57] Returning to the Pima villages on September 5, 1859, Gray spent the next forty-three days working to complete the survey, chaining nearly seventy miles of land in order to fix the limits of the reservation. Gray informed Mowry that the reservation protected "a great extent of water for their acequias."[58]

The reservation was in essence two parallelograms, each twelve and a half miles in length and connected at their ends. Each was four miles wide and, combined, they enclosed nearly twenty-six miles of the Gila River, including the "Indian gardens," "cultivated grounds," and "Pimo Villages." Glaringly absent from the reservation were the Maricopa villages and fields located downstream of Pima Butte, as well as a number of upstream Pima fields near Blackwater Spring. Mowry indirectly noted these lands, telling Greenwood, "The attention of the department is respectfully called to the necessity of an early settlement of the titles of the

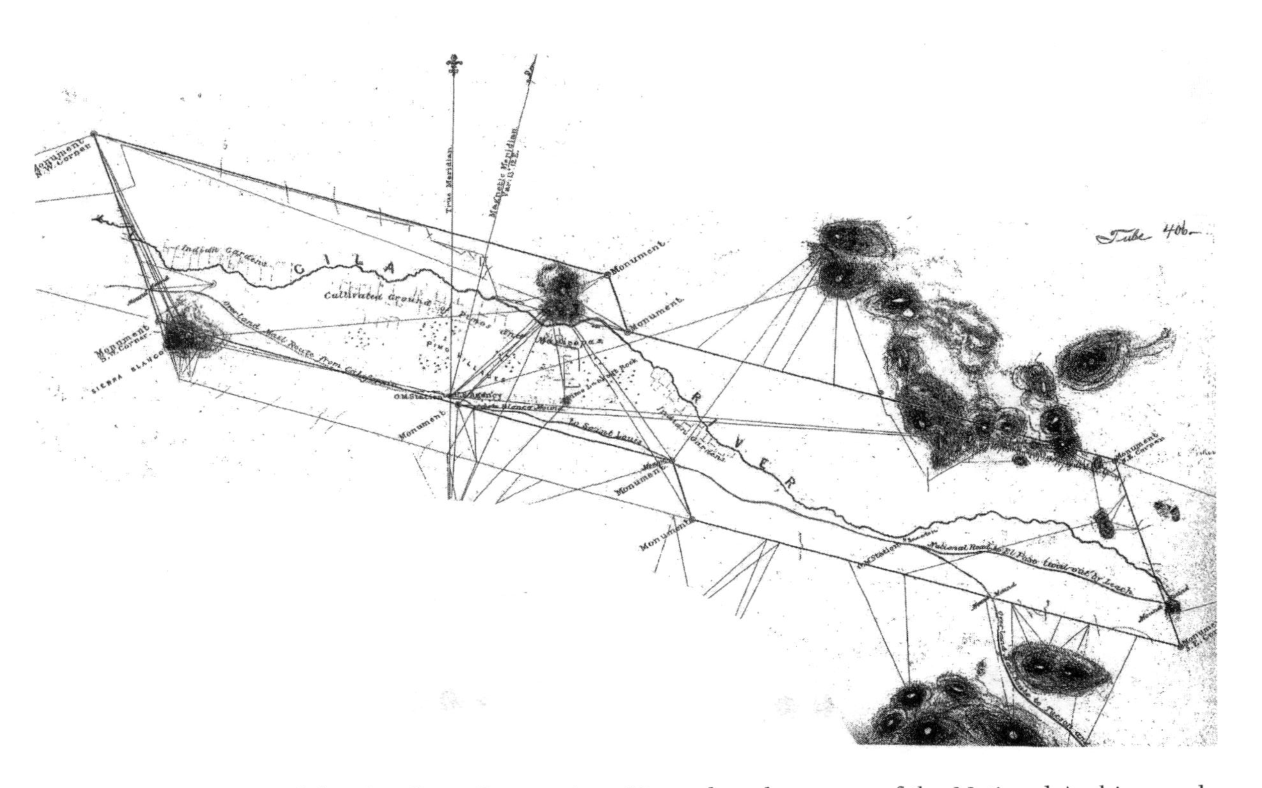

MAP 3.2. Survey map of the 1859 Pima Reservation. (Reproduced courtesy of the National Archives and Records Administration; tube 406, Central Map Files A, entry 16)

Pimo and Maricopa Indians to the lands above and below their present reservation on the Gila."[59]

As Gray surveyed the reservation, he advised Mowry he included all the water of the Pima acequias. But this was not accurate, since he failed to protect the head and upper portions of the Little Gila River and all of the Blackwater spring and slough. Also omitted were the upstream irrigated lands between the Gila and Little Gila rivers. These lands were east and north of the overland road and, although not then in cultivation, they were previously farmed. Consequently, when Gray informed Mowry he surveyed the reservation "in order to make it advantageous to the Indians," he was accurate only to the extent that he protected the wagon roads and mail stations by including them within the reservation (see map 3.3). The failure to include all of the Pima cultivated lands and the Maricopa villages and fields downstream explains why Azul and the village chiefs had difficulty in appreciating the motives behind the survey.

While the Pima were disappointed over the limits of the reservation, Mowry explained that it was not intended to limit them to sixty-four thousand acres but was, rather, designed to protect their cultivated fields, village sites, and the main transportation routes from encroachment.[60] St. John reminded Greenwood that upstream settlement would deprive the Pima of the low flow of the river, something that "would undoubtedly be a fruitfull [*sic*] source of contention and difficulty."[61]

Mowry and Greenwood recognized the gravity of appeasing the Pima and Maricopa since the Indians were the main auxiliary source of armed protection guarding the overland trails. Without controlling its own people from appropriating the land and resources of a long-time ally, the United States risked losing its alliance of peace and friendship. Any hostility would disrupt emigrant travel to the west and temporarily slow or halt national expansion. It was this geopolitical reality that the United States sought to mitigate. The development of mineral resources in southern Arizona, of which Mowry and Gray were intimately aware, was a fundamental force behind such policy.[62]

The 1859 reservation points to another important element that bears on the Pima agricultural economy. When Mowry met with the headmen in the spring of 1859, he assured them of the protection of their rights to additional land and that "full justice would be done them by the United States government in this and every other respect." Azul and the

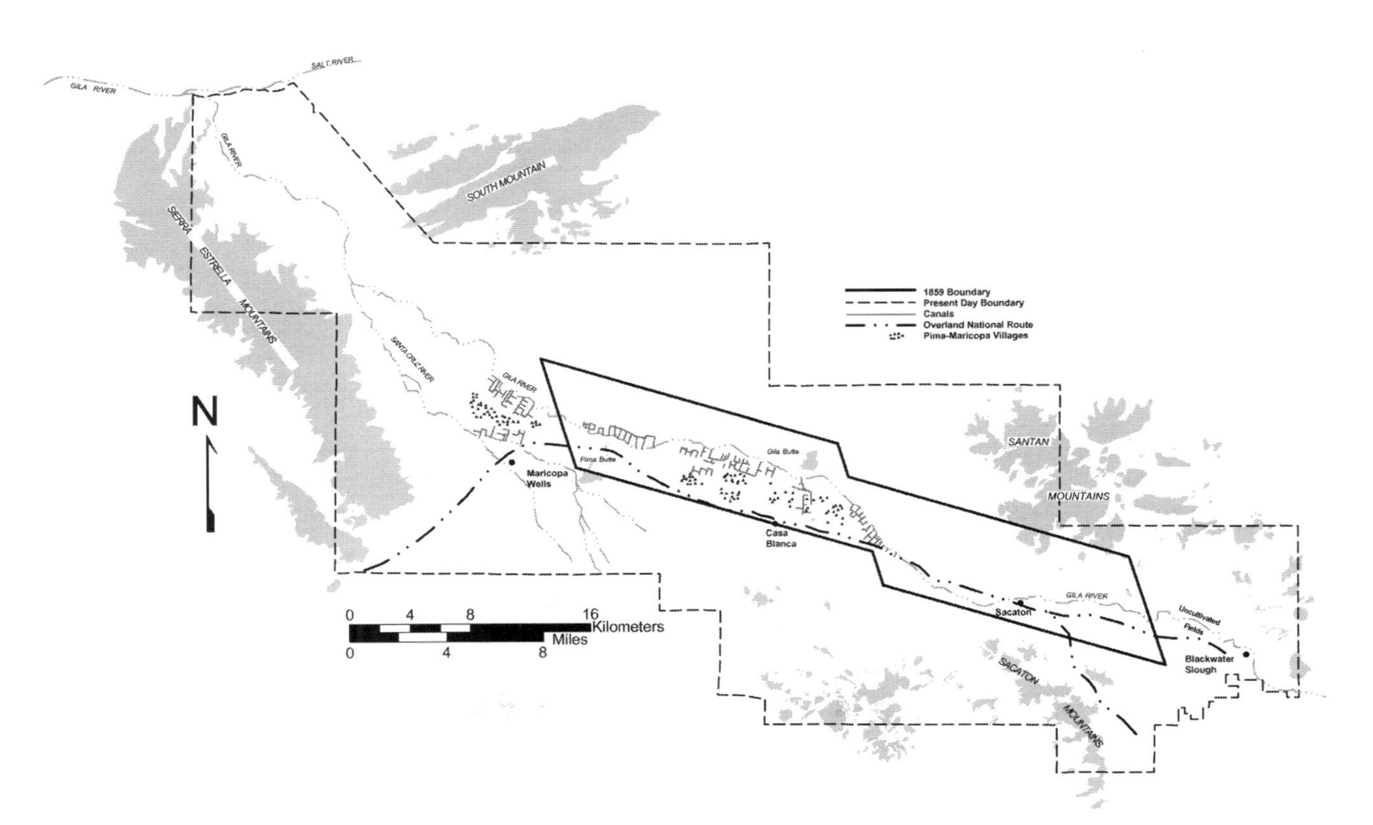

MAP 3.3. The surveyed reservation and Pima and Maricopa fields and villages, 1859.

village leaders were promised their land would be protected and that they could expect to subjugate additional land, something they did in the fall of 1859 and again in the spring of 1860.[63] Accomplishing this could occur only by expanding the 1859 reservation, protecting their water, and ensuring the viability of their economy. "Any extensive cultivation above the Indian fields will cause trouble about water for irrigation," Mowry opined, "and inevitably bring about a collision between settlers and the Indians."[64]

Throughout the 1850s, the Pima continued to enjoy economic growth. While the Indians served notice that their land and resources were under their sovereign control, in the post–Civil War years the United States encouraged settlement of the territory, and by the end of the decade, the Pima stood on the precipice of far-reaching economic and cultural change. No longer did they control their own destiny, as the rapidity of change brought about by federal policies diminished Pima sovereignty and disadvantaged the Indians, resulting in a swelling tide of emigration to central Arizona Territory.

Civil War, Settlers, and Pima Agriculture

THE PIMA VILLAGES IN 1860 were tranquil. The Pima had "a good many implements for farming and fine lands to enclose and increase their farming operations."[1] Nonetheless, Special Indian Agent Sylvester Mowry and Indian Agent John Walker focused government attention on protecting Pima water rights, as "any extensive cultivation" above the villages would create challenges for Pima water users. Charles Poston, appointed the territory's first superintendent of Indian Affairs in 1863, foresaw "discontent and disturbance" if settlers established farms and towns above the Pima villages.[2]

The beginning of the American Civil War illustrated two important themes. First, Pima grain was important to the war effort in the Southwest, both for the Confederacy and the Union. Neither could adequately control the territory without access to the Pima wheat market. Second, the Pima villages and presence were important to the war effort in Arizona. The Indians protected the communication lines, served as an auxiliary force of the territory, and, because of their hospitality and friendship, aided the United States, only to be repaid by the expropriation of their land and resources. When the war ended in 1865, the Pima were at the zenith of their agricultural economy.

The 1860 decennial census for the first time included the Pima and estimated 7,291 acres of land in cultivation within the reservation. David Miller, the census enumerator for "Arizona County," arrived in the villages in November and placed the population at 3,714, of whom 3,320 were Pima. Seven hundred thirty-six farmers cultivated an average of 9.9 acres each. The Pima cultivated more than 194,000 bushels of wheat, 252,000 bushels of corn, and 8,000 bushels of beans, representing, outside of Tucson and the Santa Cruz Valley, all the crops produced in Arizona.

Assuming Miller's enumeration included all cultivated land, the extent of agriculture in the villages was 50 percent lower than Special Agent Silas St. John's estimate of fifteen thousand acres in 1859. Miller's tabulation, however, was made in ten days, and he did not account for double-cropping, which would increase the acreage to 14,582. The Pima and Maricopa harvested 11,640,000 pounds of wheat and 15,120,000 pounds of corn in 1860. In addition, they harvested 480,000 pounds of beans, 9,200 pounds of cotton, 4,978 pounds of tobacco, 1,950 gallons of saguaro preserves, and had more than 700 cows, oxen, and cattle. Walker reported that the Pima had "extended their planting operations far beyond any previous year," suggesting Miller underestimated his count.[3] The Pima sold a minimum of 400,000 pounds of grain to the Butterfield Overland Mail Company and at least 40,000 pounds to Ammi White, a resident trader and miller who arrived in the villages in the spring of 1860.[4]

With the election of Abraham Lincoln as president, in November 1860, the Pima villages and field crops found themselves squarely in the sights of both the Confederacy and the Union. Walker left the territory in December, his political sentiments allied with the South. Territorial Superintendent of Indian Affairs James L. Collins then detailed Lorenzo Labadie to Arizona as Indian agent for the "Gadsden Purchase Indians," but he never made it to Tucson, being met by Southern sympathizers and forced to return to Santa Fe.[5] By the spring of 1861, Southern sympathizers and Apaches closed the Butterfield Overland Mail route. In July, all three federal military posts in Arizona County—Fort McLane, Fort Breckinridge, and Fort Buchanan—were abandoned.[6]

White and his business partner Ebenezer Noyes continued to operate their mill and store at Casa Blanca. Assured of his allegiance, Union Captain George Andrews solicited White's involvement to report any seditious activity.[7] Nonetheless, with federal troops withdrawn from the territory, the *Mesilla Times* hinted at the possibility of the Confederacy arming the Pima and Maricopa to protect Tucson from hostile Apaches.[8] In the meantime, the Pima planted their crops that winter, expecting a robust market in the spring.[9]

White purchased Pima wheat and corn on behalf of the California Column, Union volunteers marching east from California under the command of Colonel James H. Carleton. When Confederate troops invaded New Mexico and Arizona, in July 1861, Union Major General George McClellan ordered the volunteers into Arizona to repel the invasion, which was led by Lieutenant Colonel John R. Baylor of the Texas Mounted Rifles. Baylor appointed Captain Sherod Hunter to lead the incursion into Arizona and "secure [the] aid and goodwill" of the Pima. The Confederacy recognized it was of "utmost importance" to consummate a treaty with the Pima in order to acquire their flour, wheat, corn, and hay.[10] In February 1862, Hunter took possession of Arizona, occupying Tucson unopposed on February 28. When Union troops had withdrawn from Tucson the previous July, they had burned William Grant's flour mill and destroyed all grain fields to prevent them from falling into Confederate hands. "The smoke of burning wheat fields could be seen up and down the Santa Cruz Valley," Poston observed, "where troops were in retreat, destroying everything before and behind them."[11]

While the Santa Cruz Valley provided Hunter and his eighty mounted troops with sufficient supplies that winter, he was aware that wheat and corn at the Pima villages would enable the California Column to continue its eastward march against the Confederacy. Union Colonel Carleton, too, was aware of the importance of Pima wheat and the likelihood of its capture.[12] Controlling the Pima wheat market was critical to the Confederacy, both for its hope of holding the territory and for preventing the Union advance from securing the grain.[13]

Over the winter of 1862, the California Column assembled at Fort Yuma in anticipation of the Union advance across Arizona.[14] Major Edwin Rigg, in command of Fort Yuma with the advance troops, reported to Carleton that soldiers under Confederate Captain Hunter were in the territory aware the Pima had a "large quantity of wheat . . . and they [are] in want of it." Rigg was concerned about the wheat at White's mill, fearing it would fall into the hands of the Confederacy.[15] Carleton, meanwhile, directed White "to purchase all [available] wheat" from the Pima.[16] To alleviate Pima concerns and to secure food and forage for federal purposes, Brigadier General George Wright proposed garrisoning a subdepot at the Pima villages, to be guarded by one company of cavalry and one company of infantry. Wright believed fresh meat and flour could be secured in the villages "at fair prices."[17] White daily purchased 18,000 pounds of wheat, hourly producing 200 pounds of flour.[18]

Hunter advanced on March 3 to capture the Pima wheat supply, catching the Pima and White by surprise. White was captured and arrested for "purchasing wheat &c., for the Northern troops." While Hunter established an amiable relationship with the Pima, the Confederate captain urged General Henry Sibley to appoint an Indian agent for the two tribes to cultivate a political relationship and facilitate the purchase of all Indian wheat. For unexplained reasons, Hunter did not negotiate a treaty as Baylor expected, even though he acknowledged Pima sovereignty over their lands and villages.[19]

In the process of capturing the mill and wheat supply, Hunter controlled 150,000 pounds of wheat that White purchased for the Union advance. Lacking the means to transport it to Tucson and not wanting to destroy it for fear of alienating the Pima, Hunter returned the grain to the Indians, hoping to effect a policy of goodwill. He then occupied White's house and awaited the arrival of the rumored train of fifty federal wagons en route to collect the wheat and transport it downstream. In the meantime, Union Captain William McCleave and ten federal cavalry rode into a trap and were captured by the Texans.[20]

Carleton, hoping to catch McCleave and White before they were sent as prisoners of war to Mesilla, ordered a Union offensive on April 6, sending Captain William Calloway and 272 men up the Gila to take possession of the Pima villages. Low on grain, the Union troops took empty grain sacks to purchase wheat from the Pima. Ten thousand yards of manta (and old army uniforms) were transported to the villages to purchase wheat and other supplies. To ensure cooperation, Calloway was under strict orders to "pay promptly for anything purchased" from the Indians.[21] After a brief skirmish with the retreating Confederates at Picacho Pass, Calloway withdrew to the villages, where he wrote Rigg that he could procure supplies from the Pima "provided that we can get manta. Send us manta or we will starve."[22]

In the meantime, a combined Union force advanced up the Gila River to the Pima villages, where it constructed Fort Barrett.[23] From this vantage point, the Union Army purchased "every necessary article of subsistence and forage" for 2,350 soldiers and nearly as many animals.[24] Lieutenant Colonel J. R. West had a difficult time making the Pima "understand the magnitude of [Union] demands" and was fettered in his requests to purchase wheat and other supplies from the Pima as he had "nothing but promises" to offer in payment.[25]

Cognizant the Pima had the food and forage necessary to sustain the army, and that the military could not simply confiscate the goods without risking hostilities, West agreed to a scale of prices with the Pima: one yard of manta would be exchanged for four quarts of flour, seven quarts of wheat, four quarts of pinole, 50 pounds of hay, or 150 pounds of green fodder. The daily consumption of the advanced guard of the California volunteers was equivalent to 400 yards of manta. West quickly discovered the Pima were not willing to "trade wheat for more manta than they wanted for the moment." More importantly for military concerns, West was acutely aware that Pima and Maricopa demands for manta would decline "after 20,000 yards have been distributed," and the army already had an obligation for 3,000 yards. While at that instant seeking to purchase a standing field of wheat, West feared that if the Pima did not agree to sell more wheat, he might have "to enter their wheat fields and cut the grain for forage." In a private letter to Carleton, West reiterated an earlier request for 5,000 pounds of Indian trade goods, believing such goods "would work wonders" in securing additional wheat from the Pima.[26]

In mid-May, as West prepared to advance on Tucson via Fort Breckinridge, additional manta, calico, flannel, and drills arrived from Fort Yuma. More than 30,000 pounds of Pima wheat was purchased in one day, and all outstanding credits were redeemed. Despite the windfall, West remained concerned that there was "no guarantee how long the flow of grain [would] continue." Nonetheless, he estimated that when the wheat crop was harvested he would be able to purchase an additional 400,000 pounds. To convert the grain into flour required White's mill be repaired or that a small mill be sent from San Francisco. West further was aware of the value of arming the Pima and Maricopa in their campaign against the Apaches. "It would be of much benefit to us in our negotiations about supplies," West reminded his superior officers. Carleton agreed.[27]

When Carleton arrived in the Pima villages on May 23, he purchased an additional 143,000 pounds of wheat and expected to buy another 200,000 pounds when it matured. Having met in council with Pima Chief Antonio Azul and the village leaders, Carleton promised to send from San Francisco fifteen wagon loads of trade goods for the Indians. "The Pima and Maricopa are the finest Indians I have ever seen," Carleton waxed, "and should be afforded every advantage." To this end, he requested one hundred old percussion muskets and ten thousand rounds of buck and ball cartridges (and bullet molds) be sent to Fort Barrett to be distributed to the leading men. "This would be a great favor to this worthy people, who have always been our fast friends."[28]

From Tucson, West discovered wheat difficult to procure and, where available, its cost, six cents per pound, "exorbitant." While expecting the per pound cost to drop after an estimated 100,000 pounds was harvested in the coming weeks, West proposed introducing "a train load of wheat from the Pimas" as a show of competition to drive down the costs in the Santa Cruz Valley.[29] In the Pima villages two companies of troops guarded two hundred thousand rations and continued purchasing grain from the Pima.[30]

As the California Column moved east towards Mesilla and the Rio Grande, Carleton moved his headquarters from the Pima villages to Tucson. The demand for Pima wheat, however, did not diminish. By August, Major First Cavalry, California Volunteers, D. Fergusson dispatched Lieutenant C. P. Nichols to the villages to determine if any "Mexicans or others" were trading with the Pima. Any traders other than Ammi White were to be arrested and brought to Tucson and charged with interfering with military orders. Nichols was ordered to purchase all the wheat and flour he could and to make whatever arrangements necessary for the purchase of future wheat.[31]

While the war effort after 1862 shifted east, the Pima remained very much a part of the war effort, both through the production of wheat and other food crops and as volunteers in the army. While wheat, flour, beef, and some forage could be acquired in Sonora, most came from Arizona, with the Pima providing the bulk of the wheat and flour. In the initial months of this relationship, the California Column "trad[ed] under every disadvantage" because it lacked resources with which to purchase or trade for Pima crops.[32] Lacking resources, the federal army purchased wheat from the Pima on credit, using vouchers that were disdained by the Indians. When White began purchasing these vouchers from the Indians "at a great discount," Carleton became alarmed. White was warned to cease and desist, and Fergusson ordered Lieutenant James Coleman back to the villages to settle the vouchers since it was he who had initiated their use. The Pima expected full payment for their wheat, and Fergusson did not want White's discounted purchase of the vouchers to interrupt trade. Since Coleman completed vouchers without stating the quantity of wheat and the price the Pima were to be paid, a damaging problem resulted. This act of "stupidity," Fergusson complained to Lieutenant Benjamin C. Cutler, had to be corrected and the Indians paid as soon as possible lest they cease trading.[33] After months of delay, the Pima were paid with a new shipment of "Indian goods" that included tobacco, knives, paint, beads, needles, looking glasses, fishhooks, hoes, and other supplies distributed "in payment of the Government indebtedness in the hands of the Indians."[34]

As summer progressed, West grew increasingly desperate in securing trade goods with which to purchase wheat from the Pima, who were reluctant to accept vouchers. When the first supply of manta arrived, it was used to purchase 131,250 pounds of wheat. By the time Carleton purchased another 143,000 pounds of wheat from the Pima, he was again reduced to issuing vouchers. Special Agent J. Ross Browne reported the Pima and Maricopa sold in excess of 1,000,000 pounds of wheat in 1862, as well "green peas, green corn, pumpkins and melons." Forty percent of the Union Army, or at least one thousand soldiers, was fed with food purchased from the Indians.[35]

The spring of 1863 was as trying for Fergusson as the summer and fall of 1862. Purchases from Sonora virtually dried up as the Mexicans refused to sell more grain unless it was purchased with "gold or silver."[36] By then, Fergusson had amassed a debt of nearly $100,000. In October, Captain William Ffrench met with the leading Pima men, who informed the captain that the Indians had "an abundance of wheat on hand," but that they were hesitant to sell it due to lapses in payment.[37]

By the summer of 1863, Carleton's wheat and other food stores were running low. When no one answered a government advertisement for 500,000 pounds of grain that spring, the army contracted with trader John B. Allyn to provide grain at three cents per pound in exchange for trading privileges at the Pima villages for one year. White continued purchasing as much wheat as his mill could process. Allyn purchased 600,000 pounds in 1863, even though the Indian crop was reduced due to a damaged acequia.[38] By the spring of 1864, wheat was scarce in Arizona, with Carleton ordering troops to go on half rations.

Inspector General N. H. Davis issued an order to seize, if necessary, Pima wheat "as an act of military necessity." Superintendent Poston immediately complained to Commissioner of Indian Affairs William Dole in Washington, D.C. "A high handed outrage of this kind, perpetuated by order of the highest military authority in the territory, was not calculated to inspire the Indians with very powerful respect for the representative of their great father at Washington," Poston lamented.[39] Poston halted sales of Pima wheat under the pretense of sending the grain to the Yuma Indians. He removed Allyn as trader and fired Indian Agent Abraham Lyons.[40]

Major Theodore Coult, nonetheless, reported to Davis that he intended to purchase the grain one way or another. He did not propose taking it by force from the Pima but, rather, seizing it from White (or others who might be holding it) and issuing receipts at three cents per pound. While Poston was en route to the Pima villages, Coult sent a rider to meet Corporal John D. Walker at Bluewater and order him to advance to the villages and take possession of all the grain he could secure, an order with which the corporal fully complied.[41] Antonio Azul, however, favored the sale of all Pima grain and opposed Poston's action limiting acquisition of Pima wheat, going so far as to call Poston "a thief." Azul traveled to Tucson and complained of Poston's perceived interference in the sale of wheat.[42]

A long-standing request of the Pima had been for arms with which they might better defend themselves against the Apache. In 1860, St. John broached without success the idea of providing one hundred old Mississippi rifles for the Indians. When the California Volunteers arrived in the villages, Azul complained that the Apache had firearms, but the Pima could get none. West later requested arms for the Indians, believing it would aid in his efforts to purchase grain and other supplies, and Carleton ordered one hundred old percussion muskets and ten thousand rounds be sent to the chiefs and leading men.[43]

On December 30, 1862, Coult reported rifles were en route to the villages, although he requested the same rifles be used to raise three companies of infantry and two of cavalry to defend southern Arizona.[44] By April, Fergusson reported two sources of guns. During the winter, a shipment of arms arrived from Fort Craig and Mesilla in New Mexico and was stored in Tucson. But there was also an invoice for rifles from Fort Yuma requested by Carleton. In April, Fergusson penned a letter to Azul informing him that he would issue the headmen "arms and ammunition if they would make a campaign against the Apaches."[45] Poston also requested "some common muskets" for the Pima and Maricopa so they might serve as "valuable auxiliaries against their hereditary enemies the Apaches."[46] Unknown to Poston, arms were distributed on April 17, when Fergusson ordered Lieutenant George Burkett to proceed to the villages and distribute them.[47] When the arms from Fort Yuma arrived, Fergusson promised to distribute them as well, noting the Pima and Maricopa would be "very serviceable as auxiliaries" to the main body of U.S. troops.

By this time, the Civil War campaigns in Arizona were over. Throughout the remainder of the war, maintaining supply lines and reopening the overland mail routes required additional protection. When gold was discovered in western Arizona, prospectors flocked into Yavapai and Apache country. Joseph Pratt Allyn was delighted that many of the goldfields were close to "the granary of Arizona, the Pima villages."[48] New discoveries of gold near Prescott brought additional miners and Apache forays seeking to drive the intruders from the land. But while Apache raids increased north and west of the Pima villages, the villages were quiet.

When miners petitioned the California volunteers for protection from the Apache and Yavapai, Carleton refused. Irate miners then petitioned Territorial Governor John Goodwin to act. Goodwin requested military escorts from President Lincoln, suggesting that Pima and Maricopa volunteers be recruited for the task since they had an intimate knowledge of the land and were familiar with Apache warfare.[49]

By 1864, the quasi-settled areas of the territory, largely mining camps, were "completely paralyzed by hostile Indians." When Brigadier General John S. Mason arrived in Arizona, he found most settlers south of the Gila River had fled to Tucson, while those living north of the river had almost entirely abandoned their settlements. Exploration of the territory's mineral wealth virtually came to a halt.[50] In an attempt to open the territory, Mason proposed to blanket Arizona with light cavalry to steer hostiles into the arms of the U.S. Army. The army used this tactic with success during Kit Carson's 1863–1864 march through Canyon de Chelly and James Carleton's Gila Expedition in 1864.[51]

By 1865, the situation in Arizona was much different, as Goodwin's plan to arm the Pima and Maricopa had been approved by U.S. Provost Marshal James B. Fry. Mason now used two hundred Pima and Maricopa, more than one-quarter of the adult men, to engage the Apache.[52] Thomas Ewing, then a teamster in the Pima villages, enlisted ninety-seven Maricopa and formed Company B, with six additional Maricopa men later enlisting. John D. Walker, living among the Pima after his discharge from the California volunteers, recruited ninety-four Pima for Company C. On September 2, 1865, Companies B and C were mustered in at Maricopa Wells, with Maricopa chief Juan Cheveria serving as captain and Antonio Azul serving as sergeant (later promoted to second lieutenant).[53] The confederated tribes' primary objective was to pacify the Tonto and Pinal Apaches, for which they were to be rewarded with "Government bounty."[54] The Pima and Maricopa desired to do their part in securing Arizona Territory, believing that in so doing they were securing their own economic well-being and protecting their land and sovereignty.

In the fall of 1865, Camp McDowell was constructed with assistance from the Pima and Maricopa.[55] Situated in the heart of Apache country, the new military post enabled settlement to root along the lower Verde and Salt rivers as well as in areas upstream of the Pima Reservation. The Pima were aware their actions would encourage settlement, yet were confident of their own ability to continue cultivating and selling grain and food crops across the territory. They demonstrated this belief by demanding to trade directly with all traders. The Pima were militarily strong, enjoyed a robust economy, and saw their villages and fields as the granary of the territory. While cautious of the events around them, the Pima believed they had demonstrated their loyalty and commitment to American officials. When their military enlistments expired on September 11, 1866, each Pima and Maricopa received $50 and retained his firearm. Most of the Indians returned to their fields, although seventy chose to re-enlist in November and served as spies and scouts for the U.S. Army under Major General Irvin McDowell.[56]

Throughout the latter part of the decade, the Pima tended to their fields and grew a good article of grain. Special Agent J. Ross Browne described "large acequias tak[ing] their head near the upper boundary" of the reservation; one was on the south side of the Gila two miles below Sacaton, and the other was on the north side of the river. These canals "with their various branches, comprise[d] nearly five hundred miles of well-defined acequias and extend[ed] over a tract of land eighteen miles in length."[57] In 1864, the Pima were especially blessed with a "bountiful crop of wheat, corn, beans, melons and pumpkins." White estimated at least 1,000,000 pounds would be sold, with wheat selling for fourteen cents a pound in the mining districts of Prescott. Their supply of grain was "ample for all the citizens and a portion of the troops at present in

Arizona." The Pima used the proceeds from the sale of these goods to purchase clothing and other "articles as they require" in Tucson or from local traders.[58]

Joseph Allyn visited the villages in the summer of 1864 and estimated the amount of corn sold by the Pima and Maricopa at 250,000 pounds, in addition to the wheat they sold. Allyn speculated that Pima grain production had quadrupled since 1860.[59] Having full and complete use of the waters of the Gila River, other than minimal diversions by a handful of settlers above the reservation, the Pima cultivated additional crops without straining their water supply or their distribution system. After White's mill was reopened in 1862, Pima and Maricopa wheat, sold at three to six cents per pound, was transported to Prescott for use by the miners or sold under military contracts. *The Weekly Arizona Miner*, a Prescott newspaper, reported that "Pimo Flour, from the steam mill of White and Noyes, is now much used in Prescott. It is good and sweet, though not so white as some of the flour from the States."[60]

By mid-decade, the Pima grew and sold most of the wheat and corn supply for the new territory and served as volunteers in the territorial militia. Wheat sold for $2.00 a bushel, with sales to military contractors, miners in Prescott, and emigrants passing through the villages. While the grain was purchased by traders, who in turn processed it into flour, the Pima prospered. They were so well off economically that in 1866 they informed Indian Agent M. O. Davidson that they "want[ed] no aid at the hands of the Government, except such as will promote their education . . . in the mechanic arts, and agriculture."[61] The Pima made clear their desire to remain economically independent. When C. H. Lord, deputy agent in Tucson, visited Azul and the chiefs in May 1866, he distributed additional agricultural implements and opined there were "many well-to-do farmers" among the Pima. Lord estimated the Indians would have more than 1,500,000 pounds of grain to sell in the spring.[62] The Pima expanded their area of cultivation again, reclaiming previously irrigated land above the reservation in the Blackwater area. In 1866, they sold over 2,000,000 pounds of wheat, in addition to corn and beans.[63]

So successful was their cultivation of crops that George Hooper, a military contractor at Fort Yuma, sought a federal license to open a trading post at the Pima villages so that he, too, might profit by the sale of Pima grain. Unable to secure the required federal license, Hooper attempted to buy out White and proposed replacing the existing mill with a larger one. White was unable to process flour quickly enough, Hooper argued, with the result that "immense quantities of flour are constantly being sent into the territory."[64] Increasing the sale of wheat and flour, Hooper added, would foster settlement of the territory. Rebuffed in securing a license, Hooper purchased the interests of Henry Grinnell and, by February 1867, operated three trading posts in Maricopa Wells, Sweetwater, and Sacaton.[65] Later that same spring, White sold his interest in the Casa Blanca mill to William Bichard, who then signed a military contract to annually provide 300,000 pounds of Pima flour.[66]

The Pima's success initiated the beginnings of their downfall. Given protection by the Pima and Maricopa, miners entered the territory, affording new opportunities for the sale of Indian wheat and corn. But this also opened the door to settlers who commenced cultivating the fertile desert valleys.[67] In the process, they appropriated for their own use the water belonging to the Pima. In October 1863, Inspector General Colonel S. A. Lathroop warned Dole of "placer diggings and the copper and silver mines" in the southern portion of the territory that were attracting new prospectors. Additional deposits of gold were uncovered near Prescott.[68] Miners needed wheat and corn, which the Pima provided and the traders processed into flour. Prospectors required the protection of the military, which constructed posts in Apache country. This in turn opened the door for farmers and merchants, who sought safety in the Gila and Salt river valleys. This set the settlers on a collision course with Pima water and economic interests. Not surprisingly, Dole was warned that "the rapid influx of miners from California and elsewhere into the country occupied by these Indians necessitates immediate attention by the Government and the good policy of aiding them in agricultural pursuits by a liberal supply of seeds and agricultural implements."[69]

Poston understood what settlement meant to the Pima. In a letter to Dole, Poston discussed the rapid growth of the territory, especially the lands above the Pima villages. Any settlement here, with a diminishment of the Pima water supply, would produce discontentment.[70] The establishment of Fort McDowell and the re-garrisoning of other military posts, such as Fort Breckinridge, encouraged settlement by non-Indians.[71] Ammi White, while Indian agent for the Pima and Maricopa, also speculated in land above the reservation, where he owned a ranch. In 1864, he established Adamsville, the first non-Indian town above the villages. While composed mostly of Mexican settlers, Adamsville quickly grew into a major town in the territory, with William Bichard opening a second mill there in 1869. In May 1866, Pima Agent Levi Ruggles founded the town of Florence eight miles above the reservation. Gaining a sense of security from their proximity to the Pima Reservation, settlers arrived and irrigated land above the reservation that was then protected from hostile Apaches "by the vigilance and bravery of the Pima and Maricopa."[72] Ruggles himself soon became the largest private landowner in central Arizona Territory. In the meantime, former Confederate lieutenant Jack Swilling was attracted to the Salt River valley and the agricultural markets at Forts McDowell and Whipple. By 1871, Swilling's development efforts in the Salt River valley led to the cultivation of 2,200 acres of barley, 1,200 acres of wheat, and 700 acres of corn.[73]

In September 1866, the trouble foretold by Mowry, St. John, and Poston erupted. That month, McDowell dispatched Major Andrew Alexander to the reservation with a detachment of soldiers to quiet a land and water dispute between the settlers and the Pima. In the coming months, the dispute increased and tensions elevated. As more settlers arrived, confrontations increased.[74] Forty-two individuals each filed homestead entries for 160 acres of land, with Florence claiming 218 residents and nearby Adamsville having 400.[75] By 1868, it was apparent that the economic landscape of the Pima was rapidly changing due to the miners and farmers now pouring into central Arizona. Non-Indian grain production soon surpassed that of the Pima, with over seven million pounds grown in 1867. Over one thousand acres of land were now cultivated directly above the Pima Reservation.[76] In 1872, a colony of Mormon settlers arrived in the upper Gila River valley and founded Safford, with settlements in Thatcher, Pima, and Duncan following in rapid succession. Each wave of settlement further strained the water supply of the Gila River. While the army and first emigrants looked upon the Pima as allies and friends, with one settler commenting that "when [the Pima and Maricopa] are around one can feel a degree of safety not otherwise felt," by 1869, public opinion shifted against the Indians.[77]

While the Department of the Interior temporarily withdrew an additional 69,120 acres as reservation in 1866, settlers continued to arrive and occupy land just above the 1859 reservation, adding to the level of tension.[78] In March 1869, the Pima and Maricopa informed Colonel Thomas C. Devin that the land the settlers were appropriating was "inalienably theirs [as well as] the waters of the Gila." If these resources were not protected, the Indians would "clean out" the settlers above the reservation.[79] By fall, the tension along the Gila was due to settlers depriving the Pima and Maricopa of their water.[80]

In 1869, settlers in Florence purposefully wasted "large quantities" of water in order to deprive the Pima.[81] Lieutenant Colonel Roger Jones informed Commissioner of Indian Affairs Ely Parker that during the prior two years settlers above the reservation had "opened large acequias for the purpose of irrigation. Instead of [the water] being returned to the river after it has served its purpose, it is allowed to run waste, thereby greatly diminishing the volume of water before it reaches the Pima."[82] Such action demonstrated that the settlers saw the Pima as economic competitors and underscored the fact that the federal government would not intervene.

When Grossman held a council with Azul and leading men in October, he learned firsthand of their complaints. "We have only a few acequias filled and cannot cultivate all our land," Azul explained. The chief was tired of federal traders that took advantage of the Indians, preferring to be paid in cash or gold for their grain so the Pima could "suit ourselves and buy where we please and what we please." Maricopa Chief Juan Cheveria agreed and demanded more traders, not less, so that the Maricopa would be better compensated for the sale of their goods.[83]

The Civil War initiated the end of an era in Pima history and the beginning of another that, in coming years, dramatically affected the economic landscape of the reservation. Control of the waters of the Gila River and the Pima reputation as industrious, friendly, and hospitable cultivators of the soil slipped from their grasp. While the Indian villages had once been "the granary of Arizona," this, too, slipped away. By the end of the decade, the overall economic well-being of the Indians was threatened by declining river flows caused by upstream diversions. Settlers in the territory now farmed 14,585 acres, including 10,451 in the Salt, Gila, and Santa Cruz river valleys where wheat, barley, and corn were the dominant crops.[84] Over the course of a single decade, the Pima lost control of their own destiny.

CHAPTER 5

A Crisis on the River

AS THE 1860S CLOSED, the Pima had cause for concern. Government Indian agents Ammi White and Levi Ruggles cornered the Pima wheat market and speculated in land above the reservation.[1] The Homestead Act encouraged settlement in the Gila River valley without protecting Pima water. Lieutenant Colonel Thomas C. Devin warned his superiors that water was being taken from the Gila River upstream of the villages and that the Pima's low flow was threatened and could leave their fields without water. Furthermore, a malevolent class of Americans and Mexicans entered the reservation and demoralized the Indians with whiskey and theft.[2] Tensions escalated as more settlers drew water from the Gila River.[3]

Responding to Pima complaints of diminishing river flow, Major General E.O.C. Ord, commanding the Department of California, recommended that all land above the reservation, including the improved lands in and around Florence, be set aside as an addition to the Pima Reservation.[4] Devin warned that if the Pima failed to receive sufficient water to sustain their agricultural economy, they might well drive the settlers out of the valley. Territorial Superintendent of Indian Affairs George W. Dent notified the commissioner of Indian Affairs that "if crowded to the wall" the Pima would "fight for their rights."[5]

Despite his concern, Dent did nothing to alleviate the shortage of land and water necessary to sustain the Indian economy.[6] Commissioner of Indian Affairs Ely Parker replaced Dent with Brevet Colonel George S. Andrews and appointed Frederick E. Grossman as Pima agent to clean up the problems caused by unlicensed traders purchasing Pima wheat at fixed prices and offering shoddy trade goods.[7] Upon his arrival in October 1869, Grossman found much of the discontentment arose from the plans of White and Ruggles to develop the Gila River valley, with each receiving backing from Territorial Governor Richard C. McCormick, who recognized settlers in the valley were safe from Apache raids as long as the Pima were nearby.[8] Federal and territorial officials recognized the proximity of the Pima Reservation to Florence rendered such land "far more valuable to settlers than other lands throughout the territory."[9]

Lieutenant Colonel Roger Jones, assistant inspector general for the U.S. Army, raised the specter of war if Pima water concerns remained unaddressed. Jones predicted that in a low-flow year Pima crops "would be ruined for want of water." The continued waste of river water above the villages by settlers would "inevitably result in a collision." The Pima regarded the water "as much their property as the land they cultivate," Jones reminded Inspector General Randolph B. Marcy, and they watched the incursion of Mexicans and Americans "with an unfriendly eye."[10]

Already in June 1869, Secretary of the Interior Jacob Cox requested the U.S. Army to "remove all intruders from the reservation" and "to protect [the Pima] in their occupancy of the land, and in the right to the waters of the Gila for purposes of irrigation."[11] While the military protected Pima land and water, including the head of the Little Gila River, from encroachment, federal laws continued to encourage settlement in disregard of Pima rights.

The crisis erupted in 1869. Following a disastrous flood the previous year that destroyed three Pima villages, the Sacaton and Casa Blanca trading posts, and the Casa Blanca flour mill (Camp McDowell recorded 19.84 inches of rain during 1869), and a poor crop in 1869, the Pima openly resisted the settlers who encroached on their ancestral land above the reservation. A detachment of troops from Camp McDowell was sent to "quell the disturbance." In the fall, four hundred Indians, mainly Pima, left the reservation and claimed the fields of Mexican settlers near Adamsville.[12] Meanwhile, another group of Pima took up land above the reservation in an attempt to protect the headwaters of the Little Gila River. A third group clashed with settlers in October, demonstrating a Pima desire for the land immediately above their reservation. Diminished rainfall in 1870 left Pima crops in ruin, with Pima Chief Antonio Azul publicly admitting he could no longer preserve order among the Pima.[13] While the Pima did not war against the United States, they pressured the government to expand the reservation to include the land, water, and natural spring above the villages, each of which was fundamental to

FIGURE 5.1. Pima Chief Antonio Azul with his son Antonito and grandson Harry. (Photograph courtesy of San Carlos Irrigation Project)

their agricultural economy. Andrews sought to pacify the Pima by providing food and other goods to keep them peaceful.

By 1871, the situation was critical, with just 3.91 inches of rainfall. In October, newly appointed Pima Agent John H. Stout informed Vincent Colyer, chairman of the newly created national Board of Indian Commissioners, that no water reached the Pima fields. "The time for preparing their lands is now at hand," Stout continued, "but having no water they can do nothing."[14] While drought was a factor, the Indians blamed the settlers for diverting their water.

In despair, village captain Kihua Chinkum visited Stout and explained the challenges facing his people. For many years the Pima "lived from what they planted," but now they were facing water shortages and preparing to forcibly drive the Mexican and American settlers from the valley. After an hour of heated discussion, Stout convinced Kihua Chinkum that violence was foolish. Nevertheless, the Pima headman warned that if water was not forthcoming within the month, his people would join a number of Indian families that had settled along the Salt River. The next day, Ku-vit-ke-chin, chief of Va Vak village, announced that his village was removing to the Salt River, where water was in good supply.[15]

The water crisis created a test of goodwill between the seven hundred or so settlers above the reservation and the Pima. In August 1871, Grossman notified Herman Bendell, next in a series of territorial superintendents of Indian Affairs, that the Pima were leaving the reservation, stealing cattle and horses and destroying non-Indian crops. The only way to resolve their "just complaints" was to give the Indians "a certainty of water-privileges for irrigating purposes." This could be accomplished only by constructing "permanent dams of masonry" and "large irrigation canals, not ditches" that might direct water down both sides of the Gila so as to furnish sufficient irrigation.[16]

To ease the tensions along the Gila, Parker urged Secretary of the Interior Columbus Delano to statutorily enlarge the reservation by 81,140 acres. Although the military supported the proposition, territorial governors A.P.K. Safford and Richard C. McCormick opposed it.[17] On August 4, Andrews was ordered to survey the proposed extension. Azul stressed the return of 5,200 square miles (3,428,000 acres) of aboriginal land in central Arizona so the Pima might maintain their agricultural economy.[18]

Grossman's assessment of the situation highlighted the ongoing challenges. He informed Andrews that the Pima were promised by government agents that their claim for "more land and water" would be considered. A tone of frustration crept in when Grossman reminded his superiors that "the Indians asserted that years ago they had been promised a settlement of the water question; claimed that the whole Gila River valley had been the property of their forefathers from time immemorial, and asked that the settlers should not be allowed to occupy lands so long considered by the Indians as their property."[19] Fearing that without water the Indians would be "subject to such contingencies as may be produced by scarcity," Bendell supported Parker's idea of expanding the reservation.[20]

Government surveyors entered the field in April 1870 and surveyed an extension according to departmental limitations. Grossman reported the boundaries were "well known" to the Pima, who were anxious for Congress to act on the extension. One reason the Pima were anxious was because the proposed extension to the east encompassed the head of the

Little Gila River. This headwork was on land that settlers were cultivating, and land the Pima had to protect in order to ensure delivery of water to their lands on the south bank of the Gila.[21]

By fall, the survey was completed with every effort made to avoid "interference with the settlers and at the same time satisfy the reasonable demands of the Indians." Superintendent Andrews encouraged the Indian Service to act speedily to avoid further encroachments that would "lead to a collision." The danger was imminent that fall as the Gila River had been "very low all the season."[22]

The eastern extension included "nearly all the arable land and water privileges" proposed to be added to the reservation. In addition to "increas[ing] the Indians facilities for raising crops," the extension would also "quiet their complaints about the settlers using their water" and theoretically deprive the Pima of any reason to depredate. But while settlers along the Gila above the villages and in the Salt River valley were able to plant a second crop in the summer of 1871, downstream Pima farmers were left with inadequate water. In desperation, the Maricopa relocated off the reservation near the confluence of the Salt and Gila rivers, where they again planted their fields. The Pima drifted to the upper end of the reservation, searching for seepage water along the Gila.[23]

The Indian Service had ulterior motives for not diligently pursuing the extension of the reservation. While Parker cited the 1859 legislation recognizing the reservation as prohibiting any extension absent congressional approval, the government was working on a policy that would remove the Indians from Arizona to the Indian Territory. This policy was shaped by eastern humanitarians, public opinion, and the federal desire to develop the Gila and Salt River valleys.[24]

As the crisis intensified, public opinion shifted. No longer considered trusted allies, the Pima were called degenerate, insolent, and dangerous. The *Arizona Weekly Citizen* vowed that if the Indians did not cease their depredations in the Salt River valley there would "be such blood letting of the Pima kind as will cause a greater howl in the East than did the few drops [of Apache blood] shed near Camp Grant a short time ago."[25] Nor did the Pima view the Americans as they once had. While the Pima had taken "pleasure in feeding and assisting travelers," they were now "reserved and uncommunicative," fearing the loss of their land, economy, and water.[26]

In March 1872, Brigadier General Oliver Otis Howard arrived to initiate President Grant's Peace Policy among the Arizona tribes.[27] Pima missionary Charles H. Cook met Howard at Fort Yuma and accompanied him up the Gila and Salt rivers to Camp McDowell, where the two met with General George Crook, commander of the Department of Arizona. Howard visited the Pima Reservation on the second of May, finding the Pima restless and complaining that settlers continued diverting their water. Howard informed Delano that a large number of Pima and Maricopa had moved to the Salt River valley, causing still more problems. "Pima horses get upon a farm," Howard explained, "they are taken up or shot; retaliation comes, a house is burned, and the Pimas, as a whole, are blamed."[28] Howard suggested several possible solutions to the ongoing water problem.

Howard's first alternative was for the government to extend the eastern boundary of the reservation to include the area around Adamsville, although he advised against this as it would involve the expense of buying up existing land claims and would not resolve the water question. Second, the government could extend the reservation as far east as Florence, encompassing Adamsville as well. Again, Howard discounted this alternative due to the costs of compensating settlers for improvements they had made on the land. Third, the federal government could construct two acequias upstream, one on each bank of the Gila, with a government agent ensuring a fair division of the water to all cultivators of the land. Howard dismissed this as noble, but impractical, as it would be "too difficult of execution even with an honest and skillful agent." The only viable option, Howard remarked, was to remove the Pima from the Gila River valley. "If water continues to fail here," the general concluded, "I recommend that steps be taken to place the Pimas where there is plenty of wood, water, and good land. It can be done either inside or outside of Arizona.[29]

Indian removal and consolidation of reservations were mainstays of federal Indian policy in the post–Civil War years. Eastern humanitarians proposed removal of tribes to the Indian Territory where they would be introduced to "civilization." More importantly, removal would open millions of acres to settlement. "Many tribes may thus be collected in the Present Indian territory," Felix Brunot of the Board of Indian Commissioners explained. "The larger the number that can thus be concentrated the better for the success" of abolishing tribal status and providing for land severalty.[30]

Removal became an obsession with Delano. He hoped to concentrate all American Indians in the Indian Territory. According to his calculations, 172,000 American Indians were living on 96,155,785 acres of land, or 559 acres per capita. Another 60,000 Indians were residing on 44,154,240 acres within the Indian Territory, or 630 acres per capita. "Could the entire Indian population of the country, excluding Alaska and those scattered among the states . . . be located in the Indian Territory," Delano asserted, "there would be 180 acres of land, per capita, for the entire number, showing there is an ample area of land to afford them all comfortable homes."[31]

Delano's proposal, while feasible on paper, was nothing more than wishful thinking. Congress had abandoned removal as an official federal policy, and short of tribal nations consenting on their own accord to relocate, there was little hope of effecting such policy. Unless the Indians cooperated in these humanitarian endeavors, Delano warned, they would be crushed by the inevitable tide of white emigration. Howard's proposal to remove the Pima, therefore, was hardly unusual.

At the completion of his visit to the villages, Howard urged Stout to persuade leading Pima men to visit the Indian Territory and see for themselves the abundance of water and the absence of "bad white men." Tell them that the government intends to take all the Indians to the Indian Territory, Howard explained to Stout, "as fast as they get ready to go."[32] Stout and fourteen Pima and Maricopa chiefs and headmen met in council on May 11 to discuss sending a delegation to the Indian Territory.

The Pima faced desperate times, with Stout noting that the water crisis was so severe that some of the Pima were living in their fields "eating their grain in a semi green state." These circumstances moved Azul, who desired to ensure the welfare of his people. With some facing hunger, Azul told Stout, "If it is as you say we think we would like to live there." The village leaders, however, remained distrustful. "You say this new country is a good place and you say you have not been there, now how do you know it is a good place—if there is plenty of water there?" Azul asked.[33]

Azul's comments point to another reality: intense pressure by Stout to persuade the Pima to consent to removal. The Indian Service, as evidenced by Delano's mathematics and Howard's rhetoric, searched for an expedient solution. Stout, as the local government representative, was responsible for implementing this policy. Azul consented to listening to any proposal both out of respect and from a position of increased dependency. Pima men and women were demoralized. Desperate conditions required desperate and seemingly ignominious considerations.

Despite their cynicism, the Indians agreed to make the trip, but only after Stout agreed to three conditions. First, the Pima wished to delay their departure until after the summer harvest, returning before the advent of cold weather. Second, they demanded that Stout accompany them in order to ensure their safe return to Arizona. Finally, they requested the presence of their longtime friend, interpreter, and agency farmer John D. Walker to advise them as to the quality of the land in the Indian Territory. Azul told Stout that when the government was prepared to send a delegation of headmen to the Indian Territory, they would be prepared to go. Nonetheless, Azul told Stout, "If the President could come here, he would see what we need." The chief preferred to speak directly to President Grant and "tell him [what we need] ourselves."

When three months passed with no word from Washington, the Indian leaders again gathered in council and petitioned Stout to lead a delegation to the Indian Territory.[34] "We have not raised enough grain to keep us through the year," Azul cried, "and we are afraid we will not raise as much next year." The chief complained of unscrupulous traders, such as William Bichard, who introduced whiskey to his people and abused Pima women through prostitution. Stout immediately urged Indian Commissioner Francis Walker to initiate removal. "As it is the intention of the Government to make all of its Indians independent, they should be afforded every reasonable facility to that end." Walker, aware that American settlers were conspiring to withhold the remaining flow of the Gila from the Pima, agreed with Stout's recommendation. The Pima would have to be influenced to desire change before Walker sought "authority or appropriations" for removal from Congress.[35]

Land and water were not the only reasons the government sought removal. Cloaked in the prevailing humanitarian principles, removal was a practical solution to the broader Indian Country–wide legal problems besetting the U.S. government, which continued to encourage settlement of the land at the expense of the Pima. The federal government created a crisis on the Gila River and then proposed a self-serving solution. The social and political forces of the Indian Service effectively disenfranchised the Pima and reduced them to poverty. The assumption of federal policy makers that Pima poverty was a natural or inevitable response to liberal economic forces, however, is specious. The Pima repeatedly demonstrated a desire and the ability to adapt their economy to new forces; they requested only a level playing field. Pima deprivation and poverty did not result from a natural disposition on the part of the Pima, but rather were a direct response to government policy. The removal policy was simply a symptom of a broader effort to disenfranchise the Pima from the national and local economy.

Some Pima (principally those with families) left the reservation on their own accord to gain an honest living. Others, however, refused to give up their birthright. Lacking water to grow crops, many young Indians who were idle fell prey to the whiskey peddler. Prostitution, unknown among the tribe just a decade earlier, rivaled the effects of alcohol. Stout believed that these evils arose out of "a poverty not known within the last few years." Political expediency called for a single solution: removal "beyond the reach of these contaminating influences."[36]

Meanwhile, some Indians discovered their own solution to the water issue. Beginning in 1870, a number of Pima settled in the Blackwater district, south and east of the reservation, where an alluvial spring provided water when the natural flow of the Gila diminished or disappeared. Movement away from the Gila River, and traditional villages, to areas where seepage water was available continued with the settlement of Gila Crossing in 1873 and Maricopa Colony in 1887 (the latter two sites were added to the reservation by executive order in 1879).[37] During the summer of 1873, 300 Pima and Maricopa moved to the Salt River valley and settled on what later became the Salt River Reservation. By August of that year, 1,300 Indians were residing off the reservation.[38]

Local settlers greeted each successive move off the reservation with a chorus of protest. Residents complained that whiskey made the Pima "troublesome and dangerous neighbors," that the reservation could not support the Indians, and that the Pima were constantly at war with the Apache. A decade earlier, the Pima were praised for their military maneuvers against the Apache; now they were condemned. Settlers demanded immediate removal of the Pima. Disavowing any "selfish motives," the settlers pointed out that the reservation lands were among the poorest in the territory and "would not be occupied for years to come if the Indians were removed."[39] The *Arizona Weekly Citizen* ominously warned that if the Indians continued to bother settlers, they would have to "do it over their dead bodies."[40]

In 1873, the Board of Indian Commissioners joined other officials favoring relocation of the Pima.[41] That summer, Commissioner Edward P. Smith authorized Stout to take a delegation to inspect the Indian Territory. "Much interest has been shown by the Indians in the question of their removal," Stout reported.[42] The Pima had, in fact, frequently debated the proposition over the winter. Azul eloquently expressed their dilemma when he asked Stout: "If we cannot go to the Salt River Valley (to grow crops) then what? We have no food and you cannot feed us."[43] Nonetheless, Stout persisted. If the Pima were satisfied with the appearance of the territory and if favorable terms of removal could be agreed upon, would they prepare to emigrate? Several factors influenced the Pima: limited rainfall, upstream diversion of water, and cries of hunger from their children.[44] While limited precipitation impacted settlers as well, due to their upstream location they were able to draw water from the river when needed. Settlers in the Salt River valley were in much better condition, due to a steady flow in the Salt River.

Although Stout sought to take a delegation to the Indian Territory that spring, he was denied permission due to insufficient funding. When Delano approved funding in June, Smith authorized Stout to take five Pima and Maricopa leaders, rather than the fourteen the Indians requested.[45] Anticipating an early August departure, and arrival in the Indian Territory during "its grain producing condition," rather than when it was cold and barren, Stout and the Indians were again chagrined when the necessary funds for the trip were not available until mid-September.

On September 23, 1873, Stout accompanied John D. Walker and a delegation of five Pima and Maricopa leaders, including Antonio Azul, to the Indian Territory. There the group "prospected" a new reservation west of the Iowa and Sac and Fox agencies in central Indian Territory (see map 5.1).[46] Stout reported the delegates were "much pleased with the visit, and entirely satisfied with the appearance of the country." After selecting a "suitable reservation," the delegates returned to Arizona. But back home the following year, Stout reported that removal "had not

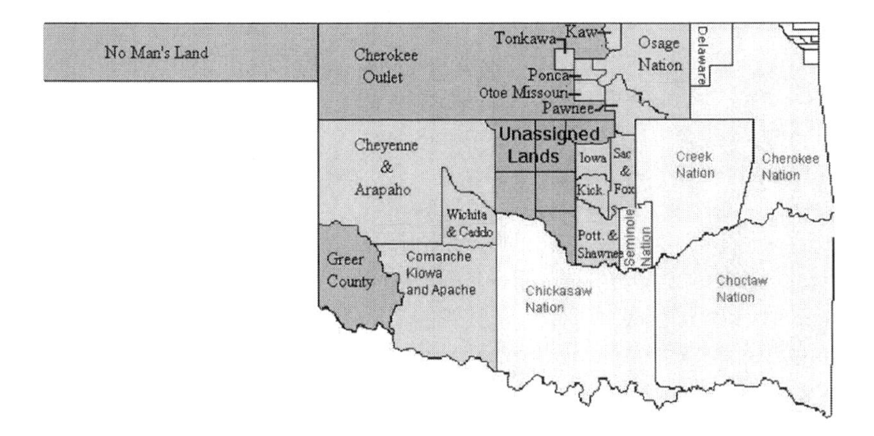

MAP 5.1. Proposed removal to the Indian Territory. In 1873, the Pima visited the unassigned lands just west of the Iowa and Sac and Fox agencies. (Oklahoma Genealogical Society, Oklahoma City, 2006)

been as generally discussed by the two tribes as would be supposed." Abundant rainfall that winter dampened the Indians' enthusiasm for abandoning their homeland, with winter flooding destroying much of the Pima's small grain crop.[47]

Many tribal members objected to removal on the grounds that the Indian Territory was too cold and distant from their present home. Tribal elders were concerned that the new country might be unhealthy or that they might die en route; removal would also mean living among strangers, far from their burial and traditional grounds. These sites intertwined the sacred nature of the spiritual landscape with the Pima conception of the cosmos, which was central in determining the physical and spiritual health of the people and providing them with sense of place anchored in the land.[48] Younger men, influenced by the stories of the traders, feared they would either freeze to death or be killed by hostile neighbors. More alarming were concerns that once the Indians gave up their reservation in Arizona, the government would renege on its promise of land in the Indian Territory. Nonetheless, "Should the Department continue its offer of removal," Stout informed Smith, "I believe that some of the Indians will go next year, and that that number will be augmented from time to time, until the entire tribes have been removed."[49]

Despite Stout's optimism, the *San Francisco Evening Bulletin* and the *Arizona Weekly Citizen* both dismissed the prospect of removal.[50] The *Bulletin* reported on December 30, 1873, that the Pima delegation had declared their present reservation "far preferable to any which they visited during their trip."[51] The *Citizen* likewise speculated that the Pima were unlikely to consent to the move.[52]

Notwithstanding Stout's assertion that some Indians were willing to emigrate, Smith notified Delano that he had been unable to secure the consent of the tribe, "or any portion of it," to remove to the Indian Territory. He went on to point out that previous removals had been effected through compulsion or affected only those tribes residing in states bordering the Indian Territory. Since the Indian Service contemplated the voluntary removal of all tribes—indeed, it was in the process of removing the Pawnees from Nebraska and seeking the consent of the Arikarees from Dakota Territory—Smith was concerned that the consent of the tribes would not be secured. He feared that "the prospect of inducing any large number of Indians [to] voluntarily . . . settle in the Indian Territory is not encouraging, and cannot safely be made the basis of any general plan for future relief or civilization of Indians."[53]

The winter of 1873–1874 witnessed a threefold increase in precipitation over the previous year, with 16.83 inches of rain in 1874. With the rain, many of the Pima who left the reservation seeking employment or relocated to the Salt River returned to tend to their crops.[54] The fall harvest produced 50,000 bushels (3,000,000 pounds) of wheat, 4,000 bushels (240,000 pounds) of barley and 500 bushels (30,000 pounds) of corn. With the sudden return of prosperity, the Pima lost interest in abandoning their farms along the Gila.

Smith then proposed that the Department of the Interior either recognize Pima water rights or remove them to the Colorado River Indian Reservation, the latter of which was endorsed by Territorial Governor Safford.[55] "This latter course is deemed entirely practical," Smith informed Delano, "if consent of the Indians can be obtained, and such legislation can be procured as will secure a fair compensation for their present reservation and afford the means necessary to establish them comfortably on the Colorado River reserve."[56]

The Pima water supply continued to be sufficient until the summer of 1875. In June, the river failed, and by the end of the month, it slowed to a trickle and on the western end of the reservation it was dry. More ominously, the recent discovery of high-grade copper east of the reservation increased the diversion of water from the river system. It would be only a matter of time, Stout warned Smith, before "the greater portion of the water of that stream will be used up by the whites, and the Indians will become dependent on the Government for support."[57] In Smith's view, rather than adopting the moral position of protecting Pima water by enforcing their rights, the mineral discoveries upstream compounded the urgency of removal.[58]

Diminished rainfall beginning in the summer of 1875 continued through 1883, adding to the hardships. While the Pima in virgin-flow conditions dealt with drought, low-flow water remained available to irrigate their crops. As upstream settlement increased, this flow dried up or was so diminished as to make ineffective the Pima irrigation system. By 1876, over two hundred Indian families were living in the Blackwater district above the reservation. In May, reports of crop failures across the reservation led to discussions of administratively adding the Blackwater lands to the reservation as the "easiest solution of the vexed question of 'water supply.'" Indian Agent Charles Hudson believed the measure would be necessary only "until these Indians form a more intelligent view of what is for their real good, and may be induced to consent to removal."[59] In August, a presidential executive order attached the nine-thousand-acre Blackwater district to the reservation, protecting the head of the Little Gila River and the Blackwater spring.[60]

Despite meager precipitation and increased diversions, the Pima cultivated "an excellent article of wheat" on seven thousand to eight thousand acres of land. The summer of 1877, however, turned into one of the warmest and driest in decades. Writing in August, Stout lamented to Commissioner of Indian Affairs Ezra Hayt that it was already too late for rain to help summer crops. "What has been planted has already dried up," he observed, "and the Indians will make no further attempt this season."[61] With the near-complete failure of summer crops, Pima grain sales ended. Stout sought permission to take twelve or fifteen of the "best practical farmers" among the Pima and examine the Colorado River Indian Reservation.[62]

The exodus from the reservation increased as the water crisis deepened. By 1877, five hundred Pima were supporting themselves on "good land and plenty of water" in the Salt River valley. Alarmed residents again petitioned the Indian Office and Congress to remove the Indians to the Gila River Reservation. When Hayt urged Stout to comply, the agent objected that to do so would cause "great suffering." Instead, Stout asked to settle these Indians on unclaimed public land under the provisions of an 1875 law that applied to Indians who abandoned their tribal relationship. Doing so, Stout asserted, would protect them in their property rights.[63] By the winter of 1878, less than one-quarter of the Pima's fields were irrigated, with no harvest projected below Sacaton.[64] Stout informed Hayt that the Indian Office had to allow the Pima to move to the Salt River valley where they could grow crops, or the government would have to feed between 1,000 and 1,500 Indians at an estimated cost of $25,000. The Pima, however, wished to remain self-sufficient, as evidenced by their movements off the reservation where they took up irrigable lands to cultivate. Their consolidation on the eastern end of the reservation further illustrated their desire to maintain an agrarian economy. "The Indians do not wish to become dependent," Stout stressed. If they were "given a chance" they would remain self-sufficient.[65]

Hayt's appointment as commissioner of Indian Affairs during the administration of Rutherford B. Hayes infused new life into the removal issue. The commissioner urged the immediate removal of all tribes from Arizona. "The government has been paying between eight and ten cents per pound for the transportation of flour and other necessaries to feed the Indians," Hayt noted, "and the total cost of maintaining the Indian tribes of Arizona for the past three years has been $1,084,000." Furthermore, Hayt viewed the Indians as "uneasy and restless" and "constantly moving about," on and off the reservation.[66]

The government's objective was twofold. By consolidating tribes in the Indian Territory, Hayt could reduce the number of agencies and the expense of maintaining the Indians. Furthermore, removal and consolidation would also "protect" the Indians' personal and property rights. Moreover, the sale of vacated lands would defray the costs of removal, with enough left over to relieve Congress of "direct appropriations" for the Indians' future support.[67] As a start, Hayt drafted a bill to remove the northern tribes to the Indian Territory and sent it to the House of Representatives Committee on Indian Affairs.

The commissioner urged Secretary of the Interior Carl Schurz to submit to Congress a bill for the removal of the Arizona, Colorado, and New Mexico tribes.[68] Hayt estimated the cost of removal at $25,000, $5,000 of which would be used to purchase agricultural implements. The proposal gained traction when the territorial assembly memorialized Congress to compel the Pima to "be removed from said Salt River" and returned to their reservation on the Gila, where they should be "forced to remain."[69]

In March 1878, Hayt dispatched Indian Inspector E. C. Watkins to the Pima Reservation. Facing the pangs of hunger, the Pima did not ask for handouts and watched the unfolding crisis with "despondent hearts." "They have never been fed by the Government," Watkins asserted, "and do not ask for it. But they do ask 'How are we to maintain our families?'" Many Pima men had taken up wage labor in the Salt River valley or Florence, while others worked in the mines or on ranches, where they were praised for their "willingness and capacity for labor." Watkins concluded that "to insist upon a strict enforcement of the policy of the government by confining these Indians to their reservations, would, under existing circumstances, be an act of inhumanity, unless they were furnished regularly with rations."[70]

That same month, Stout convened another council to obtain Pima consent to immediate removal. With almost half of the five thousand Indians residing off the reservation due to insufficient water, the agent believed the time had come for a solution to the crisis.[71] "Their only hope of salvation from a speedy extinction," Stout argued, "lies in their early exodus to the Indian Territory." Still the Indians hesitated. Several suggested that two or three tribal citizens be sent ahead to "prospect" the land, a request Stout was inclined to grant. The visit would be "timely and reasonable," and in view of the growing crisis, the agent urged the government to take every practical step to bring about the removal.[72] Hayt agreed and approved of the visit, pending a special appropriation by Congress.[73]

Although some Pima prepared to remove, Stout recognized that they would not "take kindly to the thought of leaving their old homes and haunts, and a climate to which they have become so thoroughly accustomed."[74] Moreover, some of the Indians occupied considerable tracts of land in the Salt River valley, where Stout recommended allotting them land in severalty until removal was completed. "They are in danger of losing [their farms]," he reminded Hayt, "for as these lands become valuable by cultivation, they are coveted by the white man." If the government protected their homesteads, Stout believed, the Pima "could maintain their independence until such a time as they could be removed."[75]

By the summer of 1878, the western half of the reservation was dry, with no crops raised. "If the white settlements east of this reserve increase in the next few years as they have in the past," Stout wrote to Hayt, "it will never again support the Indians." More Pima left the reservation so "that they might not hear their women and children cry for bread."[76] As a short-term solution, Stout suggested the government set aside a reservation, "temporary or otherwise," in the Salt River valley. The "Indians have some rights," he reminded Hayt, "and morally if not legally, they have a right to be where they are."[77]

In this context, the U.S. Army intervened on behalf of the Pima. Major General Irvin McDowell, having commanded Pima and Maricopa troops a decade earlier, informed the adjutant general of the army that the Indians had always "been our true steadfast friends." They had served as scouts against the Apache, protected the overland mail routes, and provided the food stores upon which the military and emigrants depended for many years. But now settlers above the reservation who knew little of their deeds had deprived them of their water. "If they have done anything wrong to any whites," McDowell explained, "I am confident they must have been driven to it by great want."[78] Secretary of War George McCrary responded by instructing General of the Army William Tecumseh Sherman to investigate Pima conditions. Sherman in turn ordered McDowell, commanding the Military Division of the Pacific, to protect the Pima "against violent actions on the part of the settlers."[79]

The task of investigating the crisis fell upon the shoulders of Captain Adna R. Chaffee, stationed at Camp McDowell. While acknowledging that the Pima wantonly traveled in the Salt River valley, Chaffee learned that settlers were planning to seize improved lands from the Indians, complete with canals and crops. This "is nothing more nor less than a legal steal," the captain reported. While the Pima were entitled to homestead on public lands, they were ignorant of filing land entries. This encouraged unscrupulous settlers to evict them from improved lands, some of which had been cultivated for years. While some "squatters" were forcibly evicted by armed Pima men protecting their property, others managed to take legal possession of the land. Still others coordinated with local officials, perpetrating a "great crime towards the Pima." More than one thousand Pima lived north of the Salt River, harvesting more than three hundred thousand pounds of wheat in 1878. On the south bank of the Salt River near the Mormon village of Lehi were twenty-eight Maricopa families cultivating the soil. Chaffee recommended 1,520 acres be set aside as a reservation for these Indians. An additional fifty-one Maricopa families lived twelve miles downstream above the confluence of the Salt and Gila rivers, where they cultivated 300 acres.[80]

On December 3, 1878, Colonel Orlando B. Willcox of Camp McDowell forwarded Chaffee's report to McDowell, adding that the deprivation of the Pima and Maricopa was a direct result of "the Government which threw open the upper Gila for settlement." The Pima, Willcox explained, "were fairly and legally entitled to the water and the diversion of it [by settlers] constitutes an act, which if done [against] citizens, would be contrary to law." In the colonel's view, the United States had to restore the water to the Pima or provide them with comparable arable land and water. Furthermore, to remove the Indians, as the Indian Service contemplated, was immoral. "Have we a right to transplant them against their wishes?" Without water, the Pima could not be "useful members of the community" and would become "vagabonds to starve or fight."[81] The only solution was to halt all sale of public land in the Salt River valley and set some portion of it aside as a reservation for the Pima and Maricopa.

A day later, Willcox telegraphed McDowell regarding the territorial water case of *Kelsey v. McAteer*. McDowell immediately forwarded the message to Sherman in Washington, D.C., adding that, according to the territorial court, the "diversion of water above prior settlements was illegal." "All public lands on the Salt River [should] be withheld from entry, sale, pre-emption or homestead," McDowell pleaded. To quiet the tension, McDowell asked Sherman for an immediate answer as to how to proceed. Territorial Governor John C. Frémont concurred with McDowell's assessment.[82]

While McDowell initially took the perspective that restoring water to the Pima was impractical because it would lead to a series of long, drawn-out lawsuits, he had a change of heart later that same day. In a second telegram to Sherman, the commanding general explained, "It may be inconvenient and cause delay as do all appearances to courts, but it would be an outrage to suffer them to be deprived of their rights." The Pima had to be restored in their rights to all that they were "lawfully and equitably entitled to."[83] The United States opened the territory above the Pima Reservation for settlement, McDowell wrote Sherman, and in the process it deprived the Indians of "their water for their farms by Act of Government."

But while it sold the land, the government did not sell the water which the Pima "had hitherto used for their lands, for it did not belong to the Government to sell." In a clear declaration of the matter, McDowell pointedly reminded Sherman that the Pima retained "a right and use [of the water] which [they] had when they came within the limits of the United States, and which they have not lost."[84] Sherman's reply was succinct: "Can you immediately support the manner in which the water can be turned back onto the reservation as appears right and just to the Indians without conflict with the whites, or without a long lawsuit?"[85]

Two days before Christmas, McDowell replied to Sherman, asking him to speak with the president regarding the protection of Pima land and water. "These Indians have been driven from their lands on the Gila," McDowell told Sherman, and according to the laws "on this coast and in Arizona [this is] illegal." Now called "renegades" and "savage intruders," the Pima must "steal or labor for their subsistence where . . . they can gain it. The United States should at once take measures by injunction or otherwise to restore to these Indians the rights to water to which they are entitled."[86]

Sherman informed McDowell that he had forwarded his letter to the secretary of the interior, who promised a decision on the matter before the end of January. "It seems he has had some plan of inducing these Indians to remove to the Indian Territory," Sherman explained.[87] McDowell then immediately appealed for justice. "We have no more right to deport them than we have to send farmers from the Connecticut Valley to Arizona." The government proposed to civilize the Indians, McDowell argued. "Well these Indians have long since taken the first giant step."[88]

McDowell persuasively argued his point, and in January 1879, President Hayes halted the sale of public land in the Salt River valley and, via executive order, added the unsold portions to the Pima Reservation. The expanded reservation extended east two miles on either bank of the Salt River from its junction with the Gila to the western boundary of the White Mountain Apache Reservation, over one hundred miles to the east and encompassing the towns of Phoenix, Tempe, and Hayden's Ferry.[89] Territorial Governor Frémont publicly joined the territorial assembly in protesting the action and called on Secretary Schurz to return the land to the public domain.[90] The territorial legislature appropriated funds to send the governor and Arizona Supreme Court Justice Charles Silent to Washington, D.C., to persuade the president to rescind his order.[91]

At the start of 1879, the Salt River valley stood on the verge of an agricultural explosion. The Southern Pacific Railroad had reached thirty miles east of Yuma and would reach Maricopa Junction by April. New lands were developed and prospects for expansion seemed unlimited. In February, the *Phoenix Herald* sounded the alarm bell: with the new reservation, settlers would be disenfranchised and liquor sales prohibited within the limits of the newly expanded reservation.[92] Even Captain Chaffee feared too much land had been reserved. "The Indians will gain nothing by holding sections, half sections, etc., of land here and there, surrounded on every side by white settlers." Fearful the land would remain "a barren waste," the captain warned "one title or the other must be extinguished, for the present, I assume, the settlers must be ousted."[93] Frémont continued to argue removal, opining "that the whole Salt River Valley and the Gila River should be left to the white people, and the Indians withdrawn to the Colorado River."[94]

In April, McDowell publicly responded to Frémont. "This proposition appears to me to bid no good to the peace of Arizona, and will, if consummated, no matter how, inflict, I believe a great wrong upon a peaceful, most friendly, hard working, self-supporting people." Depriving them of their water, McDowell argued, "was illegal." Quoting from the *Kelsey v. McAteer* decision, McDowell was adamant: "The fact that the appropriator does not irrigate all of his arable land during the first years following the appropriation does not affect his right."[95] Secretary Schurz was clear but indifferent: "The Indians must be permitted to subsist themselves—there is no appropriation for their support."

Bowing to political pressure, Hayes backed off and issued a new executive order in June that expanded the reservation northwest along the Gila River to its junction with the Salt River and then four miles up the Salt. This more-modest addition included the Maricopa village of Sacate on the Gila River and Maricopa Colony on the Salt River. Hayes also designated a separate, non-contiguous reservation on the Salt River south of Camp McDowell, encompassing the present-day Salt River Pima-Maricopa Reservation.

Despite additional land, the Pima continued to suffer from a shortage of water. In the summer of 1879, Indian Inspector John H. Hammond reported the Gila was dry and dusty. "[E]ven the increased Reservation will not prevent suffering because the laws of the Territory give the water to the oldest ditch. There is no water for the old Indian ditches."[96] Despite McDowell's plea for justice, Pima water and their agricultural economy remained in jeopardy.

Congress, meanwhile, continued debating the removal of the southwestern tribes.[97] In December 1878, Congressman James Throckmorton (D-TX) introduced an amendment to the Indian appropriation bill to prohibit the removal of any tribes from Arizona.[98] The amendment passed by a vote of seventy-one to sixty, and in February the bill became law.[99] Three years later, President Chester A. Arthur added lands south and west of the Gila River to the Pima Reservation. The following year, he issued another executive order, doubling the size of the reservation from 180,000 to 360,000 acres. However well-intentioned, the government's actions failed to address the longstanding concerns of the Pima. It was water more than land the Indians needed to sustain their economy.[100]

CHAPTER 6

Famine and Starvation

BY 1880, THE SURFACE FLOW of the Gila River was insufficient to sustain the Pima economy, with many families lacking domestic water. Half of the Indians moved off the reservation to work. Indian Agent A. B. Ludlam reported that for the first time the U.S. government purchased wheat for "destitute Indians."[1] Sixty-seven-year-old Pima elder Chir-Purtke reflected on these difficulties, noting the Pima were unable "to irrigate all our fields. We were forced to abandon them little by little."[2] The Pima had "ample lands," but lacked water and feared the destruction of their "pride as independent and self-supporting people."[3]

The Pima dealt with a variety of challenges in the latter years of the nineteenth century. Foremost among these were trespassers "who refuse[d] the Indians the use of water."[4] This was compounded as the population of the territory increased. Between 1870 and 1910 the territorial population increased twentyfold to 204,354. As importantly, the amount of improved agricultural land increased twenty-four-fold to 350,173 acres.[5] With most of these acres in the Safford, Gila River, Florence–Casa Grande, and Salt river valleys, the impact on the Pima was direct and dramatic. Indian Agent Claude Johnson opined that "considering the vast surrender of national wealth made by these Indians . . . the best aid that can be given to [them] . . . is the extension of their irrigation facilities."[6] Johnson asked that an engineer evaluate the prospects for a modern irrigation system.

U.S. Bureau of Indian Affairs Pima Agency Superintendent John B. Alexander echoed the concerns heard so often before. "The reservation contains good irrigable lands but lacks the chief essential—water."[7] One of the reasons for the diminished flow of water was the construction of the Florence Canal in 1886, which diverted nearly all the remaining surface flow of the Gila River above the reservation (see map 6.1). Upper

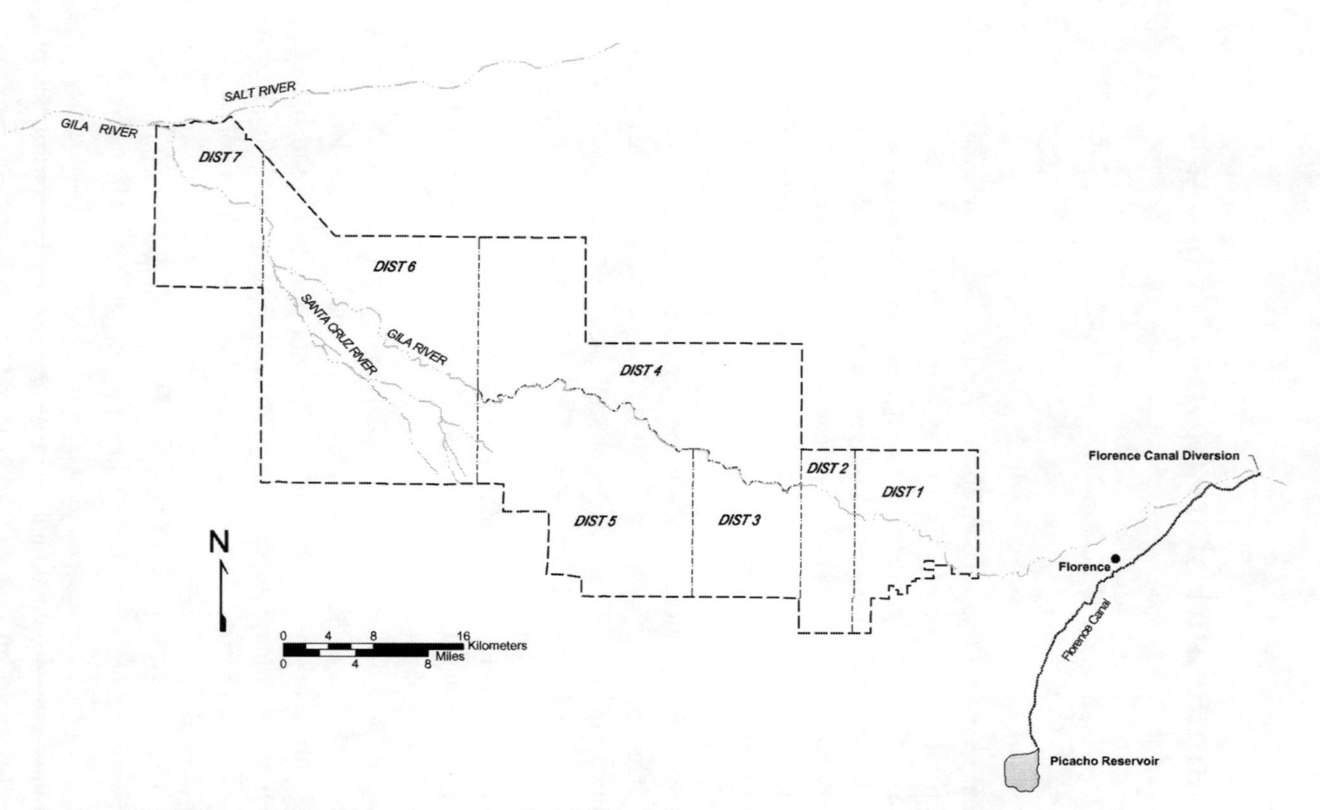

MAP 6.1. The Florence Canal and Picacho Reservoir, 1889.

Gila River valley users in Safford and Solomonville placed increasingly high demands on the waters of the river, as shown in table 6.1.[8]

Indian Inspector Robert Gardner recommended to Secretary of the Interior Henry Teller, in 1886, that the Florence Canal not be constructed since it would "benefit a few speculators to the loss and detriment of four or five thousand Indians."[9] Teller requested the U.S. Geological Survey (USGS) evaluate the situation, with the USGS concluding "if the agriculture of the Indians now on the reservation is to have normal growth [the] greater part, and perhaps the whole of the waters of the Gila will be necessary therefore." The federal agency admitted "the construction of a dam by the Florence Canal Company . . . will give the control substantially of all the water of the Gila River [to the canal company] and if the owners of the dam carry the water right also, they can deliver the water to the reservation or not, as best suits their plans." If the waters of the Gila River were cut off, Pima lands "would become uninhabitable."[10]

The Florence Canal Company, fearful of being denied a right to divert water, promised it would not diminish the amount of water currently used by the Indians. Both the USGS and the U.S. attorney general agreed to this, but did not quantify the area farmed or the amount of water used. Without this data, it was impossible to determine Pima

TABLE 6.1. Percentage Use of Gila River Natural and Floodwater Flow, Select Years, 1866–1918

Year	Pima Reservation	Florence–Casa Grande	Safford-Solomonville
1866	100.00	0.00	0.00
1878	73.60	11.23	13.57
1892	48.27	9.79	35.38
1901	42.69	10.90	36.56
1910	37.99	10.50	41.30
1914	36.38	13.00	40.71
1918	29.50	28.64	33.62

Source: "Gila River Priority Analysis, Water Distribution Chart #3," United States Indian Service, Irrigation, January 20, 1926, San Carlos Irrigation Project Archives.
Notes: Percentages do not total 100 because smaller users were omitted. Percentages were calculated by default after Florence–Casa Grande, Safford–Solomonville, and other smaller users were subtracted. This amount represents the total available flow (natural and flood), not the amount that actually reached the reservation boundary.

rights. In the meantime, the USGS admitted the natural flow of the Gila was "all appropriated now by the white settlers above" the reservation.[11]

Secretary of the Interior Lucius Q. C. Lamar requested that the U.S. attorney general "take such steps under the Federal or Territorial laws as might be necessary to protect the Indians in their rights." The U.S. district attorney for Arizona Territory did not recommend litigation be brought against the Florence Canal Company until data on acreage and water flow was quantified. It was three decades before this data was fully gathered. Rather than litigating Pima water rights, Superintendent Alexander opined that the twenty to thirty thousand dollars needed to prosecute Pima rights was too steep to warrant the effort. Commissioner of Indian Affairs William Jones concurred, and notified the attorney general that the Indian Service would pursue no further legal action.[12]

A policy of neglect followed. Since the Pima Reservation remained in communal ownership, the federal government was in no hurry to protect water rights for the tribe, desiring instead to allot land and appurtenant water rights in severalty. Without an adequate and assured supply of water to irrigate the land and make it productive, however, the reservation could not be allotted.

The allotment policy grew out of the assimilation era in the post–Civil War years. By the 1880s, it was no longer a question of whether allotment in severalty would occur, but when it would occur. The theory was premised on assigning each American Indian a tract of land, generally 160 acres in size but at the discretion of the president, with a twenty-five-year federal trust period. At the expiration of the trust period, the landowner would hold a fee simple patent to the land and be subject to all state and local authority, including property taxation. Allotment became official in 1887, when Congress enacted the General Allotment Act.

Following the lead of Congress, the Indian Service operated under the theory that reservations would be dissolved after their lands were divided in severalty. At such point, American Indians would take their place in the American polity as citizens without any special right that may have been encumbered while in tribal status. In the meantime, more farmers in the Upper Gila River valley, encouraged to acquire public domain lands under the provisions of the 1877 Desert Land Act and required to make them productive with the waters of the Gila River, diverted additional water, increasing their take of the river from 13.57

percent to 41.3 percent of the flow between 1878 and 1910. The Pima were on the brink of complete economic displacement, seeing their share of river water decline 62 percent by 1910.[13] Scores of Pima farms were abandoned or yielded "scant and uncertain returns."[14]

To the north of the reservation, settlers in the Salt River valley organized the Salt River Valley Water Storage Committee to resolve water rights conflicts, identify potential dam sites, and lobby Congress.[15] In 1901, the Maricopa County Board of Water Storage Commissioners was established to identify ways of floating county bonds to build a storage reservoir on the Salt River. Settlers in the Florence–Casa Grande valleys were convinced that the federal obligation to restore water to the Pima would ensure support for their reservoir demands. So pervasive was this belief that members of Congress believed the first federal reclamation project would be on the Gila River for the benefit of the Pima.[16]

Congress debated the role and extent of federal support for, and involvement in, financing reclamation projects across the West. While a series of reclamation bills was introduced in Congress, none provided direct federal support to construct storage reservoirs. The Carey Act became law in 1894 and provided grants of federal land to individual states, which sold the land and used the proceeds to finance reclamation projects.[17] Territorial Governor Nathan Oakes Murphy was a catalyst in such grants, opposing direct federal involvement, fearing it would impede local control.[18]

Congress also authorized water resource investigations of western streams. The USGS set out to quantify water supplies, identify potential reservoir sites, and map areas that could potentially be irrigated. In 1890, hydrologist Frederick Newell arrived in Arizona to consider reservoir sites in the Salt and Gila river basins. By 1893, he teamed up with Charles Walcott, director of the USGS, and Arthur Davis, a hydrologic engineer, and formulated a national irrigation policy that was conspicuous in that it did not include Indian Country. While the Indian Service encouraged Indian agriculture, it did little to secure or protect the water necessary for its success.[19]

In 1895, Congress appropriated $3,500 for the USGS to conduct an irrigation study for the Pima Reservation. Newell assigned Davis to head the study and, in his report to Walcott, Davis noted that outside of forcing upstream water users to "turn back into the river an amount of water equal to that formerly employed by the Indians," the only real option to providing water to the Pima was to build a masonry dam at a site on the Gila River capable of storing at least 200,000 acre-feet of water. While considering a site on Queen Creek, a storage capacity of just 27,000 acre-feet doomed the proposal. More appropriate was consideration of a site at The Buttes, twenty-five miles above the reservation on the Gila River, with an estimated storage capacity of 208,000 acre-feet, enough to provide water for the Pima and "leave a large surplus to be sold to settlers on Government lands under the canal system," demonstrating the liberal nature of government policies that advocated settlement before addressing issues of Indian water rights. Davis further illustrated this when he opined that it was impractical to return the flow of the river to the Pima. "The Government has taken no steps to protect the prior claims of the Indians to the water," Davis argued, "and, on the other hand, has acquiesced in its diversions to the lands which it has disposed to other parties along the stream." There were then some seven thousand acres irrigated under the Florence Canal above the reservation. This land, Davis noted, "would be rendered barren by its being deprived of water."[20]

At the same time, the New York–based Hudson Reservoir and Canal Company secured a right of way across the reservation to deliver Salt River water to the Casa Grande Valley.[21] As part of its right-of-way agreement with the federal government, the company agreed to deliver water to Pima farmers whose lands abutted the canal.[22] Despite grand plans, a national depression and the difficulty in raising $3,000,000 in capital forced the company to abandon the site.[23]

A number of territorial and federal officials sought and expected federal support for a dam on the Gila River. While for the benefit of the Pima, such a project would also encourage the development of off-reservation lands.[24] Territorial Governor Louis C. Hughes energetically encouraged the United States to construct a storage dam on the Gila River. Playing on the water needs of the Pima, Hughes envisioned a project that would irrigate five hundred thousand acres of land in the Gila River and Casa Grande valleys. This would "supply all the land required by these Indians for all time to come" and allow "a bonus" of off-reservation land to be "served with water from the proposed reservoir." Hughes foresaw more than four million families making their homes in Arizona.[25]

Indian Inspector William Junkin recommended the Indian Service protect Pima water rights "before encroachments of the white men have deprived [them] of their prior rights." Special Agent Franklin Armstrong reminded Secretary of the Interior Ethan Allen Hitchcock the Pima "must have water for irrigation or starve."[26] While Congress appropriated $20,000 for the USGS to evaluate and study two proposed dam sites, it refused to commit to any project.[27] "Until the time comes when the Government is ready and willing to come to the assistance of [the Pima]," Indian Agent J. Roe Young complained, "I consider any further discussion of the subject unnecessary."[28] Even Walcott noted the "matter of obtaining a permanent [water] supply for these Indians is one which has been before the Department in one form or another for fourteen years." While Congress introduced a bill appropriating $1,000,000 to study the San Carlos site, it failed to enact it, instead appropriating another $30,000 for the "support of the Indians at the Pima Agency."[29]

The $30,000 appropriation was critical because of events both upstream of, and far removed from, the reservation. The entire Gila watershed was undergoing an ecologic transformation. Beginning with the near extinction of the beaver from the watershed, erosion, gullying, and silting had significantly increased with the loss of upstream mountainous forest canopies. Other factors impacting the flow of water and disrupting its natural recharge included forest fires and the destruction of native grasses through overgrazing.[30]

But there were other changes adding to the stress of the Pima. Using available surface water, the Pima grew sufficient food on which to subsist, but they were completely marginalized from the local economy. Hay, or alfalfa, was becoming the primary cash crop in central Arizona, with barley the main cereal crop. With the Salt River valley having access to outside markets by rail and with wheat now grown in the valley, the Pima wheat market declined. The Pima, unaware of these changes, continued to cultivate wheat.[31]

After 1890, the Pima were limited to a single winter crop. The completion of the Florence Canal in 1889 left the Pima dependent on tailwater and the river's underflow that was forced to the surface in various locations. The largest of these underground springs was near Blackwater; this explains why many Pima moved to the eastern end of the reservation at this time. Seepage water, also found at Sweetwater near the center of the reservation and Komatke on the western end, was "not very good" and resulted in reduced yields.[32] The Pima grew less than two-thirds of their normal crop.[33]

While drought was not a new phenomenon, the fact that in the 1890s it was prefaced with increasing upstream diversions made conditions on the reservation harsher. Between 1889 and 1901, upstream settlers added 14,654 acres of new irrigated farmland, representing 86 percent of the new land developed (see table 6.2). What water was left in the river increasingly failed to flow on the reservation or came as floods in short ephemeral bursts. Seepage into the sandy alluvium claimed more water than what arrived on the reservation.[34] Summer crops failed eleven times between 1892 and 1904, and winter crops failed five times between 1899 and 1904, marking the years between 1892 and 1904 as the years of starvation. A Pima calendar stick for 1898–1899 noted: "There was no crop this year."

By 1900, Pima Agency physician George J. Fanning reported "more than the usual number of deaths among the Indians during the past year, owing, I believe, to a lack of water." The result was an increased "state

TABLE 6.2. New Acres with Priority Rights to Water, 1889–1901

Year	Florence–Casa Grande	Safford-Solomonville	Pima Reservation
1889	205	1,919	130
1890	143	865	233
1891	974	888	110
1892	400	603	105
1893	326	372	105
1894	192	240	105
1895	740	568	473
1896	310	993	90
1897	0	1,110	90
1898	38	790	90
1899	5	690	90
1900	0	1,074	340
1901	40	668	155
Total	3,373	10,781	2,116

Source: "Gila River Priority Analysis, Water Distribution Chart #1 and #2," United States Indian Service, Irrigation, January 20, 1926, San Carlos Irrigation Project Archives.

of semi-starvation and scurvy."[35] While not completely dependent on cultivated crops for food, the Pima diet was rapidly changing. Pima children suffered from malnutrition and nutritional deficiencies. More than one elderly couple was found dead in their home without any food in their storehouse. As proud people, the Pima "preferred to starve rather than beg."[36]

Diversions compounded by drought conditions became acute in the spring of 1891 after a disastrous winter flood in 1890–1891. While the Pima grew six million pounds (one hundred thousand bushels) of winter grain in 1889–1890, they grew just half that amount in 1890–1891. Conditions were serious enough that Inspector Junkin recommended the purchase of thirteen thousand pounds of flour and twenty-five hundred pounds of bacon for "destitute Indians."[37] By the fall of 1891, Arizona ranchers were shipping hundreds of thousands of cattle and horses out of the territory.[38] Nonetheless, more than twenty thousand head of steers were driven into the Salt River valley to forage on irrigated alfalfa, suggesting there was plenty of water in that valley.[39] Conditions on the Pima Reservation deteriorated to the point that the first large-scale cutting of mesquite trees began.

Every year after 1892, lasting through 1904, the Pima grew insufficient crops to sustain themselves. Indian Agent Cornelius Crouse estimated that one thousand Indians would raise no grain at all in 1893 and asked for departmental authority to purchase three hundred thousand pounds of wheat for subsistence and seed. About 5,000 acres of land were fenced and prepared for cultivation in 1895, but because of the "scarcity of water," the Pima could not sow their grain, even though they prepared an additional 473 acres for crops.[40] The Pima required fifty thousand bushels (three million pounds) of wheat to subsist (based on two pounds per person per day for pinole and tortillas). The starving years had begun, even though other areas in southern Arizona continued to grow crops.[41]

By the mid-1890s, conditions were so severe on the reservation that Indian Agent J. R. Young requested permission to purchase an additional 225,000 pounds of wheat "to prevent starvation." Young predicted the government would have to increase purchases of food annually for the Pima due to development above the reservation.[42] In 1894, more than 2,100 new acres were improved above the reservation in Florence, bringing the total acreage of improved land in Florence to 26,343.[43] There were 6,520 acres actually irrigated in Florence and 19,239 acres irrigated in the Upper Gila River valley, meaning 25,759 acres above the reservation were irrigated from the river.[44]

The Gila River ceased flowing on the reservation on April 10, 1895, a month earlier than 1894. Summer crops failed, and the Pima faced hunger, prompting Young to inform Commissioner of Indian Affairs Daniel Browning that "a large number of these Indians" would have to be fed during the coming winter. "They made a strong effort to make a crop and would have done so had the water supply not given out. Again this year they must have subsistence or suffer the pangs of hunger."[45]

In a sign of the times, a Pima father was convicted of grand larceny in the territorial district court. Wee Paps was arrested, tried, and convicted of stealing horses and trading them for food. Upon his conviction to serve one year in the territorial penitentiary, Wee Paps explained the Pima's challenge: "Until the past few years we have always had plenty of water to irrigate our farms, and we never knew what want was. We always had grain stored up for a full year's supply. . . . The Government refuses to give us food and we do not ask for it; we only ask for water, for we prefer to earn our own living if we can. I am no thief, and I will not beg, but my wife and children were hungry, and I must either steal or they must starve. So I took the horses and traded them for grain, and the hunger of my family was satisfied."[46]

The water gave out earlier in 1896, compelling Young to arrange work for more than two hundred Pima men on the Southern Pacific Railroad.[47] In July, Territorial Governor Benjamin J. Franklin reported "the reservoirs and canals [of the territory were] bank full and there will be no scarcity of water during the hot season."[48] Yet, on the Pima Reservation little progress was made in supplying the Indians with water. Consequently, the Pima were left "destitute and [in] much poverty and distress."[49] Given a fair water supply, the reservation would be a prosperous community, as demonstrated by the small parcels cultivated by the Pima that resulted in some thirty to forty bushels of wheat per acre. Having farmed 15,000 acres in 1859, the Pima now farmed fewer than 4,000.[50]

Conditions turned deadly in 1899, when Pima winter crops also failed. The river ceased flowing across the reservation in February. With no rainfall between February and July, "crops that bid fair with a good start in January were an entire failure." "Taking an average not more than half

FIGURE 6.1. Many Pima families faced difficult times during the years of famine. Children and the elderly were especially vulnerable. (Photograph courtesy of the San Carlos Irrigation Project)

a crop of wheat was harvested this year," Indian Agent Elwood Hadley explained.[51] While the summer rain arrived, allowing the Pima to raise some corn, beans, and squash, that summer proved to be especially difficult.[52] Some of the Pima, "driven by hunger," crossed into Mexico on marauding expeditions. Facing starvation, the Indians were overtaken by "an insidious blight" of poverty. With each successive crop failure, they planted less. Each planting yielded less. Expecting less, they "scaled down accordingly the standard of their existence." More farms were abandoned, while others were only partially cultivated, "yielding scant and uncertain returns." As the "lines [of despair] have tightened about the Indians," some of the men congregated at the Pima Agency in Sacaton hoping to find work or news of the return of their water.[53]

As bad as conditions were, they grew worse in 1900. S. M. McCowan, superintendent of Phoenix Indian School, visited the reservation in May and described many Pima families having "nothing to eat now but mescal and old mesquite beans. Last year's crop of wheat is entirely exhausted and the new crop will not be ripe for weeks. And the worst of it is that when the new crop ripens there will be so little of it, owing to the drouth [*sic*], that a very few weeks will see it all gone." The Pima were in a "deplorable condition. Never before in the history of the tribe [had] they been so destitute nor the prospects for immediate improvement more discouraging." Just one-fifth of the Pima grain crop was harvested, with their cattle "dying in large numbers."[54]

The national media broadcast the predicament of the Pima in the summer of 1900, but not due to any particular moral culpability on the part of the American people. In 1893, the National Irrigation Association was formed in Chicago to advocate federal reclamation. While the association found limited success with the Carey Act, the law had no effect in Arizona Territory. What the association needed was a strong moral argument and a national poster child to represent this need. The association looked no further than the Pima Reservation, where a strong moral and legal case demonstrated the necessity of federal subsidies for reclamation. Only the federal government could resolve Pima water needs and in the process open the door to a national policy of reclamation.

The National Irrigation Association encouraged the publication in 1900 and 1901 of sympathetic media articles. Dozens of newspapers, including those in Los Angeles, New York, Chicago, Washington, D.C., and places in between, carried stories of Pima privation. The *Chicago Tribune*, for instance, reported: "This statement of the pitiable condition of the friendly and industrious Pimas is old news to western readers, and the case is one of the most shameful and outrageous instances of neglect and betrayal on the part of the United States of an ally, worthy and true. That 6,000 Pima Indians, always the consistent and active friends of the white man, should be reduced from a condition of wealth and great prosperity to actual starvation through neglect of the federal government," the newspaper opined, "while the adjacent Apaches, always the white man's foes and causing more trouble, pillage and loss of life than any western tribe, should be today sleek and well-fed at the hands of the same government, seems a rewarding of enemies and killing of friends." The *Tribune* implored, "Cannot some of our friends, who have anon professed such interest in the poor red man come to his assistance now and see that he may be accorded simple justice? The cause is worthy, the means are at hand; the interest alone is lacking."[55]

The *New York Tribune* carried a similar story. "About 6,000 of these Indians are dependent for their subsistence upon the lands of the reservation which contains 350,000 acres, while the water supply in the Gila last year, owing to use for lands above, has not been sufficient to irrigate 1,000 acres belonging to the Indians. Fully half the crops planted have not produced enough for seed, notwithstanding the great fertility of the soil."[56]

Recognizing that Pima Agent J. B. Alexander's assertion that the reports of starvation were exaggerated and used by the National Irrigation Association to further their own cause, stories of Pima starvation circulated in newspapers across the country.[57] Territorial Governor Murphy acknowledged that the growth of the Gila River valley above the reservation had "been disastrous to the [Pima]."[58] Presbyterian ministers Sheldon Jackson and George L. Spinning released a report of their investigation of the Pima situation in 1900. Distributed to churches, charities, and philanthropists across the nation, Jackson and Spinning painted an austere picture of the severity of the crisis. "Of 586 families recently visited, of whose number 1,428 are males and 1,425 are females," the Presbyterians explained, "only 7 families have been able to get a full crop; 17 have raised three-fourths of a crop; 39 have secured about half the regular crop; 91 families have got only one-sixth to one-fourth of a crop; and 432 families of industrious Indians eager to work have not been able to raise any crop at all for lack of water."[59]

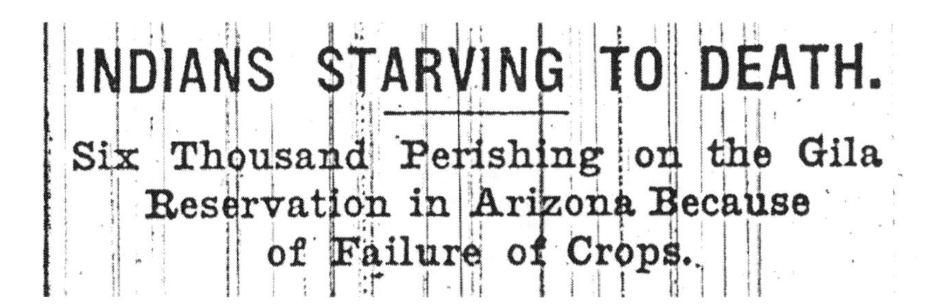
INDIANS STARVING TO DEATH.

Six Thousand Perishing on the Gila Reservation in Arizona Because of Failure of Crops.

FIGURE 6.2. The National Irrigation Association used the Pima as its national poster child in its efforts to persuade Congress to adopt a national reclamation act. Scores of newspapers ran similar articles. (*Chicago Tribune*, June 18, 1900)

The summer monsoons began in the middle of July 1900. But despite an inch of rain in Florence on July 19, the drought was too far along. On July 21, the *Florence Tribune* reported the Pima were busy "hauling away their dead cattle and horses."[60] More than one hundred fifty pounds of wheat and five thousand pounds of beans were distributed that summer, and Hadley continued to distribute to "the needy and helpless." Some Pima resorted to gleaning grain from off-reservation fields. "[M]any of the Indians, by permission of the owners of the lands, gleaned the fields and gathered many lbs. of which greatly aided in their sustenance," Hadley informed Jones.[61]

While the Pima suffered from drought, groundwater could still be found from ten to thirty feet deep in wells across the reservation. There was no reason, Hadley asserted, "why the Indians cannot provide water for their stock with a little labor." This truth reflected the fact that, while the surface waters of the Gila River dried up, the subsurface flow remained. The introduction of off-reservation groundwater wells, nonetheless, impacted the underground flow, with Crouse reporting the water table had already dropped between five and eight feet in Sacaton.

To survive the crisis, the Pima cut large quantities of mesquite to sell as a cash crop. More than nineteen thousand cords of mesquite were cut and sold in 1900.[62] The Pima had cut and sold mesquite since 1891 when drought first began. In the span of a few years, what had once been a dense mesquite *bosque* stretching more than sixty-five miles along the Gila River and its tributaries was nearly destroyed. An 1896–1897 Pima calendar stick noted "the Blackwater Indians were forced to leave home to sell wood." A year earlier, nearly five hundred cords were cut and sold "by Indians whose crops had failed."[63] By the summer of 1900, the *Arizona Gazette* reported more than thirty thousand cords of firewood, "cut and piled between Maricopa Junction and Phoenix," were waiting to be transported to towns north of the reservation.[64] But while providing a cash income to some Pima families, the cutting and selling of mesquite was not a boom to the Pima economy, as it left ecological and environmental degradation behind.

In December 1899, Commissioner Jones approved of a plan to cut "dead and down wood" within the reservation, although there was no way to prevent individuals from cutting live trees to meet the needs of their families. Hadley attempted to restrict the cutting of mesquite to an area west of the Maricopa and Phoenix Railroad (in the Santa Cruz River drainage southwest of Pima Butte). The railroad even built a special switching yard to accommodate the Indians who sold wood.[65] Between 1900 and 1905, more than fifty thousand cords of mesquite were cut and sold for use off the reservation, destroying an estimated sixty-four thousand acres of mesquite lands.[66] In the dozen years of famine, nearly one hundred thousand acres of mesquite was cut and sold as firewood (see table 6.3).[67]

The Pima were increasingly dependent on the government for support. In 1898 the Board of Indian Commissioners expressed grave concern over President William McKinley's lack of attention to Pima rights. "We regret that so little progress has been made toward supplying the

TABLE 6.3. Grain Production vs. Cords of Mesquite Cut, 1887–1904

Year	Winter grain grown (bushels)	Corn (bushels)	Wood cut (cords)[a]	Acres[b]
1887	105,000	5,000	—	—
1888	110,000	2,700	—	—
1889	144,000	3,600	—	—
1890	114,000	3,000	—	—
1891	50,000	—	200	256
1892	110,000	5,500	300	384
1893	76,000	3,000	350	448
1894	62,000	0	1,000	1,280
1895	70,950	500	1,500	1,920
1896	51,250	0	4,000	5,120
1897	51,250	0	1,500	1,920
1898	117,819	0	1,500	1,920
1899	34,488	1,072	5,000	6,400
1900	12,980	180	19,000	24,320
1901	25,417	36	11,000	14,080
1902	16,955	18	14,896	19,066
1903	42,051	18	10,600	13,568
1904	12,000	500	5,300	6,784

Source: U.S. Bureau of Indian Affairs. *Annual Report of the Commissioner of Indian Affairs*, (Pima Agency), 1887–1905.

[a]Based on an average of 128 cubic feet of mesquite per cord.

[b]Based on 100 cubic feet of three—inch diameter or greater wood per acre.

FIGURE 6.3. Antonio Azul standing in front of cut mesquite at Sacaton Station, ca. 1900. (Photograph courtesy of the San Carlos Irrigation Project)

Pima" with water, the board wrote. "A plan for their relief has been proposed, and we urged Congress to appropriate a sufficient fund to carry it out, but all we could get was a grant of $20,000 for a preliminary survey and estimate of the cost of the work."[68] In 1901, the board pleaded for the president to act. "White settlers on the river above them have recently diverted this water. This *they would not have been allowed to do* without protest and legal protection *if the earlier irrigators had been whites and not Indians*. . . . These Indians are now in danger of starving because the water has been taken from them and all their crops fail."[69] The Pima grew just 12,980 bushels (779,000 pounds) of wheat in 1900, enough for just 1,067 people to subsist. The six-year average (1899–1904) for grain crops totaled 23,982 bushels, less than the 25,000 bushels needed for subsistence. In addition, the Pima needed 25,000 bushels of corn, with the same period yielding just 340 bushels annually. More than four thousand Pima faced some level of hunger. The Board of Indian Commissioners recommended President Theodore Roosevelt provide the Pima with adequate irrigation, lest government neglect drive "toward hopeless pauperism and laziness the largest body of skilled and trained agriculturalists ever known in the history of our Indian tribes."[70]

While the board's report circulated in Washington, D.C., the Pima continued to starve. Hitchcock dispatched Indian Inspector Walter Graves to the reservation in the summer of 1900 to "ascertain the feasibility of a limited system of irrigation." Graves, however, was limited to an expenditure not exceeding $30,000, an amount too small with which to build an irrigation system and too large to waste on a system that would wash out with the first flood. Instead of a limited system, Graves suggested the development of a project to bring the "underground waters" of the Gila River to the surface.[71]

The Gila River flowed until May 1901, giving the Pima hope that they might harvest a sustaining crop. But the water again gave out before the wheat matured. "[T]he wheat shriveled up," Hadley lamented, "and much of the grain failed to mature at all." Some 25,000 bushels of wheat were harvested that summer. While the summer rains began to fall in July, they were insufficient to sustain Pima crops. "Unless the government provides ways to work them and help the old and disabled of which there are a large number, starvation awaits them."[72] Congress appropriated $40,000 to feed the Pima that year, but the people missed "their beans, bacon, coffee, and sugar," to which they had grown accustomed during the good years.[73] About nine hundred Pima managed to make a living at Gila Crossing, one of the few areas within the reservation that had water. Pima farmers cultivated fewer than 3,600 acres in 1900.[74]

Conditions were so poor in 1902 that Pima Chief Antonio Azul and twelve village leaders petitioned Commissioner Jones to provide them with work. "We have had very poor or no crops for the past three years," Azul wrote. "About two thousand of us are not likely to raise any wheat this year, because we have no water. . . . Our Horses and cattle are dying for want of food and [having] nothing to feed them we cannot work them. . . . Many of our people have not enough to eat and to wear and don't know what to do for a living."[75] Some "of the older Indians who were once self-supporting are now drawing rations," sixty-eight-year-old Pima Juan Jose added, "while some of the Pimas are living on what little they can make by selling wood."[76] In April 1902, Congress formally acknowledged a measure of culpability for the condition of the Pima. The federal government must "provide for these Indians who have supported themselves by means of irrigation and cultivating the land from time immemorial," a Senate committee stressed, "in as much as the action of the Government in disposing of lands to settlers higher up the river has deprived them of the means of subsistence."[77]

The following year, Azul appealed directly to President Roosevelt. Noting the Pima's historic assistance to American emigrants and his people's long history of irrigation farming in the desert, Azul informed the president of their desire to remain self-sufficient. In recent years, the aged chief told Roosevelt, "our water supply during low water has been taken from us by whites, and there has been much suffering for the necessaries of life." Furthermore, Azul lamented, the Pima experienced an economic loss of crops totaling "over $100,000."[78]

Roosevelt assembled a committee to examine the complaints of the Pima, concluding "the conditions of these people has [*sic*] been one of grinding poverty and that there has been extreme and wide-spread suffering among them." While they managed to retain "their self-respect and have endeavored to eke out a living," the president acknowledged the United States was responsible for the "deprivation of their water," which was the cause of their condition. For all intents and purposes, there had been "no crops for six years and most cattle herds had been sold for subsistence."[79] Eleven years of crop failures, including five consecutive years of failed winter and summer crops, reduced the Pima to a position of government charity.

While the worst of conditions ended in 1904, the Pima continued to suffer.[80] They were now dependent on federal assistance. They had cut tens of thousands of cords of mesquite. A dying river and declining water table were destroying one of the few resources the Pima retained. The drought and upstream diversions not only changed the course of the Gila River but, combined with episodic floods, also deepened the river's channel, rendering the Pima irrigation system obsolete and unusable. The Pima economy, once strong and vibrant, had been destroyed. Discouraged and lacking water, the Pima could neither feed themselves nor compete with the local economy.

The Pima grew bitter "at living in the knowledge that the white man far up the river was stealing his water which had once given life to fields of grain and had established a land of plenty."[81] The results of the loss of their water were the Pima were completely displaced from the market and their economy was on the verge of destruction. There was little hope they could join the growing economy of central Arizona, and without protection and restoration of their water, their very existence was in doubt. Only a modern irrigation system to replace the one that had been destroyed and abandoned due to water loss could restore their economy.

CHAPTER 7

Allotment of the Pima Reservation

THE PASSAGE OF THE National Reclamation Act of 1902 set off a showdown over control of Indian land and resources in central Arizona. On the north boundary of the Pima Reservation was Maricopa County's Salt River valley, which increased in population from 20,487 in 1900 to 34,488 in 1910. The number of farms within the county more than doubled to 2,229, with the value of farm property increasing 312 percent to $33,879,281, which was more than double the territorial average of 150 percent. Graham, Maricopa, and Pinal counties, the three counties impacting Pima access to water and agricultural development, represented 58 percent of the farm value in Arizona (see table 7.1). For the territory as a whole, 96.1 percent of the water used for agriculture was from stream flows, with 2.4 percent coming from wells. The U.S. Reclamation Service served 138,364 of the 320,051 acres of irrigated land in Arizona, or 43 percent of the irrigated land in 1909.[1]

In a microcosm, powerful economic and speculative forces in the Salt River valley were pitted against the survival of local Indian tribes. At the center of these activities was the division of Indian land in severalty. While tribes in Arizona were among the last to face land severalty, allotment took on a new focus in the territory, one directed at water as much as at land.

Allotment in central Arizona did not commence until Roosevelt Dam neared completion and the eligible acres of irrigated farm land in Maricopa County increased to 199,052 acres.[2] But, rather than adhering to the gradualist policy envisioned by severalty's framers in the 1880s, government officials and speculators now viewed that policy as undermining the economic growth of the West and the assimilation of the Indians. Land ownership was no longer a defining point in the "civilization" of the Indian; it was now a pawn in the economic integration of Indian resources and labor.

TABLE 7.1. County Population and Farm Size and Value, 1900 and 1910

County	Population		Average farm size (acres)	Number of farms		Farm value in 1910
	1900	1910		1900	1910	
Graham	14,168	23,999	81.8	509	1,028	$7,669,553
Maricopa	20,487	34,488	111.4	1,089	2,229	$33,879,281
Pinal	7,779	9,045	70.4	243	609	$2,306,782
Arizona	122,931	204,354	135.1	5,809	9,227	$75,123,970

Source: U.S. Bureau of the Census. *Thirteenth Census of the United States*, 1910, vol. 6: *Agriculture*.

As Congress debated the Reclamation Act, it assumed the first federal reclamation project would be for the relief of the Pima. Yet, no sooner had the bill become law than political maneuvering in the Salt River valley and Washington, D.C., persuaded Reclamation officials to support the Salt River project.[3] Popular writer Charles F. Lummis could not overlook this irony. "Everyone remembers, of course, that the very forefront of National Reclamation was the San Carlos Reservoir. It was urged and urged with all the eloquence of the irrigation crusade, and with the added plea of humanity. It was not only to be a great exemplar of the noble National Irrigation policy of reclaiming arid public lands in order that home-seekers might find homes," Lummis wrote in 1903, "it was also to succor something like 7,000 Pima Indians . . . who are starving because deprived of their water by white settlers." If it had not been for the Pima, Lummis added, "it is not too much to say that the whole National Irrigation movement would have been handicapped by several years."[4]

After 1902, tribal economic and political sovereignty was under attack from all levels of government. Congress enacted numerous bills restricting tribal authority, and the U.S. Supreme Court followed suit. In 1903, the court ruled in *Lone Wolf v. Hitchcock* that Congress had plenary authority to unilaterally change the terms of Indian treaties and agreements, opening the door for further erosion of tribal rights and authority. Locally, speculators, railroad corporations, timber and mineral interests, and agriculturalists clamored for control of Indian land, lobbying for changes in the General Allotment Act to open additional Indian land for settlement. It was a time for Indians to fend for themselves; if they could not adjust to the evolving policy of economic integration, popular theory prescribed, they "would remain on the fringes of American society—behind and below their enterprising new neighbors."[5]

The Arizona Territorial Legislature memorialized Congress, seeking federal support to allot in severalty the lands of tribal nations within the territory. In a supposedly altruistic gesture, territorial officials pledged their support that Indians should "be furnished with farming implements and an inexhaustible supply of water for irrigation of their lands."[6] Within two years, a plan was afoot to restore water to the Pima and divide their land in severalty. To pay for this scheme, the Indians were to give up 180,000 acres of land. Owing to the influence of irrigation engineer William H. Code, the Indian Service believed the water supply for the reservation, a precursor to allotment, would come not from the Gila River but rather from groundwater drawn to the surface by electric pumps.[7]

Dispatched to the U.S. Bureau of Indian Affairs Pima Agency as Indian inspector in 1902, Code soon became chief irrigation engineer for the Indian Service. A former irrigation engineer employed by Dr. A. J. Chandler and vice president of Chandler's Mesa Bank, Code had connections to hydrologist Frederick Newell and Secretary of the Interior Richard Ballinger, who was a good friend of President Theodore Roosevelt. Code served as "the engineer member" of the Salt River Valley Water Users Association (SRVWUA), which met weekly to consider means of securing water for the Salt River valley. Code was adamant that groundwater was the only means of restoring water to the Pima, and it was at his behest the Indian Service no longer recommended construction of a dam at San Carlos, which Code saw as "wasteful and unsuitable."[8]

Working with Louis Hill and Frederick Newell of the Reclamation Service, Code proposed wells in place of water stored in the San Carlos Reservoir. Using their influence, the three men laid out a scheme that was deleterious to the Pima. Code met with Arthur Davis of the U.S. Geological Survey (USGS) immediately after the passage of the Reclamation Act to see if a way could be found to secure water to benefit the Pima. Code badgered Davis until he finally offered a solution: water could be had at the cost of 180,000 acres of land. If Davis would recommend the cession, Code promised to see to it that it was approved.[9] It was at this time, Presbyterian missionary Charles Cook opined, that the

Reclamation Service went into the hands of big speculators.[10] Secretary of the Interior Ethan Allen Hitchcock had already gone on record supporting the San Carlos site, although with Code no longer encouraging construction at San Carlos, support for the first federal reclamation project in Arizona quietly transferred to the Tonto site.[11]

With the passage of the Indian Appropriation Act of 1903, Congress provided $150,000 for general irrigation works on Indian lands. These funds were administered under the authority and at the discretion of the secretary of the interior. Using this authority, the drilling of wells on the reservation began. The master plan was to construct ten pump stations, "each furnishing sufficient water for the irrigation of about 1,000 acres of land." The cost of these wells was around $80,000, with $460,000 needed to construct a power plant in the Salt River valley, making a total appropriation of $540,000 necessary. Since these funds were reimbursable, the Pima would repay these costs after they received fee simple title to their land.

Code recommended approval of a plan to sink four or five wells at the Sacaton school farm and install a "first class pumping plant" capable of irrigating six hundred acres of land. Code kept this request from the Pima, fearing they would not support his scheme. Designed as a precursor to the ten large pumps to be installed at Santan, Code received permission from Commissioner of Indian Affairs William Jones in December 1902 to install five smaller wells. The pumping plant (five wells combined) was operational by the winter of 1904 and, by summer, provided two thousand gallons per minute, enough to irrigate 250 acres of land (600 acres if the pumps ran 24 hours a day).[12] The quality of water, Code assured the commissioner, was "much superior" to the water pumped in the Salt River valley. In May, Pima Agency Superintendent John B. Alexander was authorized to spend $4,000 to increase the size of the existing plant and evaluate the prospects for sinking two more wells.

That same year, J. R. Meskimons, superintendent of irrigation for the reservation, proposed developing the seepage waters of the Gila River to put on a self-supporting basis "about one-half of the Indians that depend upon the Gila River water."[13] These plans were forwarded to Code, who agreed there were 1,400 miner's inches (35 cubic feet per second) of water at Gila Crossing, but claimed the Pima were irresponsible farmers, irrigating just 1,035 acres of crops when they could have

FIGURE 7.1. The round-roofed Sacaton pumping plant, shown in the center of this photo, as it appeared in 1915. (Reproduced courtesy of the National Archives and Records Administration)

been irrigating more than 4,000. "Until the present water supply is used by these Indians in a proper manner and made to irrigate every acre it can successfully provide for," Code informed Commissioner of Indian Affairs Francis Leupp, "I would not recommend spending large sums of money in this locality."[14]

In the meantime, Alexander, having been requested by the U.S. district attorney through Jones to provide information relative to Pima water rights, informed the commissioner there were 960 water users above the reservation. While he believed Pima water rights could be "prosecuted to a favorable ending," Alexander informed Jones that non-Indian interests upstream were varied and that the water was diverted by settlers as far as two hundred miles above the Indian's point of diversion. It "would be impossible," Alexander argued, "for the court to enforce" any decree of rights.[15]

Leupp agreed that the federal courts were not the proper means to secure water for the Pima, despite the fact that the territorial court in 1903 upheld Maricopa rights to water from the Salt River in the Haggard Decree.[16] In reality, Leupp and his successor Robert Valentine subscribed to the theory that the Pima no longer had any rights to the waters of the Gila River. Valentine opined "the Pima Indians lost substantially all of their water rights except to the flood waters . . . by the beneficial use of the water [by non-Indians] above them."[17] Government negligence in failing to protect Pima water would be alleviated not by restoring water but by confirming upstream users in their junior rights to the water. The Justice Department allowed the matter to drop.[18] Although the 1908 *Winters v. United States* Supreme Court ruling recognized Gros Ventre and Assiniboine reserved rights to water, the Indian Service operated on the belief that Indians had to demonstrate beneficial use as did non-Indians, a proposition that was upheld by a federal court in 1916.[19]

Code "had as much authority, and probably more, than anybody else in the field" over water matters. Despite being charged with providing the Pima with water, he "never regarded it as feasible to attempt to fight for water rights that had been taken away so many years before." In his view, it was impossible for the Pima to recover their "low water rights." Groundwater was the only option.[20] In the process, Code sought to redefine Pima water rights according to the beneficial use doctrine as set forth in local law, seriously undermining Pima sovereignty over their water resources.

The Pima did not desire groundwater, believing it caused bowel and kidney problems and killed cattle and horses.[21] In a letter to Secretary Hitchcock and Commissioner Leupp, Pima Chief Antonio Azul requested stored water from the Salt River Project. This water could be transported by canal to Pima lands, the chief informed the two men, through a highline canal.[22] Code did not share Azul's view and he did not wish to include Pima land in the SRVWUA, seeking instead to have the government construct a power plant on the Salt River and deliver electrical power to the reservation. As a backup energy supply, Code solicited approval to build an auxiliary 500-kilowatt steam plant on the reservation to generate power.

The $540,000 Code requested for ten wells and electrical power would pay a substantial portion of the hydroelectric power plant below

Roosevelt Dam. Code was more than "willing to pay the [Pima's] proportionate part" of the Salt River Project using Pima funds.[23] Leupp agreed, since he believed any water rights the Pima had would be permanently lost if the water were not quickly put to beneficial use under local law.

The Sacaton Contract, as the power agreement came to be known, spelled potential doom for the Pima. Signed by Secretary of the Interior James Garfield on behalf of the Pima and Benjamin Fowler and Frank Parker on behalf of the SRVWUA, the contract provided the association with a significant customer for its surplus electrical power. The success of the Pima, and the protection of their water, was now dependent on the completion of Roosevelt Dam and the generation of electrical power in the Salt River valley. The contract itself provided for the sale of 1,000 horsepower of electricity to the Pima for $300,000. But this was simply the right to use electrical power: it still had to be purchased. And this power was available only "out of the excess power over and above that which may be needed by the members of the Association."[24] The Indian Service immediately transferred $100,000 to the U.S. Reclamation Service.

Under the Sacaton Contract, 10,000 acres of reservation land was to be part of the Salt River Project for determining costs (and the Pima paid their proportionate share), but the Indians were not made members of the SRVWUA, although the contract included the caveat that once the Indians became owners severally in fee simple, and at the discretion of the secretary of the interior, their lands could be made part of the association. Under no circumstances was water to be furnished to the reservation. Former Territorial Governor and Judge Joseph Kibbey, who drafted the document, admitted non-Indians would not have entered into such a contract.[25] Nonetheless, Code approved it. By so doing, the Indian Service committed itself to a policy that complemented the scheme laid out by Code. Once the groundwater project was initiated, the Pima would be unable to pay the costs associated with repaying the construction and operation and maintenance charges of the project, forcing them to sell a large portion of their reservation.

With the contract in hand, the well project continued and provided Code with a legal means of detaching the western half of the reservation and throwing it open to non-Indian speculators. With the completion of the Salt River Project, this land would become valuable, as it was susceptible to irrigation from the Salt River. Since the Sacaton Project (as the reservation project became known) obligated the Indians to repay $540,000, Code now recommended the sale of 180,000 acres of the reservation at $3 per acre, even though land with water was selling at more than $100 per acre.

In January 1905, the Senate Subcommittee on Indian Affairs met to discuss the Sacaton Project. Testifying before the subcommittee, Newell explained that a power plant along the Salt River was essential to the project, as it would produce electricity to "pump water for the Pima Indians from beneath the surface of their own land." Newell underscored the fact that funds by law would have to be repaid. This could be done only by opening to sale a portion of the reservation "not now utilized or occupied by the Indians, [but] which may have some value in the future." Newell assured the senators that groundwater was "the only feasible proposition for supplying these Indians with water."[26]

Davis concurred with Newell's position that the project would have to be repaid through the sale of unallotted lands. When Leupp was informed, he referred the matter to Code, who, having devised the plan, believed the matter "extremely favorable to the Indians." Code did make two exemptions to the land to be sold. He excluded 1,500 acres at Maricopa Colony (with Salt River Haggard Decree water rights) and 5,000 acres near Gila Crossing (with seepage water).[27]

Code sought to irrigate 10,000 acres on the north side of the river at Santan. Even with exemptions at Maricopa Colony and Gila Crossing, 10,000 acres at Santan were too few to meet the needs of the Pima. Newell admitted this in 1905, but opined that Pima farmers needed only an "average of 4 or 5 acres of good irrigated land" to support their families. This was clearly discriminatory, as non-Indians could acquire 160 acres of land under the Homestead Act or 320 acres under the Desert Land Act. The Indian Service, however, opposed larger allotments, fearing it would have to provide water to all allottees. With nearly five thousand Pima eligible to receive an allotment, 800,000 acres would have to be allotted, with some portion of each allotment provided with water if each Pima were to receive a 160-acre homestead. This was twice the size of the reservation and would require all the water of the Gila River, a plan government officials rejected as impractical and limiting efficient use of the water by non-Indians. Newell, not surprisingly, sought small

Indian allotments that would keep irrigation costs to a minimum and at the same time protect water for off-reservation use.[28]

Newell, meanwhile, submitted to Charles Walcott, director of the USGS, a report on potential groundwater development on the reservation.[29] While a perpetual water supply on the western end of the reservation remained from the subflow of the river, by 1903 the river rarely flowed across the eastern half of the reservation except during flood season. With local precipitation insufficient to maintain the underflow, the water came from the subsurface flow of the river and its tributaries. The subflow above the reservation was 237 cubic feet per second, while forty miles downstream the flow was 430 cubic feet per second, clearly indicating that other sources of water were added to the underflow. This underflow was important to the Pima wetlands, in addition to providing irrigation water. Hill estimated the subsurface flow of the Gila River to be "of an indefinite" quantity.[30] The quantity of water that could be pumped each year was somewhere between 35,830 and 278,256 acre-feet. "There is enough water," USGS engineer Willis Lee concluded, "at present within pumping distance of the surface to supply the Indians for *twenty-eight to forty-nine years*."[31]

Lee did not favor seepage ditches as the means of securing water for the Pima, preferring pumping plants. Ten such plants could furnish 64,350 acre-feet of water annually, more than the 40,000 acre-feet the Indian Service deemed necessary for the Pima. Based on these calculations, it was probable that water could "be drawn from the underflow of the Gila River valley, not only to supply the needs of the Indians but also to materially extend the cultivated area [of non-Indians] without exhausting the available supply." The Pima dismissed the report, claiming Lee "made assertions that cannot be verified."[32]

Lee correctly observed the best location to pump water was on the western end of the reservation, where "the most promising conditions are to be expected." These conditions, water near the surface, a large return flow of water into the underflow, and the freedom of movement in the underflow, suggested that wells would be more likely to succeed here than any other location. But wells on the western end of the reservation were not acceptable to Code. The western-end lands included fertile land with easy access to well and Salt River water. Wells at Santan and the consolidation of the Pima at that location were the only means of opening up the lands on the western end of the reservation and getting at the water west of Chandler Ranch.

Assured that there was an adequate source of water for the Pima, Congress appropriated $50,000 for the Sacaton Project on March 3, 1905.[33] In January 1906, John Granville arrived on the reservation to begin a preliminary survey in advance of allotment. With the Sacaton Contract in place, work began on constructing an electrical line to the north boundary of the reservation. In April 1908, Congress gave the secretary of the interior the authority to enter into agreements with the U.S. Reclamation Service to build Indian irrigation projects.[34] Using this authority, work on the first well for the pumping plant began on April 20, 1908.

The Sacaton Project included water from the ten irrigation wells and any floodwater that might come down the Gila River. The project included the construction of three irrigation canals. The first would carry floodwater from the Gila River beginning at a point 3.5 miles east of Sacaton. The head of this floodwater canal was at the future site of the Sacaton Diversion Dam (and Olberg Bridge), authorized in 1916. A second, smaller canal was to branch off the first canal and carry well water only. A third canal was to be constructed on the south bank and supply a limited amount of water near Casa Blanca.[35]

The Pima questioned the new floodwater canal. In their view, its "intake on the Gila River was at a higher level than necessary for the Indian lands to be irrigated."[36] This appeared to the Pima to be what was necessary to convey water to the reservation lands west of Chandler Ranch, land that Code proposed to sell. The canal itself ran along a high ridge in the north-central part of the reservation before dropping through a series of grades. But then it mysteriously forked, with a smaller branch heading toward Santan and the larger fork continuing west in the direction of Chandler Ranch.[37]

The Pima first learned of the Code scheme in 1904, and "it came," Cook scolded Leupp, "like a thunder clap out of the clear sky." At first the Pima refused to believe Cook's claims. Then the Indians learned "the plot had been laid secretly." Any scheme to rob the Pima of their land would be opposed, as the land proposed to be sold "can be irrigated from the Tonto Reservoir and the Gila and Salt rivers," a fact "well understood by those who advocate the sale of these lands." This "explain[ed Code's] haste and secret endeavors," Cook chided the commissioner.[38] The Pima refused to move to such lands.[39]

The Pima also rejected Code's proposed five-acre allotments, as some Pima growers cultivated sixty or more acres.[40] In March 1906, Antonio Azul informed Leupp the Pima needed "enough water to irrigate from 25–30 acres to the family" and additional land to grow crops to sell and pastureland for their animals. Leupp responded the Indian Service was "doing all in its power to get irrigation for that amount of land for each family." Nonetheless, Leupp was surprised to learn the Pima still opposed groundwater. "I beg to assure you that if water cannot be procured through pumping," Leupp warned the chief, "it will be impossible to obtain irrigation for the Pimas." The commissioner further informed Azul he was "not aware of any movement on behalf of whites to take your land. Unless it can be irrigated by pumped water, it is not worth the taking."[41]

The following year, Azul informed Secretary Garfield that the Pima needed thirty or more irrigated acres of land for each family.[42] Hugh Patten, a Pima businessman and former school teacher, dispatched a letter to Leupp on behalf of Azul and the village chiefs, again requesting river water that would fertilize the land and produce good crops. In response to the cession of land, the chiefs explained the Pima had "no land to spare as Mr. Code thinks."[43]

Azul penned another letter to Garfield, expressing his view that the Pima were "willing to pay our share for good river water." Nonetheless, the aged chief opined, government engineers had sent in false reports "in order to rob us of our lands."[44] When Patten and fellow Pima Lewis Nelson planned to travel to Washington, D.C., in 1908, to personally object to groundwater and allotment, they were forbidden to leave the reservation. Assistant Commissioner of Indian Affairs A. C. Tonner told the men, "The Indian Office [will] look after [your] interests." The men were disallowed "to meet with and talk to Government officials who came to our reservation." Government officials effectively disenfranchised the Pima. Garfield did, however, agree to postpone allotment. "In the future," the secretary promised, "when the extent to which the lands can be irrigated is made known the question of separate allotments can be taken up in council with your tribe."[45]

The Pima stood on another precipice in 1908, fearing not only the loss of 180,000 acres of land and their rights to the low-water flow of the Gila River but also the ability to restore their agricultural economy. Having grown increasingly frustrated at the lack of responsiveness of the Indian Service, nine Pima men sent a petition to the Indian Rights Association seeking its assistance in defining Pima water rights. Within their petition, the men declared their steadfast opposition to being "moved from our homes," seeking instead to have "water supplied to our farms as they are at present situated." They also demanded that their rights to the "natural low-water mark flow" of the Gila River, or as much "as we were accustomed before it was all stolen from us," be protected.[46]

As importantly, the chiefs requested their sovereignty be respected and that a representative of the U.S. government "confer with us . . . to examine the conditions pertaining to land and water on this reservation." To date, Antonito Azul, the Pima chief's son, and Sacaton Flats Chief John Hays complained, "we have had no voice in the matter at all," having been "continually overreached by Engineer W. H. Code, who has attempted to force a system of irrigation upon us."[47] On December 16, 1911, Antonito Azul appealed directly to the U.S. Congress. "Some 20 years ago and all the time before that date we, the Pimas, had all the water needed to irrigate our farms, and we had no difficulty in making our living. Since that time, unless the rainfall was great, we have had to suffer more or less for the necessaries of life." After the assassination of President William McKinley, Azul continued, William H. Code "persuaded [the] Government to build the Tonto (also called the Roosevelt) Reservoir at a great cost. [He] also persuaded the Government to build electric power pumping plants, at a great cost, in order to supply [us] with worse than worthless well water." The Pima understood what the alkali-impregnated groundwater would do to their farms. They had water samples analyzed and sent Nelson and Patten to Washington, D.C., only to discover the Indian Service and the U.S. Reclamation Service "would not listen to our people."[48]

Two weeks later, Azul penned "An Appeal for Justice" to the "People of the United States," describing how Superintendent Alexander "place[d] himself across the Pimas' path, between him and his river water." Soon after, Code was appointed irrigation engineer. "We have not the papers to show just what the speculators and politicians of the Salt River valley had to do with the appointments of Agent Alexander and Engineer Code, but the events which followed speak loudly." The appeal then described how the Phoenix schemers "decided upon . . . the Salt River Valley instead of the Gila River Valley" for the first reclamation project. After the Indians were promised water from the Salt River Project, Code immediately began speaking of groundwater for the Pima, failing to tell the Indians of their "right to good river water without expense." Azul appealed to Congress and the American people to "come to our aid."[49]

At the request of the Pima, Samuel M. Brosius, of the Indian Rights Association, encouraged the House of Representatives to investigate the activities of Newell and Code, as well as the general expenditure of irrigation funds on behalf of the Pima. Brosius explained how Code sought to allot land in Gila Crossing, but then changed his mind with "the completion of the Roosevelt Reservoir [as] all the cultivable land . . . at Gila Crossing can now be supplied with Salt River impounded water." Once considered of little value, the land had "much speculative value."[50]

Brosius distrusted Code, questioning why he "want[ed] the [Gila Crossing] Indians to abandon [1,500 miner's inches of water] in order to get a similar amount of pumped water from the wells at Santan." Furthermore, seepage water at Gila Crossing and Maricopa Colony was equivalent to the output of seven pumps in Santan. With the cost of each pump at $10,000, why was this money not used to extend the electrical power line and "augment the natural supply of water at Gila Crossing with three or four wells?" As Brosius reasoned, the wells were put in at Santan and not Gila Crossing so that non-Indians would "get the natural flow of good river water and the Indians [would] get the electricity" to pump inferior-quality groundwater. Through the "aid of some unscrupulous officials," the Pima stood to lose much more than their land.[51]

With regard to the "Casa Blanca Indians," there was a concern they, too, might be relocated to Santan. While Code initially agreed they should receive allotments at Casa Blanca, by 1909 he was of the opinion they should remove to Santan, with children potentially receiving allotments on the south side of the river near Casa Blanca.[52] Code added that even "the Blackwater Indians would have to be moved," going so far as to threaten the Indians that if they refused to go "there are many Indians (i.e., Papago) who would be glad to come."[53]

The Pima were not amused with this scheme. In the summer of 1909, Antonio Azul convened another meeting of the village leaders "for the purpose of sending in a strong protest to Washington." Azul and village chiefs Juan Jackson and Slurn Vanico continued to protest to Garfield. The chiefs' objection was the uncertainty of water in the Gila River. They understood that the proposed allotments were insufficient to enable them to make a living by agriculture and stock raising as they had done heretofore. Pima protests to the Indian Service made clear they wished to remain self-sufficient. Azul explained the Pima were willing to part with surplus land as soon as the government demonstrated "that we can make a decent living without such lands." Otherwise, Azul stressed, "We object to being made paupers and ration Indians merely to benefit a few bad white men."[54]

Despite Pima concerns, Commissioner of Indian Affairs Robert Valentine, who succeeded Leupp in 1909, ordered allotting agent Charles E. Roblin to allot each family ten acres, five for married men and five for married women. This was rationalized on the basis that limited water supplies could be spread across smaller allotments. Minor children would be allotted in the future unless considerations should "cause such course to be impractical."[55] This ambiguity caused the Pima more concern, leading many to conclude that children would not be allotted at all. In the meantime, Cook informed the Presbyterian Board of Home Missions that he "had more calls from the hungry than at any [other time in the] twenty years during my stay here."[56] The conservative Board of Indian Commissioners even adopted the position of encouraging Valentine to restore the natural flow of the Gila River so as to enable the Pima to once again farm the land, "regardless of any injustice or alleged injustice to whites farther up the river."[57]

Nelson lamented how Code (or Alexander; they each blamed the other) ordered the closing of the Little Gila River in 1904, denying water to Pima farmers south of the Gila River. The Little Gila for centuries had served as the main conveyance channel delivering water to the fields between Blackwater and Sweetwater. Its head on the Gila was low and allowed the low-water flow to enter its bed to be carried west fifteen miles to fields south of the river. By closing the Little Gila, Code hoped to persuade the Pima they were without water and that groundwater in Santan was their only option. He disguised his scheme by ordering the closure of the Little Gila as a matter of public safety. Both the Pima Agency farmer and experimental farmer characterized the closing "as an outrage." Loss of this important water conduit caused more distrust, but it did not persuade the Pima to accept the pump scheme.[58]

In July, in response to continued Pima complaints, the Indian Service withdrew its preliminary allotment plan. "The Indians at Gila Crossing and Casa Blanca will be permitted to take allotments where they are now located," Assistant Commissioner of Indian Affairs C. F. Hauke informed Alexander. "But if they want allotments where water is now developed they can be allotted [at Santan]. Please make it clear to everyone that the place of allotment for each Indian is within his or her selection." In a follow-up letter, Hauke stressed that wherever there were "settlements of Indians in large numbers enough and under favorable agricultural and irrigable conditions, every effort possible will be made to bring water to them where it can be done at a cost that would not be nugatory of all other efforts."[59]

Herbert Marten, an outspoken advocate of Pima rights and financial clerk at the Pima Agency, played an important role in informing Congress about irrigation matters on the reservation. Contrary to what Code stated, Marten told the House of Representatives Committee on Indian Affairs surface water could "be conducted down [canals] for the irrigation of Indian lands on the reservation." Despite congressional beliefs that all the Pima had been or soon would be provided with water, Marten informed the committee that only about eight hundred Pima had access to water. Nearly 80 percent were without water.[60]

Furthermore, while $540,000 had already been appropriated for wells and electrical power, Marten estimated that another $1,000,000 would be needed to complete the Sacaton Project. Add in the estimated $35,500 annual operating expense (estimated at $3.55 per acre), and the costs were staggering. "It will be a great hardship and it is believed a practical impossibility for the Indians to meet the annual payments for electricity alone." When maintenance charges were factored in, "instead of being made self-supporting, as the government contemplates, [the Pima were] likely to be pauperized and ruined." Cook estimated these consequences cost the Pima $380,000 per year.[61]

As to the groundwater scheme, Marten suggested the water was not only expensive but also "contain[ed] dangerous quantities of alkali." If it were used exclusively, groundwater would "ruin the land" within a few years.[62] Nelson, writing to Congressman John H. Stephens (D-TX), a member of the House of Representatives Committee on Indian Affairs, asked why the Pima should be asked to experiment with groundwater "when the Gila River water, to which we are already entitled, would make experiment unnecessary." Surface water, Nelson reasoned, "is in no way an impossibility, and we know that it is the best and most practical system." The Pima will "some day stand side by side with our white brother in thrift and culture," Nelson added. "To place us at a disadvantage now may mean the loss of hope, and when hope is dead the man is dead."[63]

To support their assertion, the Pima contacted Professor W. H. Ross of the University of Arizona to conduct an analysis of the water. Ross concluded that "water containing 100 parts . . . of soluble salts per 100,000 parts of water would carry on to the land 8,167 pounds of salts per acre in one year." Based on his analysis, groundwater would damage the soil in "a very few years."[64] Even as little as 68 parts per 100,000 could damage the soil. Two of seven wells tested exceeded this level, with the remaining five averaging 52 parts per 100,000.[65] Could it be, Marten inquired, that the pumping scheme was more for the "interests of the [Salt River Valley] Water User's Association than of the Government or Indians?" Besides, "It would have been equally feasible to have bought impounded water from the Roosevelt Reservoir for the Indians' lands . . . as to have bought electricity."[66]

Valentine was unconvinced and informed the House of Representatives that the reports indicated the absolute safety of using groundwater. Hill admitted the groundwater was salty but otherwise safe for irrigation purposes, especially if mixed with floodwaters. By 1911, Valentine reported that over 4,500 acres were being irrigated on the north bank of the river in the Santan district and that "the main canals are now built above 10,000 acres." The U.S. Reclamation Service noted that while the Indians "with few exceptions refused to use well water" in 1912, when river water ran low in 1913, they used it with "remarkable success."[67] Use of the water restored some confidence, but while the Pima were forced to use groundwater, they continued to oppose it. Tribal leaders Kisto Morago, Lewis Nelson, Harvey Cawker, and Jackson Thomas complained that they had no voice in the pumping scheme. "The water rights in the Gila River appear by consensus of legal opinion to be still ours, and such water would cost us nothing," the men argued. A month earlier, 444 Pima signed a petition appealing to the Senate to restore "our river water."[68]

Three months later, the House of Representatives Committee on Expenditures in the Department of the Interior launched its investigation of the reclamation activities in the Gila and Salt River valleys. Besides implicating A. J. Chandler and a score of other Salt River valley speculators, the committee concluded the U.S. Reclamation Service had indeed gone "into the hands of big land speculators." Almost immediately, the U.S. Reclamation Service turned over its Indian Country activities to the Indian Irrigation Service.[69]

Marten testified before the subcommittee, which listened as the Pima questioned the intent of the new Santan Floodwater Canal, which they believed was heading toward Chandler Ranch. From the Pima perspective, the $286,126 Santan Floodwater Canal was a waste of money unless it was designed to provide "a large supply of water" to Chandler Ranch.[70] The Sacaton Contract was particularly scrutinized as it seemed "to render

FIGURE 7.2. The Santan Floodwater Canal, ca. 1915. Water diverted from the Gila River was to irrigate 10,000 acres. (Reproduced courtesy of the National Archives and Records Administration)

all of the reservation, with the exception of 10,000 acres, entirely valueless to the Indians so that they will in self-defense have to sell this excess." To fulfill the contract would be a burden. Rather than testify, Code resigned from government work.

The Sacaton Contract, despite its shortcomings, brought 4,500 acres in Santan under irrigation by 1911. Despite irrigating this land, however, water shortages were still acute. The drought ameliorated, but upstream diversions continued. To provide current users with water and restore water to the Pima, the Indian Service continued evaluating a storage dam on the Gila River to impound floodwater that could not otherwise be used. The work of evaluating the physical location of the San Carlos Reservoir and the maximum acreage it could support fell to the USGS.

In 1909, M. O. Leighton, chief hydrographer of the USGS, turned the idea of reclamation upside down, suggesting the factor that determined the feasibility of an irrigation project was not the "abundant but the scarce years of water supply." Leighton did not recommend a project be built to irrigate more land than the average irrigated acreage during the drought of 1900 to 1904. Anything beyond this would risk insufficient water. With the average water use on the middle Gila River during these years just 140,200 acre-feet, Leighton recommended no more than 40,000 acres of land be irrigated from San Carlos.[71] Engineer F. E. Herrmann cautiously concluded the actual safe yield was just 24,000 acres of land.[72]

While the USGS adopted a conservative approach to reclamation, consulting engineers James Schuyler and H. Hawgood did not. In dry years, when storage water was low, Schuyler argued, groundwater pumping could supplement the reservoir supply.[73] Other studies supported a maximum water use of 260,000 acre-feet and no more than 65,000 acres. Most of these studies assigned the Pima one-third of the water, since "there is known to be a copious supply of underground water" on the reservation.[74] The government continued to assume that beneficial use of the water by non-Indians had preempted Pima rights. Nonetheless, the USGS concluded that the Sacaton Project, which utilized groundwater and floodwater (when available), could irrigate 12,000 acres, with approximately 21,500 additional allotted acres irrigated with stored water, bringing the potentially irrigated lands on the reservation to 33,500 acres.[75] Schuyler was of the opinion that the Florence Canal could convey a maximum of 108,000 acre-feet of water seven years out of ten, enough to irrigate just 12,000 to 25,000 acres of land.[76]

When Congress directed the U.S. Army Corps of Engineers to evaluate the San Carlos site in 1912, the Corps concluded that a 180-foot-tall dam could impound 709,626 acre-feet of water at a cost of $2,104,000.[77] The Corps calculated the average annual discharge at San Carlos at 346,568 acre-feet. A low volume of 99,936 acre-feet occurred in 1902, with a high mark of 1,011,082 acre-feet in 1905. The low average runoff and the extremes between high and low volume concerned engineers. But of far greater concern was the length of time during which the annual run-offs were “continuously below” the average. The years 1898–1904 and 1908–1910 all had below-average flows. While the dam could store more than 310,000 acre-feet of water, the Corps did not believe it prudent to plan more than that amount being stored in any given year. Using conservative estimates, no more than 200,000 acre-feet should be used annually, with 2 acre-feet of water allocated per acre.[78]

With water to support 90,000 acres of cultivation, the Corps of Engineers recommended 122,222 acre-feet of water be set aside for 55,000 acres of land south and east of the reservation and 77,778 acre-feet of water be assigned to the Pima Reservation. The Corps adopted a plan to irrigate 40,000 acres on the reservation. Of this, 10,000 acres were under the Sacaton Project, with 20,000 acres to be supplied with stored water on the south side of the river. Since the Santan area had groundwater, an additional 10,000 acres on the north side of the river was to receive just 1 acre-foot of water per acre.[79]

In the spring of 1910, Alexander proposed ten-acre allotments for the reservation.[80] Seeking to limit the expense of a costly irrigation system, the federal government advanced ten-acre allotments, with each allottee receiving an irrigable tract of land to provide for his needs. Such lands, however, would provide only subsistence cropping rather than enabling the Pima to reenter the market economy they enjoyed when they had sufficient water. In November, the Indian Service tentatively adopted a plan to allot each Pima five acres with assured water rights, five acres with tentative water rights, and forty acres of grazing lands.[81]

By the spring of 1911, Valentine, desperately wishing to allot the land and emancipate the Pima from federal supervision, made preliminary plans for irrigable allotments. In April, he dispatched a letter to new allotting agent Charles E. Roblin directing him to "bring sufficient irrigable land within the reservation under ditch to afford allotments . . . of at least 5 acres." Allotments would be given to heads of families, their spouses, and adult children only. Those not old enough to use their allotment would have their right protected and receive land in severalty at a later date from land "not yet under water."[82]

Concerns over water again postponed allotment, and it was not until 1914, after the U.S. Army Corps of Engineers certified the feasibility of San Carlos Reservoir (and assured water for irrigable allotments), that the first temporary allotments were made. That year there were 1,661 allotments made, totaling 16,632 acres of land. In 1915, another 1,492 allotments for 14,920 acres of land were made, and 1,733 allotments totaling 23,930 acres were made the following year. In 1917, 3,407 allotments for 33,737 acres of mostly grazing land were made. By the end of 1917, 4,886 irrigable allotments were made. None were yet approved, pending confirmation of water rights. Secondary, non-irrigable allotments (grazing) were being prepared "as rapidly as possible."[83] When the allotments were made, they were forced on the Pima. "No consideration was taken by the allotting agent," Pima elder Lloyd Allison remembered, as "to the location the Indians had lived and farmed in." The allotments were simply drawn up on paper. Most Pima did not object to moving to an allotment, but feared the allotment process.[84] It was what was on the "other side of the allotment paper" that concerned the Pima. Since many Pima were assigned land that was already occupied by others, they agreed to informal exchanges with "the new allottee [being] charged whatever the old owner thought the crop, wire, fences, etc., on the land they left was worth."[85]

By 1916, Pima Agency Superintendent Ralph Ward optimistically reported young Pima farmers "making all haste to get these new allotments under cultivation." But in the first sign of the changing economics of Pima farming, there was a growing need for capital resources. Ward noted the Pima were "handicapped in this matter considerably." The Pima, expecting to have time to transition from years of deprivation and quasi-traditional methods of farming, were rapidly being thrown into the foray of intensive agriculture needed to compete with their non-Indian neighbors. Needing capital to compete, the Pima discovered it was difficult to farm under the new system. As allottees died, the already small allotments were fractured, with heirship compounding the matter. Not withstanding

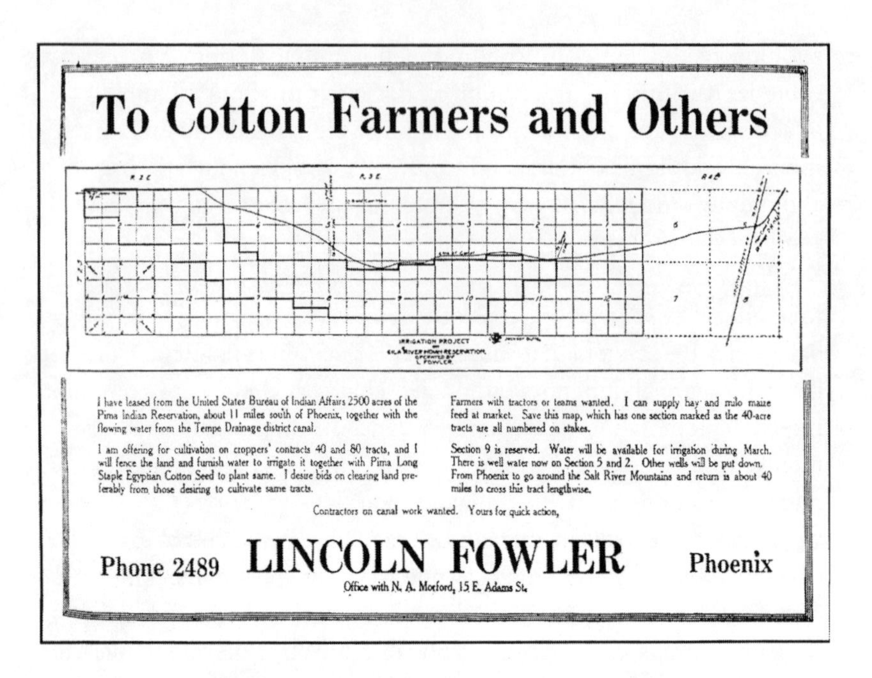

FIGURE 7.3. The Fowler lease was the first on the reservation. It set the pattern of land leasing facilitated by the 1910 amendments to the General Allotment Act. (*Arizona Republic*, March 10, 1918)

challenges, two Pima farmers leased land "outside the reservation." As of yet, none of the reservation land was leased.[86]

The leasing situation changed in 1917, when Lincoln Fowler, a Phoenix farmer and entrepreneur, leased allotted land along the northern boundary of the reservation near Tempe. War-time demands for cotton led to a dramatic increase in cotton acreage in central Arizona. To cash in on this bonanza, Fowler, with the assistance of former Pima Agency Superintendent Frank Thackery, leased 250 ten-acre allotments made at the direction of Commissioner of Indian Affairs Cato Sells in 1917. Aware that Maricopa County Drainage District (MCDD) No. 1 (Tempe) had incorporated in 1914 for the purpose of draining groundwater and tailwater from land being reclaimed in south Tempe, Fowler worked out the details of the lease with Sells, Thackery, and Congressman Carl Hayden. With the war-time agricultural boom in the Salt River valley, land was at a premium, with the remaining sloughs and other wetlands drained by 1915. By 1916, 212,836 acres were irrigated within the Salt River Project alone, with speculators and farmers seeking to reclaim all irrigable land.[87] The water from MCDD No. 1 was drained via what came to be known as Fowler's ditch (now Gila Drain).[88]

The drainage ditch was completed in May 1917, and on September 20, Sells signed an agreement with MCDD No. 1 giving the U.S. government control of the drainage water. Since Pima allotments could be leased under the 1910 amendments to the General Allotment Act, the era of leasing Indian land began. Fowler proposed the Tempe drainage water be used on the 2,500 acres he subleased to non-Indian farmers in the area due north of Lone Butte. Superintendent Ward then signed eight-year leases on behalf of the Pima landowners, and by March 1918, work on the Fowler ditch began.[89]

The Fowler lease demonstrated the changing nature of land severalty and tribal economics. Rather than benefit Pima landowners as the original severalty act intended, the allotment act was manipulated, in light of the National Reclamation Act initiating a race to put all arable land under irrigation, by speculators, who then asserted rights to the water from the Salt River valley to benefit Fowler (and eventually sub-lessees). Pima land, rather than being farmed by and for the benefit of the Pima, was instead leased and made productive by non-Indians to the benefit of the local economy.

Allotment was completed by 1920, with the first trust patent issued to Antonio B. Juan on June 25, 1921.[90] By 1922, 4,894 Pima and Maricopa (and some Papago) received trust patents to two ten-acre allotments within the reservation.[91] The first was for a ten-acre irrigable allotment referred to as an A, or primary, allotment with rights to water. The second was for a ten-acre non-irrigable grazing allotment referred to as a B, or secondary, allotment with no assurance of water. Because of the restricted status, the land could not be sold, mortgaged, taxed, or otherwise encumbered for twenty-five years.

When the severalty book was closed on the reservation, more than 96,000 acres were allotted. Just 7,693 acres were farmed (less than half the 1859 acreage), with an additional 18,500 acres waiting for water. By 1922, 1,654 allotments were "under ditch."[92] The largest Pima farms were Jose Mendoza (100 acres), Jack Stone (96 acres), Lewis Porter (60 acres), Frank Armstrong (55 acres), Pancho Lopez (54 acres), Joseph Smith (52 acres),

FIGURE 7.4. A Pima farmer, ca. 1920. Allotment and the loss of water marginalized the Pima economy. (Photograph courtesy of San Carlos Irrigation Project)

John Jones (50 acres), Jose Kalka (50 acres), and Ed Wood (50 acres). Many others farmed between 30 and 50 acres, growing wheat, barley, alfalfa, corn, cotton, beans, squash, and a variety of garden crops.[93]

While the Pima were willing to work the land once canals and ditches were constructed, nearly half of the irrigable allotments for which ditches and turnouts were constructed were "unfit for the purpose for which [they] had been allotted." Soil analyses indicated these lands contained "excessive amounts of alkali" and were condemned.[94] Pima Agency Superintendent Albert Kneale admitted that allotment and the irrigation system were "idle gestures." The Indian Office, Kneale opined, "must have known in advance that neither singly [n]or collectively could they have any effect upon the water situation or upon the financial status of the tribe."[95] Excessive alkali necessitated a survey to locate an additional 25,000 irrigable acres of in-lieu land so allottees that lost some or all of their original irrigable allotment could exchange it.

Some Pima allottees received two ten-acre allotments within an area designated as irrigable, while some received two non-irrigable allotments. Since every eligible member was entitled to ten acres of irrigable land, the only solution offered by the Indian Service was to "effect exchanges of allotments," something that was accomplished with "an immense amount of labor." With the exchanges came another expense: "the enlargement and revamping of the entire irrigation system."[96]

While the Pima successfully thwarted Code's scheme to "rob them of their land," they were unable to stop the economic transformation occurring within the reservation. Rather than follow existing land divisions and local land customs, allotting agents laid new subdivision lines that followed the township structure. Rarely did an allotment correspond with the old system of fields and canals. Areas that had been farmed with river water for centuries, such as Sacate and Snaketown, were without water as the new canals and irrigation system were built. Families living in these traditional farming areas had little choice but to "go from place to place" looking for work. Nearly 7,000 acres of cleared allotted land were without water, and a crop, in 1922.[97] Overall, the amount of land in production after allotment decreased 2,600 acres, a great source of discouragement to the Pima.[98]

Despite hardships, some 575 Pima and Maricopa farmers cultivated 11,860 acres of land in 1923 using ground-, flood-, and seepage water. Owing to drought conditions and new canals bypassing old fields, Pima farmers in Sweetwater, Bapchule, Sacate, and Snaketown, once the heart of the Pima agricultural economy, "were unable to farm their land."[99] In Casa Blanca, 2,571 acres were planted, but no crop grew, due to insufficient water. While farmers in the Santan area managed to plant a crop, their grain yield was poor. In Santa Cruz, 1,500 acres of productive land were divided into 75 twenty-acre farms, but lack of water prevented its development, much to the chagrin of the Indians.[100]

The economic structure of the reservation had clearly shifted. Once in control of all their lands, the Pima now owned land in severalty. Pressure to farm using modern farming methods proved costly. While development of a new irrigation system was designed to make the Indians self-sufficient, in reality it made them more dependent. The Indian Service expected to see a return on the investment it had made in the land. Congress wanted the expense of the irrigation project repaid. Indeed, the U.S.

Army Corps of Engineers recommended in 1914 that all eligible Indian land not farmed by the Pima be "leased to white farmers or otherwise farmed."[101]

The Pima opposed the leasing of their land for fear they would become vagabonds in their own homeland. Some allottees prophetically saw the day when non-Indians would one day farm their land because of the Pima's lack of financial resources. Having survived the years of starvation, the Pima did not desire federal paternalism. They did not seek to abandon "habits of thrift," and they did not wish to drift into "indolence and crime" because of the changing reservation economy.[102] While the Pima were unified in their opposition to leasing their lands, powerful social and political forces remained at work. If the Pima could adapt to this changing reality, they would survive. If they could not, their resources would be turned over to someone who could.

CHAPTER 8

The Pima Adjudication Survey

AT THE TURN OF THE TWENTIETH CENTURY, settlers lived above and adjacent to the Pima Reservation and cultivated 142,322 acres in the Salt River valley, 35,000 acres between Florence and Casa Grande, and 18,000 acres in the Casa Grande Valley.[1] Federal legislation assisted settlers in acquiring and developing the land and required them to make bona fide application of water in order to perfect their land titles. These federal requirements put settlers in direct competition with tribal nations over control and use of the waters of western streams. In the end, the rights of tribal nations were rendered *n'importe*, as politically well-heeled settlers, government bureaucrats, and congressional allies asserted control over the water.[2]

In the midst of these activities, the Indian Service made a belated attempt to assert Pima rights. In 1914, an adjudication survey quantified Pima irrigated lands in an effort to protect their water. This assertion of rights was tied to a plan to benefit local agricultural interests, as Congress tied support for Pima water rights and development to the broader policy of incorporating the Indians into the American polity. Not surprisingly, congressmen such as Carl Hayden (D-AZ) saw an opportunity to cultivate these sentiments to benefit all farmers along the Gila River, especially those in Pinal County.[3]

In 1913, irrigation engineer Charles Olberg proposed surveying the reservation to determine the current and previous level of cultivation. This would quantify an amount of water the government could claim on behalf of the Pima. Confident congressional sympathies would side with the Pima, Arizona's congressional delegation sought to use the survey to propose a legislative package that would extend the benefits of an irrigation system to settlers as well. The responsibility of conducting this survey fell to Clay H. Southworth, a thirty-three-year-old Indian Service engineer.

Southworth made this survey in 1914 using relatively simple technology: a field survey using the standard triangulation system, a visual analysis of the land, and the oral testimony gathered from thirty-four Pima elders.[4] Using this oral testimony and technology provides a qualitative and quantitative means of analyzing the adjudication survey not available to Southworth and not possible with a simple visual analysis of the maps. While not altering the general findings of Southworth, a modern analysis identifies specific crop patterns on the reservation that illustrate the effect of water loss and aid in understanding the depth of economic deprivation and the adaptation the Pima were forced to make a century ago.

The Indian Irrigation Service assembled a set of maps identifying current and previously irrigated lands on the reservation as a precursor to both the passage of federal legislation authorizing the Florence–Casa Grande Project (FCGP) and the anticipated adjudication of Gila River water rights. Using data extracted from these maps, the Indian Service intended to protect water for the Pima under the local doctrine of prior appropriation. With a conservative population estimate of 3,500 adults, the Indian Service projected 35,000 irrigable acres with water rights.

With the survey, the Indian Service instituted an action encouraged by the U.S. Army Corps of Engineers. A bill in Congress contemplated a federal project to restore Pima rights "to the use of the water." This project was predicated on a joint-use irrigation system that would benefit all farmers and integrate the reservation economy with that of Pinal County.[5] A corollary measure was to facilitate the final allotment of the reservation. From a political and practical perspective, Pima tribal water rights would have little relevance following land severalty since the federal consensus supported the theory that Indian water rights followed the doctrine of prior appropriation. Scarcity of water materially reduced the number of Pima acres farmed, as shown in table 8.1, which indicates 33.6 percent of all fields were abandoned (not in cultivation or having been previously irrigated) due to insufficient water in 1914 (36.7 percent of all acres).[6] As compelling, the mean abandoned field size was 21 percent larger than the mean 1,914 cultivated fields.

In 1912, two years before the survey, the Pima had cause for optimism when Congressman John H. Stephens (D-TX) introduced into the House of Representatives a bill authorizing federal action on Pima water rights. Assigned to the Committee on Indian Affairs, the bill had the support of

TABLE 8.1. Mean Field Size of Abandoned and 1914 Cultivated Pima Lands

Category	Abandoned	1914
Fields	1,066	2,112
Acres	6,998	12,069
Mean field size	6.57	5.16

Source: Adapted from the Southworth maps, 1914, San Carlos Irrigation Project Archives.

a number of eastern "friends of the Indians" who could expend political capital on Indian causes without fear of voter insurgency. Some members of Congress, including Stephens, Senator Joseph Taylor Robinson (D-AR), and Senator Carroll Page (R-VT), were familiar with the Pima's grievances. Western politicians, having voting constituents competing with Indians for federal reclamation, generally opposed Indian irrigation projects. Hayden, a member of the House of Representatives Committee on Indian Affairs, was no exception. Litigation, the first-year congressman and son of a former trader on the Pima Reservation argued, would not provide Pima lands with "as much moisture as was to be found in the ink of the signature of the judge who would sign such a decree." A judge could not make it rain, and no judge could stop the river from flooding. Besides, Hayden reasoned, the loss of Pima water was "not due in any great measure to diversions," but resulted from environmental changes within the Gila watershed.[7] Hayden convinced the committee to kill the bill and instead worked to gain support for a joint-use reclamation project on the Gila River that would rival Roosevelt Dam on the Salt River. With the bill dead in committee, Hayden secured legislation authorizing the Corps of Engineers to conduct a feasibility study of the San Carlos dam site.

Heavy flooding along the Gila River in the spring of 1912 destroyed the brush diversion dams used by the Pima to divert what natural flow remained in the river. By the time the necessary repairs were made, the floodwaters receded and the Pima again lacked water. Special Indian Agent Charles L. Ellis wrote Commissioner of Indian Affairs Robert Valentine suggesting the efficacy of building an inexpensive diversion dam on the eastern end of the reservation to harness floodwater. If water was not restored soon, the Pima might not "ever regain their past confidence."[8]

Without protection of their water, Olberg opined, the Pima would be unable to "cultivate as much land as they formerly did."[9]

After 1912, Indian water cases overwhelmed the U.S. Department of Justice. Well-publicized suits from the Fort Belknap Gros Ventre–Assiniboine in Montana, Pyramid Lake Paiute in Nevada, Yakima in Washington, Uintah and Ouray Ute in Utah, and the Gila River Pima dominated congressional Indian Affairs committees. Nevertheless, challenges remained in prosecuting these cases. Indian Service chief engineer Wendell Reed complained to Commissioner of Indian Affairs Cato Sells in 1913 that the Justice Department litigated Indian cases, but it did not "get out and secure the evidence" needed to prosecute successfully such claims. It "simply fights with the ammunition that is brought to [it]." Opponents of the Indians hired "good lawyers" and "leave no stone unturned" in gathering the evidence needed to support their position. While the Justice Department assigned two water rights attorneys to handle Indian cases, it did not provide any resources to research Indian claims.[10] Such unresponsiveness forced the Indian Service to change its tactics. To protect Indian water rights and provide the Indians with an equal chance to succeed in the local and national economy, the Indian Service needed data that substantiated tribal claims.

Olberg informed Sells of the importance of survey maps in documenting the extent of Pima land then under cultivation and having priority rights to water. With Sells's support, Olberg proposed putting four men in the field conducting "adjudication surveys," two gathering data on the reservation, and two above it. He then assigned John S. Layne to examine land records in Pinal, Pima, and Graham counties regarding "water appropriations that might have some bearing" on adjudication hearings. Assistant engineer F. R. Schanck stressed the propriety of a survey to determine the extent and quantity of water used by the Indians.[11] Until this information was gathered, Olberg was unable to "guess within a couple thousand acres" how much Pima land was or could be under irrigation.[12]

Olberg did not believe it proper to take water from upstream users, after they had put it to beneficial use with the blessing and approval of the U.S. government, and restore it to the Pima. In an effort to mitigate this conflict, Olberg recommended constructing two diversion dams on the river, believing they would "be of material and immediate benefit" to the Pima and "absolutely essential" to the success of irrigated agriculture on the reservation.[13] When the Corps of Engineers declared feasible the proposed San Carlos Project in 1914, it recommended the construction of a diversion dam above Florence. This would better utilize floodwaters that could then be transported through a thirty-one-mile-long canal "to improve irrigation conditions on the Pima Reservation." If the Florence diversion dam were not politically possible, then at a minimum a diversion dam was to be built at the head of the Little Gila River to capture the return flow from upstream users near Florence to be used beneficially by Pima farmers on the eastern end of the reservation.[14]

By spring, some members of Congress were convinced of the propriety of a reclamation project on the Gila River and remained open to the idea of constructing a diversion dam if it would benefit Pima farmers.[15] Hayden and Senator Henry F. Ashurst (D-AZ), determined to use this sentiment to the advantage of all Pinal County farmers, sought a joint-use system that would enable the Pima and their non-Indian neighbors to put their water to beneficial use and thereby protect it under state prior appropriation laws. Distributing the benefits of reclamation through a joint-use project was socially and politically more palatable than reallocating water, leading Hayden to support the more conservative and expedient course.[16]

In June, Hayden and Ashurst co-introduced legislation calling for construction of the San Carlos dam and a joint-use irrigation project. Facing opposition from western congressmen who believed Arizona already had its share of federal reclamation (i.e., the Salt River Project), Hayden and Ashurst initiated a public relations campaign designed to shape opinion for the San Carlos Project. "Our best, and in fact our only, avenue of approach is by reason of the fact that the Pima Indians will be benefited," Hayden noted.[17] The Pima, meanwhile, initiated their own public relations blitz, with the Pima First Presbyterian Church in Sacaton writing members of Congress seeking support for a reclamation project on the Gila.[18] John Truesdell, assistant U.S. attorney representing the Pima, also broadcast Pima water rights in speeches and articles to local communities, pushing for an "early adjustment" of Gila River water rights by court decree.[19]

Ashurst, chairman of the Senate Indian Affairs Committee, immediately requested that Secretary of the Interior Franklin Lane prepare a position paper outlining the views of the Indian Service regarding a smaller joint-use diversion dam above Florence, a concept viewed as more feasible after a series of floods in the winter of 1914–1915. "Certain it is," assistant engineer Nicholas W. Irsfeld wrote Southworth from Sacaton in February, "more acres of land went downstream with the last flood."[20] The torrent left several canals on the reservation in "very bad condition," with the wing dam at the head of the Little Gila River completely destroyed. While upstream farmers might be able to build a permanent diversion dam above Florence to protect them from flooding and better utilize the water, Lane told Ashurst, the government would have to oppose them "in order to protect the water right now claimed by the Indians." Lane consented to the proposed project but only if it would "give the Indians an advantage of location that they have not heretofore enjoyed."[21]

Reed proceeded cautiously, seeking to protect Pima water through the politically conservative "beneficial use" approach. Writing to Sells, Reed stressed the desirability of increasing Indian irrigation as a means of self-support and for "the preservation of undisputed legal rights to the water." Showing his deference for prior appropriation, Reed informed Sells that such use of the water was more in accordance with the "law in arid states" and "cooperation with state officials is encouraged by acting in harmony with this plan."[22] Already in February 1914, Reed dispatched a letter to Olberg stressing the importance of demonstrating actual number of acres cultivated by the Indians. "I find that Congressmen simply go up in the air when they question [me] and find that a considerable amount [of money] has been expended in irrigation projects and [I am] unable to show any tangible beneficial results."[23] Olberg responded by explaining again that the "amount of land irrigated [by the Pima] changes from year to year," depending on water availability. While currently unable to quantify the acreage under irrigation, Olberg promised Reed when the present surveys were completed he could quantify the acreage to within "a fraction of an acre."[24]

While the Corps of Engineers recommended adjudication of Gila River water rights as a precursor to any irrigation project, litigation made Hayden- and Florence–Casa Grande–area farmers uneasy, especially if Congress authorized federal action. Desiring to restore water to the Pima and provide for his voting constituents, Hayden encouraged Pinal County water leaders to settle any water adjudication matter in a friendly manner rather than "quarrel over the meager supply." Water then going to waste in times of flood made little sense, when it could be harnessed to benefit all farmers in the Gila River valley.[25]

In anticipation of adjudication proceedings, Sells approved Olberg's request to survey the reservation and determine the extent of Pima agriculture. Schanck suggested Olberg not only survey the reservation but also include the upstream lands so as to "limit and define the quantity of water" being used above the reservation.[26] Assistant Commissioner of Indian Affairs Edgar Merritt authorized $3,000 to install and maintain gauging stations on the Gila to chart the flow of water and effects of upstream diversions. At Olberg's request, six of these stations were placed on the Gila River, one on the Santa Cruz River, and one on the San Pedro River. In an attempt to keep water hearings out of federal court, Pinal County water users initiated a friendly complaint in Florence on December 9, 1913. Olberg immediately begged Reed to do all he could to "stave off the adjudication a few months longer [so] we will be in a position to present the claims of the Indians."[27]

Reed delayed adjudication hearings in the *Lobb v. Avenente* complaint until June 10, 1914, when Cochise County Judge A. C. Lockwood commenced hearings on the complaint that sidestepped Pima water rights and focused on the rights of water users in Pinal County. As noncitizen wards of the government, the Pima were neither present in the Florence courthouse nor were their interests represented. Hayden convinced Lockwood to limit the proceedings to Pinal County, believing that keeping Upper Gila River valley users in Gila County out of court would best serve all parties.[28]

Meanwhile, Reed agreed with Olberg's request to survey all the middle Gila River valley in order to quantify the current and formerly irrigated lands of the Pima and Maricopa as well as their non-Indian neighbors, both above and below the reservation. Olberg then assigned Southworth to conduct the surveys. Southworth and a crew of Pima instrument men went about surveying and mapping all irrigated and previously irrigated lands within the reservation, producing a graphic representation of the historic parameters of agriculture on the reservation.

The maps illustrate in detail the land then irrigated, that previously irrigated, and that susceptible of irrigation, as well as the "various kinds of crops to which the land was planted." The survey clearly shows the abandonment of scores of Pima farms due to water loss, with entire villages shifted or deserted.[29] There were 3,766.19 acres not in cultivation and 3,231.81 acres giving evidence of having been previously irrigated, leaving a total of 6,998 acres (36.7 percent) abandoned in 1914. Other farms were "only partially cultivated, yielding scant and uncertain returns."[30] This is substantiated by Pima farmer George Pablo, who complained that many of his people "had to leave our farms and move up the river" where seepage water was available. Pima elder James Hollen added, "Our fathers were forced to leave their old fields in the District of Sacaton Siding [Sranuka] where they built homes and cultivated lands. We felt the decrease of water first as we were the last to take out our water from the river." Whole villages, including Pablo's Mount Top village, simply disappeared as the water dried up.[31]

The Southworth survey demonstrated the geomorphology of Pima agriculture. Of the eight village clusters shown on map 8.1, half were of recent origin or had shifted location, i.e., Gila Crossing (1873), Santa Cruz (1875), Santan (1877), Maricopa (1887), and Cooperative (1900). All but Santan were downstream of the historic center of the Pima villages (Casa Blanca area) and close to the confluence of the Santa Cruz, Gila, and Salt rivers. Furthermore, several village clusters abandoned canals and fields after the first upstream diversions of water, including Blackwater, Sacaton, and Casa Blanca, all older, established villages. In addition to currently cultivated lands, each village demonstrated evidence of previous agriculture (abandoned fields due to lack of water) and lands not then in cultivation (due to the inability to get water to the land). Blackwater, Sacaton, and Casa Blanca exhibited the largest percentage of abandoned fields (38 percent, 36 percent, and 37 percent, respectively).[32]

The easternmost cluster centered around Blackwater, which was dependent on floodwater and a limited supply of seepage water for its crops. Seepage posed problems, although Pima farmer Juan Enas "felt obliged to use it anyway in order to keep our families alive," despite the fact that it reduced yields on vegetable crops.[33] During the 1890s, Blackwater farmers harvested few crops, due to insufficient water. Water failure doomed the Old Woman's Mouth ditch to abandonment by 1905, although the Blackwater Island ditch still irrigated 1,029 acres in 1914. The Padilla ditch on the south bank (heading above the reservation) irrigated

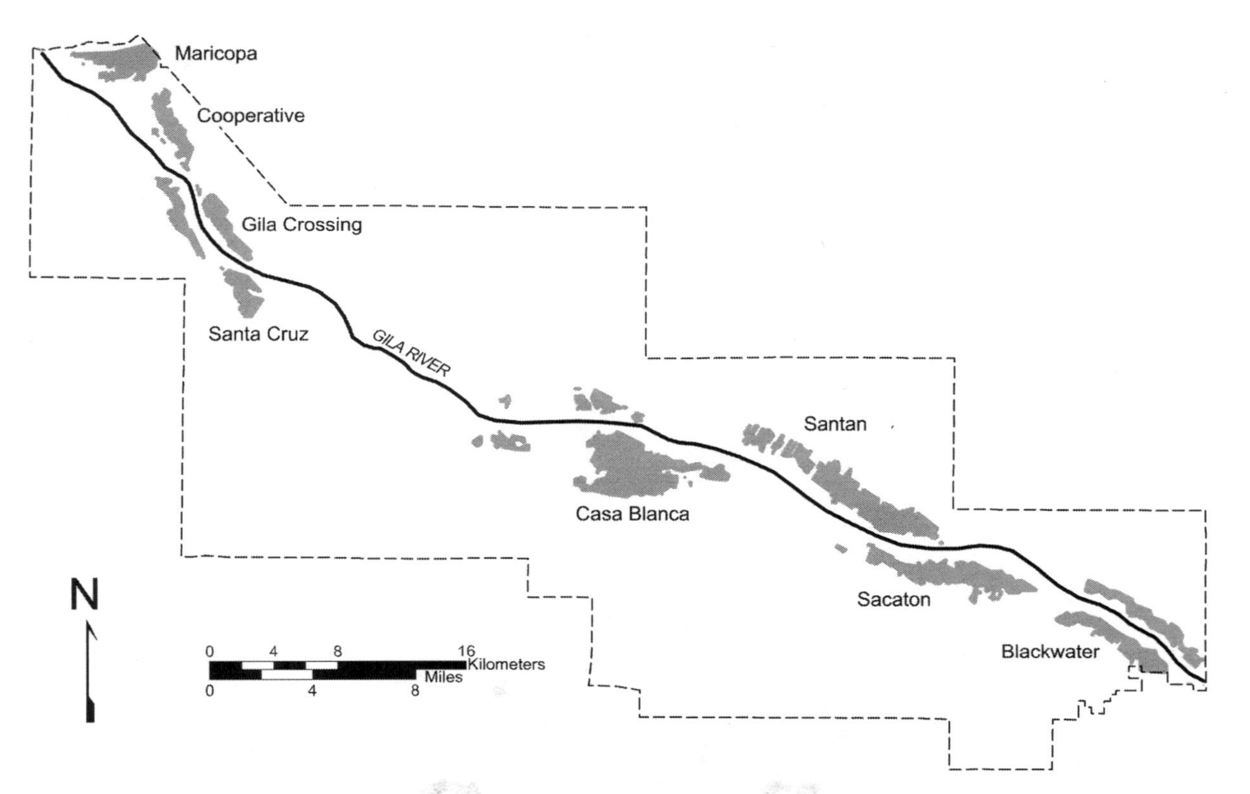

MAP 8.1. Village clusters and agricultural lands within the Pima Reservation, 1914.

just 44 acres of reservation land. A scarcity of water in the Cayah ditch led to the downstream establishment of the Santan district in the 1870s. The Cholla Mountain ditch irrigated 941 acres in 1914. Despite existing ditches, some farmers did not harvest any crop due to water shortages. Southworth estimated 2,761 acres in cultivation or abandoned in the Blackwater cluster.[34]

Downstream from Blackwater was the Sacaton cluster, which included the villages of Sacaton and Sacaton Flats. Six ditches served the area that included the U.S. Bureau of Indian Affairs Pima Agency and agency farm, as well as the U.S. Department of Agriculture's Sacaton Cooperative Extension Agricultural Experiment Station. The Yaqui ditch irrigated just 44 acres before it was abandoned in 1902 and replaced by a larger ditch to convey water from Blackwater slough via the Little Gila River for use downstream. Although abandoned in 1885 due to inadequate water, the Old Santan ditch at one time irrigated 1,272 acres. The Sacaton Flats Canal and the Cottonwood ditch served 899 and 819 acres, respectively, at the time of the survey. The Hendricks ditch irrigated just 76 acres, while the Old Maricopa ditch no longer served any land. Sixty-seven-year-old Antonito Azul lamented the abandonment of 123 acres of land he and his father, Pima Chief Antonio Azul, once cultivated under the Cottonwood ditch, "not because we cannot work, but because there is no water to irrigate with."[35] George Pablo abandoned 30 of his 45 acres of land due to lack of water.[36] Southworth estimated the current and abandoned cultivated land in the Sacaton cluster at 4,348 acres.[37]

Directly north of Sacaton was the Santan cluster, which included the Santan Indian Canal and the Lower Santan Canal, both of which were on the north bank of the Gila River. When water grew scarce under the upstream Cayah ditch, these canals served families that moved downstream, where Juan Jose recalled their "purpose was to get and work more land" than what was then available upstream.[38] The Lower Santan Canal was eventually absorbed into the Santan Indian Canal, with irrigated fields located on either side of it. The Santan cluster was unique in that its fields were rectangular and served by multiple lateral ditches conveying water from the Old Santan Canal. This anomaly is a reflection of missionary Charles Cook who surveyed the canal and the lands served by it in 1877. There were 3,520 cultivated or abandoned acres in the Santan cluster.[39]

Downstream was the Casa Blanca cluster, which included the waning villages of Snaketown and Stotonic, as well as Bapchule, Sacate, Wet Camp, and Vah Ki. Two ditches served Snaketown, including the ancient Sratuka that historically irrigated 1,273 acres and the Snaketown, under which 354 acres were cultivated. Pima farmers under these ditches moved to the Salt River in 1872 due to insufficient water. Directly opposite Snaketown was the Ancient Stotonic ditch, which once served 590 acres. Abandoned because of shifting in the head of the canal precipitated by reduced water flows, the Stotonic ditch replaced it and irrigated 1,559 acres. The New Mount Top ditch replaced the Old Mount Top ditch, before it, too, was abandoned. Below the Stotonic was the Bapchule Canal, serving 1,937 acres.[40]

Just to the west, but still part of the Casa Blanca cluster, were four smaller ditches. The Bridlestood Canal was abandoned in the late 1880s due to insufficient stream flow. Farther west was the Ancient Maricopa ditch, which was abandoned in the 1870s when river flows declined. The Sranuka ditch once irrigated 736 acres, with Pima farmers under these ditches moving downstream to Gila Crossing in the late 1870s.[41] A portion of this ditch remained in use and was renamed the Alkali Camp Canal, which served 198 acres of land. The Old Santa Cruz Canal was abandoned when most of the villagers moved west to the Santa Cruz River in the 1870s. Once the epicenter of Pima agriculture with 11,222 acres in production, Casa Blanca farmers cultivated just 4,048 acres in 1914.[42]

A fifth cluster centered around the village of Santa Cruz, located between the Santa Cruz and Gila rivers and established in 1875 by farmers from the Old Santa Cruz Canal. Two ditches served the village, with the Simon Webb ditch serving 660 acres.[43] The more southerly Breckinridge ditch diverted water from the Santa Cruz River, but irrigated just 5 acres. Crops under this ditch fared poorly, Pima farmer Juan Lagons recalled, because of seepage water, again indicating reduced productivity when loss of the river mandated dependence on seepage. Only because of episodic floodwater, Lagons continued, were the fields kept alive as "otherwise they would have been useless long ago." There were 665 cultivated and 31 abandoned acres in the Santa Cruz cluster in 1914.[44]

Downstream from Santa Cruz was the Gila Crossing cluster, served by three ditches that irrigated fields on both banks of the Gila. The Hoover ditch, constructed to supply water to a group of Pima farmers who moved downstream in 1873, served 954 acres. To the west and on the south bank of the river was the John Thomas Canal, which irrigated 587 acres. The Joseph Head Canal and the John Thomas ditch were consolidated and irrigated 139 acres in 1914. Within the Gila Crossing cluster, there were 1,680 cultivated and 138 abandoned acres.[45]

The final village cluster irrigated by the Gila River was Cooperative village, served by the Cooperative Canal. Seventy-two Pima heads of families worked cooperatively in 1900 to develop the land and utilize seepage water that rose to the surface in the Gila just below the Hoover ditch heading. While once irrigating 984 acres, the three-and-a-half-mile-long Cooperative ditch irrigated just 594 acres in 1914. The Oscar Walker ditch also served the Cooperative cluster, but irrigated just 13 acres. This latter ditch was the lowest taking water out of the Gila River. At the time of the survey, there were 1,042 acres prepared for irrigation, although just 607 were cultivated.[46]

The eighth and final village cluster was the Maricopa, which took water out of the Salt River four miles upstream from its confluence with the Gila. The Maricopa, once irrigating along the middle Gila upstream, abandoned their fields and moved to the Salt River because of a growing scarcity of water in the 1880s. Maricopa village, established in 1887 and served by the Maricopa Canal, irrigated 1,271 acres. An additional 219 acres were abandoned, and another 144 acres had been fenced and cleared but were not irrigated. Fields under this canal were entitled to water from the Salt River under the 1903 Haggard Decree.

The village clusters indicate that at least one-third of the peak Pima agricultural lands were abandoned and not irrigated in 1914 due to insufficient water and the lack of a modern irrigation delivery system to convey water to lands that, due to the geomorphology of the Gila River, were not capable of receiving irrigation water. Nearly two-thirds of the agricultural lands once served with water, or 12,069 acres, had access to water, largely due to excess water available during the wet years of 1914–1915.

Reservation vs. state-wide crop patterns provide a measurement of the health and vitality of the reservation economy.[47] This is an important consideration, given that the Indian Service was prepared to allot the reservation. If the Indian Service sought to provide the Pima with an "equal chance" to compete in the national economy, as it suggested with its allotment policy, then it was incumbent upon the department to ensure the Indians were actually in a position to compete with non-Indians.

In considering the maps, there are several caveats to mind. Southworth spent six months (January through June) in the field conducting the survey. This is significant in that, under normal conditions, it might be skewed toward winter crops with an accounting of only some summer crops (i.e., fields surveyed in May or June). While summer crops would have been planted and winter crops would be nearing maturation in Santa Cruz, Blackwater, Gila Crossing, Cooperative, and Maricopa, the fact that not all villages were surveyed during the spring precluded some from being adequately represented on the survey map, particularly Sacaton, Santan, and Casa Blanca. Since Pima agriculture historically was seasonal, with grains the dominant winter crop and cotton, corn, and squash dominant in the summer, the data may be skewed towards the former. This limitation, however, is mitigated in that insufficient water limited most fields to one crop per year, as Pima farmers Juan Thomas, Havelena, and John Makil explained in 1914.[48]

Another factor is that off-reservation crop data for the State of Arizona, while reflecting an accurate picture of all crops grown, provide values taken from the 1910 and 1920 U.S. Census Bureau crop census. The State of Arizona did not collect crop statistics in 1914. Consequently, local cropping patterns cannot be directly compared with reservation patterns. This challenge is mitigated by using averaged data from 1910 and 1920 to reflect the condition of Arizona agriculture in 1914. Census data, however, limits crop patterns to total acres and proportions only, not specific field (or farm) sizes and number of fields planted to specific crops, something the adjudication survey does provide. Because the Southworth data are for fields (not necessarily farms) and the Arizona data are for farms (not fields), no direct comparison can be made of farm sizes, although the average of the former was estimated by Southworth at between 10 and 15 acres, while the latter was 135.1 acres.[49]

Furthermore, Southworth listed each Pima field as planted to a single crop when this was not likely the case. Pima farmers frequently planted "a portion of each field . . . to pumpkins, squash, and melons" each year. Other smaller plots of vegetables were planted, but fail to show up in the survey. Fruit production was minimal and, as Wendell Reed explained, would have been "confined to small orchards in connection with individual farms."[50] This might explain why there were only eleven fields marked "orchards" out of the 3,178 fields. While the map scale is detailed and shows fields smaller than one acre, Southworth omitted small garden plots or simply consolidated them with the more dominant crop.

A final consideration is the variance of crop selection from one village cluster to another. Two clusters stand out: Sacaton and Santan. These village clusters were the most diverse in terms of cropping patterns, which was likely a reflection of the U.S. Department of Agriculture having a field research station in Sacaton, which was just across the river from the Santan district. Farmers in these clusters had greater access to markets and experimental crop seeds than those in remote village clusters. These latter clusters grew a greater percentage of grains, as shown in table 8.2. Sacaton was also the agency center with a bustle of government activity and influences from the agency farmer, and Santan was the recipient of the first federal reclamation project on the reservation.

To demonstrate that the Pima were pushed into a subsistence economy requires a comparison of cropping patterns on the reservation with those off the reservation. A graph was constructed (not shown) to display the value of each crop, although this pointed only to the difference between the reservation and the state. Proportional values were then calculated for the reservation based on a per capita distribution of crops across the state. Population data was secured from the 1910 U.S. census

TABLE 8.2. Field Cropping Patterns by Village Clusters, 1914

Cluster	Hay	Corn	Cotton	Grains	Other	None	Total
Blackwater	17	3	4	215	1	146	386
Sacaton	57	47	9	152	4	147	416
Santan	34	42	18	290	2	152	538
Casa Blanca	0	58	0	391	2	262	713
Santa Cruz	49	0	0	123	1	74	247
Gila Crossing	65	3	0	221	1	82	372
Cooperative	27	4	0	76	4	114	225
Maricopa	14	9	19	148	2	89	281
Total	263	166	50	1,616	17	1,066	3,178

Source: Adapted from Southworth maps, 1914, San Carlos Irrigation Project Archives.

for Arizona and a 1904 Indian Service census for the reservation. While suppositional, table 8.3 reflects the actual and proportionally calculated values.

Based on population and geographic area, Arizona had larger crop acreage and greater totals by crop. However, when examining 1914 Pima cultivation and comparing it with what might have been grown if a uniform state-to-reservation ratio of acres to population was true, significant differences appear. Based on a uniform ratio, the reservation would have an increased acreage of hay, cotton, and other crops (vegetables), a decreased acreage of corn, and 82 percent less grain. In other words, based on average need and crop selection, the Pima would be expected to grow more fiber crops and less food crops.

This disparity lends support to the belief that Pima farmers expended more energy on growing grain, since it would not only provide subsistence for their people but also required the least amount of water. Pima farmer George Pablo supported this hypothesis when he reported that some Pima farmers fed grain to their cattle in 1914, "after convincing themselves that there will be no maturity of their planted wheat this year" due to insufficient water. Ho-Ke Wilson, another Pima farmer, opined the "uncertainty of water and this alkaline seepage water" either caused grain not to mature or reduced its yield.[51]

This disproportionate grain production was a product of insufficient water. Table 8.4 shows the proportion of crops grown by village cluster. Analyis of this distribution by village cluster points to several patterns. First, there were clear shifts in a number of villages and scores of farms by 1914, as whole groups of Indians simply abandoned one location and sought to reestablish themselves in another. Overall prospects for water

TABLE 8.3. Actual and Expected Acreage of Pima Crops versus Arizona Crops, 1914

Location	Hay	Corn	Cotton	Grain	Other	Total
Pima actual	1,001	920	164	9,910	72	12,067
Pima expected	2,361	357	1,004	1,828	268	5,818
Difference	(1,360)	563	(840)	8,082	(196)	6,249
Arizona	124,922	18,877	53,151	96,722	14,196	307,869

Source: Adapted from Southworth maps, 1914, San Carlos Irrigation Project Archives.

to irrigate crops were unpredictable at best, leading farmers to abandon their fields or plant fewer acres. Many families left their villages and moved to places where seepage water was available. Fields in the central and eastern, traditionally farmed, areas of the reservation were abandoned due to a dry river channel. This included the villages of Snaketown, Old Stotonic, Mount Top, and North Blackwater. Some farmers were no longer able to grow sufficient food for their needs.[52]

The overall proportion of grain grown on the reservation was significantly higher than the statewide proportion, as shown in table 8.3. Reed believed this disparity was attributed to a lack of water. "Wheat and barley are the staple crops," Reed informed the House Committee on Indian Affairs. "While the grains are the least profitable, yet they require the least water for irrigation and this consideration is responsible for the selection of these particular crops." Reed further noted the Pima grew some corn and garden produce, but such crops were "not a safe proposition under the gravity system," due to the inability to get water on the crops at the right time. "When [the farmer] is supplied with water," Reed concluded, he "will make a living and a surplus."[53]

To understand better the effects of water loss requires an examination of changes in field size by village cluster. Larger mean field sizes are found on the eastern half of the reservation. Since water was the primary

TABLE 8.4. Proportion of Fields Sown to Grain, by Acres, Based on GIS Analysis

Village	Acres of grain	Cultivated acres	Proportion in grain
Blackwater	1,495.38	1,619.68	92.3%
Sacaton	853.40	1,396.36	61.1
Santan	2,114.61	2,670.98	79.2
Casa Blanca	2,747.92	3,092.45	88.9
Santa Cruz	472.38	581.39	81.3
Gila Crossing	953.27	1,140.76	83.6
Cooperative	317.42	451.37	70.3
Maricopa	956.10	1,114.95	85.8
Pima totals	9,910.48	12,067.93	82.1
Arizona	96,722.50	307,869.50	31.8

Source: Adapted from Southworth maps, 1914, San Carlos Irrigation Project Archives.

limiting factor, it might be assumed that larger cultivated fields would be located in areas where seepage water was more likely to be available or in those villages on the downstream portion of the reservation. However, this is not the case. The largest cultivated mean field sizes in acres (6.92 in Santan and 6.86 in Casa Blanca) were in areas where the river was dry. In areas where the river still contained some water, mean field sizes in acres were the smallest (3.36 in Santa Cruz, 3.93 in Gila Crossing, and 4.07 in Cooperative), as shown in table 8.5.

When all fields are analyzed (including those abandoned and cultivated), traditional farming areas retain the largest mean field size. The largest mean field sizes in acres were found in Blackwater (7.67), Casa Blanca (7.26), and Sacaton (5.78). Santan, established in 1877, had a mean field size of 6.82 acres. Newly established villages such as Santa Cruz (3.21), Gila Crossing (3.74), Cooperative (4.75), and Maricopa (5.73) all had smaller mean field sizes in acres. Since the latter villages were of recent origin in 1914, it appears that, as water deprivation increased, villages not only moved downstream nearer the confluence of the Salt River but also were reestablished with smaller fields that were more likely to support a subsistence economy.

The larger mean field sizes of Casa Blanca, Sacaton, and Blackwater were in older villages, reflecting the pinnacle of Pima agriculture (1845–1870) when they annually sold millions of pounds of surplus grain, corn, and vegetables to military expeditions, government contractors, and

TABLE 8.5. Cultivated Mean Field Size by Village Cluster

Village	Fields	Mean	Standard deviation	Variance
Blackwater	240	6.75	4.80	23.03
Sacaton	269	5.19	5.26	27.67
Santan	386	6.92	4.38	19.16
Casa Blanca	451	6.86	5.00	25.00
Santa Cruz	173	3.36	2.69	7.26
Gila Crossing	290	3.93	2.56	5.72
Cooperative	111	4.07	2.39	2.39
Maricopa	192	5.81	3.94	15.55
Total	2,112	5.99	5.85	34.25

Source: Adapted from Southworth maps, 1914, San Carlos Irrigation Project Archives.

California-bound emigrants. This is substantiated by the Pima, who tell the story of villagers constructing canals downstream in new districts to irrigate smaller fields with the limited seepage water available. Having little time to build ditches and having little expectation of planting larger fields, heads of families reestablished their farms downstream in areas where they believed limited amounts of water would sustain them.[54]

The variance in field size and water availability did not escape officials within the Indian Service. A farmer in Gila Crossing stated the Pima once "had an ample water supply for from 4,000–6,000 acres," even though they were then cultivating less than one-quarter that amount. In Sacaton, the "Indians have had little water since 1890." Farms that were productive before that time were now idle. While ephemeral floodwaters or localized storm events enabled the cultivation of a crop, the uncertainty over water resulted in most Indians "ceas[ing] to prepare their fields" for production or sowing them to grain. They also planted smaller fields.[55]

That the Pima faced difficult and uncertain times is clear. Pima farmers had already reduced their mean field size by more than one-fifth, and more than one-third of all their fields were out of production. The older and more established villages on the eastern portion of the reservation exhibited a pattern of land going fallow and no longer being productive. In fact, these eastern villages show the greatest percentage of fields abandoned. Blackwater had abandoned 40 percent of its irrigation ditches, Sacaton 50 percent, and Casa Blanca 58 percent. Family groups from the North Blackwater area moved downstream to the newly created Santan district in the late 1870s. Whole villages within the Casa Blanca cluster abandoned their fields and were reestablished downstream or moved to the Salt River.

The degree of water deprivation is evident by comparing differences in reservation and statewide cropping patterns. These differences are so distinct that they are not likely to occur under normal conditions. Intervillage analyses demonstrate grain was the most dominant crop in the eastern villages, supporting the belief these villages were hard hit by water loss. While isolated Pima farmers grew an abundance of crops in 1914, most grew little beyond their own subsistence needs.

The comparative analysis with state patterns points to two final factors. First, the Pima were preeminent farmers. Using state per capita crop production ratios, Pima cropping patterns indicate they should have cultivated no more than 5,818 acres, yet they attempted to cultivate more than twice that amount and desired to cultivate still more. Second, by preparing over 12,000 acres for crops in 1914, the Pima remained committed to an agrarian way of life, one fully compatible with their social, cultural, and economic heritage. Once players in the market economy, the Pima were now subsistence farmers struggling to support their families.

CHAPTER 9

The Florence—Casa Grande Project

WITH THE COMPLETION OF THE adjudication survey in 1914 and the 1916 Lockwood Decree, which prioritized Pima water rights for 35,000 acres of land, Congress addressed Pima water rights by enacting into law the Florence–Casa Grande Project (FCGP), believing it would "thoroughly safeguard" Pima rights.[1] Envisioned as an integral component of the larger, still-hoped-for San Carlos Project, the FCGP instituted a joint-use irrigation system designed to facilitate the economic integration of the Pima Reservation with the surrounding economy and encourage efficient utilization of the remaining water of the Gila River. With speculators and farmers in the Salt River valley having already won the race for the first federally financed reclamation project, farmers in the Florence–Casa Grande Valley learned important lessons. Politically involved and enfranchised, these farmers aligned themselves with the politically impotent and disenfranchised Pima to generate a strong moral and legal rationale for development of the valley's water resources.

Arizonans predicated their rights to the use of water on the doctrine of prior appropriation, which conflicted with the Pima's reserved rights. While the U.S. Supreme Court opined that tribal nations had "reserved rights" to the water, neither Congress nor the Indian Service gave much credence to the ruling. Lacking resources to develop a competitive and modern irrigation system, the Pima struggled to put water to beneficial use as defined by local law. Much to the consternation of the western tribes, the Indian Service "waver[ed] between near panic and lackadaisical awareness" of their rights.[2]

In the meantime, the amount of land irrigated by the Pima declined, dropping to 7,693 acres in 1916. Statewide, the amount of Indian land irrigated by the Indian Irrigation Service plummeted to 8,733 acres from 19,386 acres. Non-Indian irrigated acreage, however, increased 46.1

percent to 467,565 acres.[3] Of this acreage, 247,260 acres were north of the reservation in the Salt River valley. Another 76,982 acres were irrigated along the Gila River above the reservation, with 33,019 acres irrigated upstream of the Pima along the Santa Cruz River. As telling, capital improvements along the Gila River and its tributaries (including the Salt River) increased 509.1 percent between passage of the Reclamation Act in 1902 and 1919, jumping to $25,165,814 (see table 9.1). Of this, U.S. Reclamation Service improvements totaled $20,277,919, while Indian Irrigation Service improvements totaled just $585,029.[4]

The mobilizing forces to develop an irrigation project for the Pima stemmed not only from a congressional desire to integrate the reservation economy with that of Pinal County but also from the long-standing goal of assimilation. With Congress moving in one direction for political reasons, the federal courts moved in another, collision-bound course. The question was whether the Pima would have the water needed to restore their economy and compete in the market or be relegated to the fringes of society.[5]

The Pima grew increasingly frustrated by the government's inattention to their water resources. Unable to restore water on their own accord, the Indians were forced to rely on the government for redress of their grievances. The lack of federal action affected the integrity of the tribe. "Following a year of plenty of water," Indian Service chief engineer Wendell Reed lamented, "the Indians take heart . . . and cultivate a large part of the land." But when water was scarce, they became discouraged and "the next year they will not farm so much."[6] Loss of water not only encouraged the Pima to abandon their agrarian heritage—and this at a time when it was official federal policy to promote agriculture among

TABLE 9.1. Irrigated Acres and Capital Improvements for Select River Basins, 1902 and 1919

	Acres		Capital	
Basin	1902	1919	1902	1919
Gila River	55,973	76,982	$1,203,882	$2,891,526
Salt River	140,642	247,260	$2,697,189	$14,939,034
Santa Cruz	10,606	33,019	$79,686	$5,168,524

Source: U.S. Bureau of the Census. *Fourteenth Census of the United States*, 1920, vol. 7.

the Indians—but it also tested their faith in the commitment of the government to restore their water.[7]

New concerns over water were raised when U.S. Bureau of Indian Affairs Pima Agency Superintendent Frank Thackery alerted Commissioner of Indian Affairs Robert Valentine that landowners near Florence intended to build yet another canal. The Pinal Mutual Irrigation Company of Florence had incorporated in 1911 with plans to head a new canal above and parallel to the Florence Canal. While it sought to secure federal funds for construction, Pinal Mutual targeted putting as much water as possible under prior appropriation and pushing forward with its plan without federal involvement. Consulting engineer James Schuyler, who earlier had evaluated Pima water projects, believed there was enough water to irrigate 25,000 acres above the reservation. This canal would further jeopardize Pima water. More ominously, Schuyler recommended Pinal Mutual sink twenty 15-inch groundwater wells.[8]

As in many parts of the Indian West, the Pima were fighting not only to hold onto the remaining floodwaters of the Gila River but also to restore natural-flowing water to which they had been deprived. The federal government, the agency to which settlers turned for reclamation assistance, was the same government responsible for protecting Indian resources. Frederick Newell, director of the Reclamation Service, was cognizant of this conflict. "The history of . . . Indians on arid lands has shown that unless protected with great care the rights to the use of water on Indian lands has been gradually lost through neglect or oversight." Without careful protection, "the future use of the necessary water has resulted disastrously to the Indians."[9] As legal guardians of the Pima, the U.S. government had a fiduciary obligation to protect their water. The federal government was in the ambiguous position of "enforcing a contradictory and inconsistent set of water laws."[10]

Congress was deliberate in considering the impact of the reserved rights doctrine. Western congressmen staunchly opposed the doctrine, while eastern legislators were amenable to it if it quantified a time frame for existence (until allotment was completed). Most did not understand or were unaware of the Supreme Court's ruling, including Senator Marcos Smith (D-AZ), who admitted he had never heard of the *Winters v. United States* (1908) tribal water rights case. Senator Carroll Page (R-VT), a proponent of Indian reserved rights, explained the challenges facing

Indian Country. While encouraged to farm and make beneficial use of their water: "The Indian says, 'I have no money; I have no horses; and I have no wagons. I have no plows. Help me to the wherewith and I will do it.' Our reply to him is substantially this: 'No sir, we are going to tie your hands. We will not give you anything to work with; and yet if you do not make beneficial use of this water within three years your rights'" will be taken away.[11]

Smith was antagonistic to Pima reserved rights, viewing any issue of water rights as a matter of states' rights (and prior appropriation). Assistant Commissioner of Indian Affairs Edgar Merritt prophetically explained that Congress, by not dealing with the inherent conflicts in water law, would one day see tribes taking "their water rights status to the courts for determination."[12]

The Indian Service poorly understood the meaning of reserved rights. Commissioner of Indian Affairs Cato Sells believed Indian water rights were in jeopardy and that the "legal right to the use of water" by Indians was "of primary importance." This right, the commissioner explained, rested "upon common-law riparian rights in some cases, and in others [upon] beneficial use of water." While noting the court's implied reservation of water, Sells believed this applied only to tribal lands and did not "involve the rights of any individual Indian." The Indian Service adopted the view that reserved rights applied to tribes up to the point of severalty, at which time individual Indians fell under prior appropriation laws.[13] Sells saw "no danger of immediate loss of [Indian] water rights." With the Indian Service failing to recognize the need to legitimize Indian water rights, Congress felt little compunction to do so. Representative Franklin Mondell (R-WY) was quick to point out this lack of urgency. If the Indian Service saw no danger to Indian water rights, then Congress had no reason to statutorily protect Pima rights.[14]

When heavy property damage resulted from flooding in the winter of 1914–1915, Congressman Carl Hayden (D-AZ) believed it was the time for Congress to control the river. Recognizing Congress would not approve of the costly San Carlos Project, Hayden and Senator Henry F. Ashurst (D-AZ) focused on gaining approval to build a smaller project for the "benefit of the Indians." It was advantageous, Hayden argued, to have a portion of the Florence diversion dam charged to private landowners since they would also benefit from it. The Pima and their neighbors received water from the same source, Hayden reasoned, and had a common interest that would bind them "for all time to come."[15]

Ashurst worked to secure an amendment to the bill, adding a second diversion dam to be located on the reservation. Reed urged Sells to approve of the plan to build the second dam with a superstructure bridge over top. Irrigation engineer Charles Olberg explained a bridge was "badly needed by the Indians and the white people."[16] Furthermore, the dam was needed to divert water into the Santan Floodwater Canal, a proposition that depended at the time on brush dams (see map 9.1). While ostensibly a means to provide the Indians with transportation over the river, the bridge was more the desire of A. J. Chandler, who sought to influence the development of a state highway connecting Phoenix and Tucson through his growing agricultural community to the north.[17]

The Senate Committee on Indian Affairs was skeptical of the real intent of the FCGP, fearing another "white man's proposition" designed to deprive the Pima of their water. Senator Harry Lane (D-OR) explained that Indians rarely "benefit from water . . . if the white man has the first opportunity." Despite the *Winters* decision upholding Indian water rights on the Fort Belknap Reservation, upstream users continued to appropriate the waters of the Milk River. How would it be any different on the Pima Reservation, Lane inquired.[18]

Senator Lane invited Samuel Brosius of the Indian Rights Association (IRA) to address the committee. Brosius recommended committee support for the bill but only if it guaranteed the enforcement of the prior rights of the Indians through the insertion of a clause clearly spelling out Pima water rights to forty thousand acres of land. Any water remaining after the Pima received theirs would be available to neighboring farmers.[19]

Hayden opposed legislation delineating Pima water rights. He and Merritt resisted specific quantities and acreage, fearing they would bind the Indian Service so that it "could not do what was best." Senator Joseph Taylor Robinson (D-AR) feared the omission of a dedicated water supply for the Pima, arguing that if the government agreed the Pima had prior water rights then "why should it not be incorporated in the bill?" Robinson further feared that by not including clear language protecting Pima water rights, the Indian Service at a later date might "be forced to exercise a discretion that it might not want to exercise."[20]

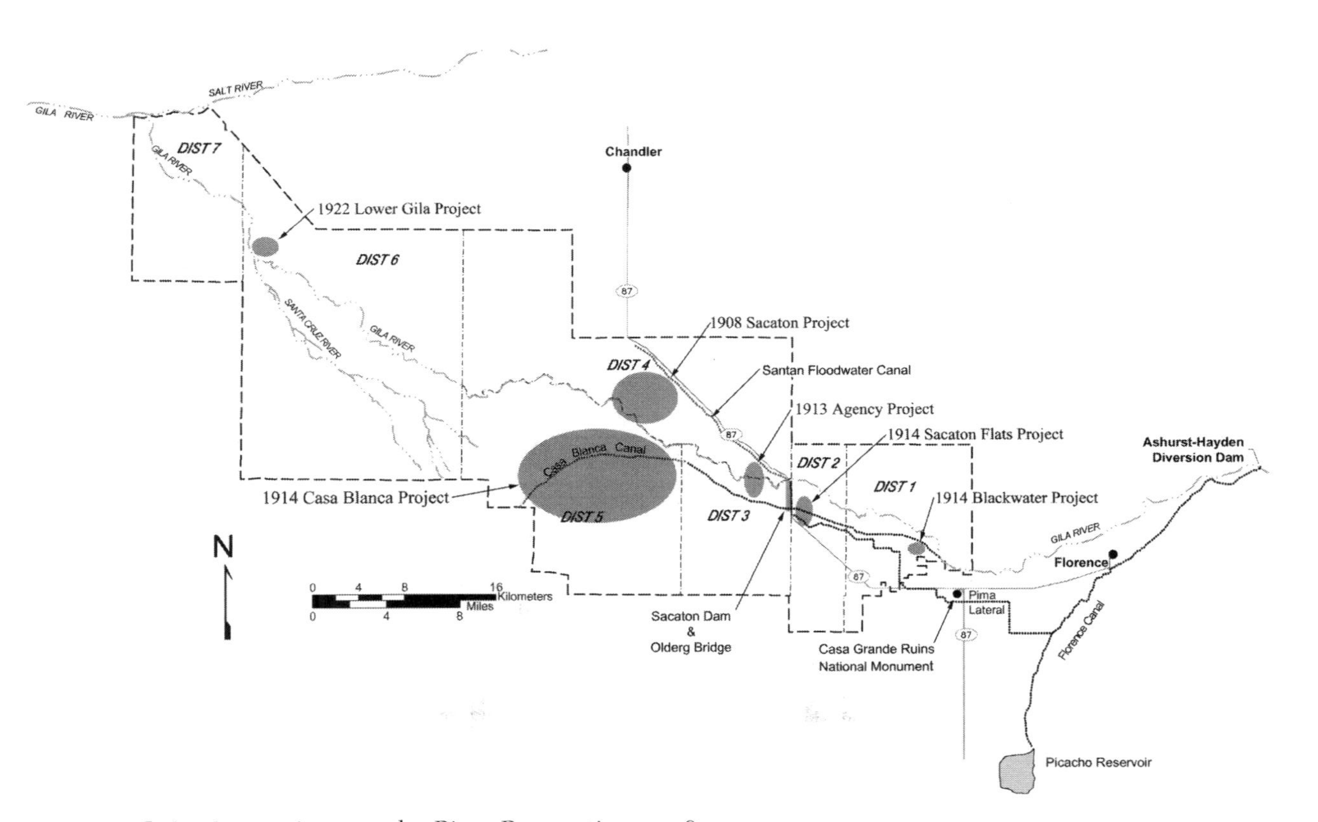

MAP 9.1. Irrigation projects on the Pima Reservation, 1908–1922.

Senator Lane badgered Hayden on the quantity of Pima land that could be irrigated with construction of the FCGP. Acres under ditch and potentially irrigated acres were crucial data needed to demonstrate allocation of water. Hayden, wanting the project approved, played his "Indian card." The Pima's current diversion of water was "below the white diversion," but passage of the FCGP would "carry the Indian diversion up the river so that he will get an equal chance to obtain his share of the water."[21] Hayden sought to ensure the appropriation of water for the reservation, but without addressing reserved rights. Since Hayden believed it was senseless to build a second canal to deliver water to the reservation, he proposed using the existing off-reservation distribution canal and constructing a lateral to convey water to the reservation.

To deliver water to the reservation, the United States would have to purchase the Florence Canal. Any lateral extension would cross private and public lands. While the 1890 Canal Act reserved such rights, Hayden preferred an exchange for the right-of-way, with the government allowing non-Indian farmers to divert water from the same system. Only if the government built and controlled the diversion dam on the Gila River and operated the distribution and lateral canals would the Pima be assured of receiving their water.[22] Ashurst was so confident the project

FIGURE 9.1. Pima farmer Richard Pablo cutting grain in his field, ca. 1920. (Photograph courtesy of the San Carlos Irrigation Project)

would protect Pima water rights that he boasted in Arizona one had to be "an Indian to secure . . . your rights."[23] Despite lacking a consensus on the meaning of Indian water rights, the House of Representatives and the Senate agreed the most expedient means of resolving the dispute was to build a joint-use irrigation system that would distribute the benefits and costs of the project. In March 1915, the Senate Indian Affairs Committee recommended an appropriation not to exceed $175,000 to construct the Florence diversion dam. A House of Representatives filibuster, however, prevented the bill from passing, and it died.

After five years of discussion and debate, it was apparent that neither the Indian Service nor Congress understood or cared to pursue the matter of Indian reserved rights. The Indian Irrigation Service, meanwhile, continued to gather data in preparation for land severalty and to demonstrate Pima utilization of the water. Congress considered legislation but only within the context of a joint-use system based on prior appropriation rights. To appease the friends of the Indians, Hayden and Ashurst had to clearly show that the Pima were the primary beneficiaries of the project.

To this end, the Indian Service began work on a series of reservation irrigation projects designed to protect existing Pima water and demonstrate that the Pima could farm the land with protection of their water rights. The centerpiece of the emerging irrigation system was the Sacaton (sometimes called Santan) Project. This project was designed to irrigate ten thousand acres on the north bank of the Gila River between Sacaton and Stotonic, and centered around the construction of the Santan Floodwater Canal and the introduction of groundwater pumping on the reservation. The canal, which headed on the Gila River 3.5 miles east of Sacaton, was to convey episodic floodwater from the river onto land targeted for allotment. Ten pumping plants would supply the majority of water for irrigation.

Valentine optimistically reported over 4,500 acres irrigated in the Sacaton Project in 1911, with "the main canals . . . now built above 10,000 acres."[24] But when the IRA publicized the Pima cause, Congress was compelled to examine more closely irrigation matters in central Arizona, with the House of Representatives Committee on Expenditures in the Interior Department opening hearings on the matter. Irrigation engineer William H. Code opined that it was impossible for the Pima to recover their low-water rights now that the water had been used by upstream farmers for more than twenty-five years. Code did not regard it "as feasible to attempt to fight for water rights that had been taken away so many years before."[25]

By the spring of 1913, Olberg began constructing laterals to convey water to 9,090 acres staked and scheduled for allotment within the Sacaton Project. Nearly 7,800 acres were to be served with groundwater. Head gates and check structures were installed and new culverts and bridges constructed. By 1915, nearly sixty miles of laterals were constructed, irrigating 3,319 acres with ground and episodic floodwater. Despite high hopes, Olberg was forced to acknowledge that, at most, 6,000 acres could be served by the project, just 60 percent of the Reclamation Service estimates.[26]

While a portion of the floodwater canal was completed, the means of diverting floodwaters from the Gila River into the canal were not. Lacking a permanent diversion dam, Olberg built a temporary brush dam across the river in an attempt to push water into the floodwater canal. The Pima, having built their own brush dam to channel water into the old Santan Canal, objected.[27] The new canal crosscut the old one, making it impossible to use both systems concurrently. Concerns over allotment, groundwater use, incompatible delivery systems, and insufficient floodwater resulted in the Santan Floodwater Canal becoming "completely choke[d]" with silt and impossible to operate "until a diversion dam" could be built.[28]

By 1915, the Sacaton Project extended west of Stotonic, where new problems arose, including well casings filling with silt. Winter flooding damaged both the laterals and the main canal. Olberg saw little value in repairing the damage unless a permanent diversion dam could be built at the head of the canal on the Gila River. To provide water to the allotments in the interim, Olberg capitulated to the demands of the Pima and diverted water through the old Santan Canal. Flood- and groundwater from eight wells irrigated just 1,740 acres under the Sacaton Project by 1915.[29]

To put additional water to beneficial use, and in anticipation of land severalty on the south bank of the river, Olberg initiated the Little Gila Project in February 1913. This project was designed to restore irrigation south of the main channel of the Gila River extending from Blackwater to Casa Blanca. The Little Gila, closed by the Indian Irrigation Service in 1903, for centuries had been used by the Pima to convey water from the main channel of the Gila River onto lands south of the river.[30]

The Little Gila reopened in the fall of 1913 "to safeguard the interests of the Indians in the waters of the Gila." Before Olberg began work, he reconstructed a small lateral the Pima built to irrigate a limited area of land in Blackwater after the Little Gila closed. To protect their rights to this water, Olberg constructed a flume to carry the ditch over the Little Gila into the Blackwater Island District and then re-excavated the river and installed two wing dams to divert the natural flow of the Gila River onto Pima farmland on the south bank. The Little Gila now carried three hundred cubic feet per second of water west for a distance of twenty miles.[31] By fall, Olberg expected to irrigate one thousand acres of land with natural flow water in Blackwater.

The floods of 1914–1915 damaged the Little Gila, with silt and driftwood plugging the channel and destroying the Blackwater flume.[32] Three wagon bridges were damaged, and a half-mile of embankment on the south side of the Gila near Sacaton Flats washed away. More than a mile of the Sacaton Flats Canal was replaced in what Olberg coined the Sacaton Flats Project. More than nine hundred acres of agriculture were restored as a result of this project.[33] Additional flood damage in Blackwater resulted in the Blackwater Project, designed "to retain the Indians'

FIGURE 9.2. The Blackwater flume carried water from the Little Gila River, seen flowing under the flume, to Blackwater Island, ca. 1914. (Reproduced courtesy of the National Archives and Records Administration)

rights to water." Olberg, wishing to demonstrate actual Pima water utilization, rebuilt over 27,000 feet of ditch in Blackwater, reflecting the importance the Indian Service placed on beneficial use as a means of protecting Pima water rights. By 1915, the Blackwater Project was completed, with two thousand acres prepared for cultivation.[34] Winter flooding limited full development of the Blackwater Project and pointed to a continuing need for "a permanent diversion dam" if the Pima were to use their water beneficially.[35]

In November 1913, Olberg surveyed land north of the Pima Agency on the Agency Project. This project was designed to put water to beneficial use on 1,870 acres two miles above Sacaton and lying on an island between the Gila and Little Gila rivers. Construction of nearly three miles of laterals began in January 1914. The land under these laterals was farmed until the opening of the Florence Canal thirty years before when, for lack of water, the land "was abandoned." The Indian Service scheduled the land for allotment once the laterals were constructed. Difficulties crossing the agency grounds, however, left just eight hundred acres with irrigation.[36]

In the spring of 1914, Olberg made plans to construct the largest irrigation project then attempted on the reservation. The Casa Blanca Project was designed to irrigate up to 35,000 acres with water channeled through the Little Gila River. While more land than necessary to "furnish 10 acres for each individual now living in the district," Olberg informed Reed, the grandiose scale of the project was necessary "to keep the costs per acre as low as possible." Olberg admitted cost was only part of the consideration. By allotting land in Casa Blanca to those Pima and Maricopa living downriver in the villages of Santa Cruz, Gila Crossing, Komatke, and Maricopa Colony, the Indian Service could avoid "the losses that would occur if the water was used lower down the river."[37]

Olberg recognized the advantage of utilizing as much water as possible as a means of protecting it under the beneficial use doctrine.[38] Nicholas W. Irsfeld, engineer in charge of the Casa Blanca Project, proposed heading a fifteen-mile-long canal on the Little Gila River to irrigate the land.[39] While not yet surveyed, Olberg requested $15,000 to begin the project, which encompassed the villages of Sweetwater, Bapchule, Alkali, Wet Camp, and Casa Blanca.[40]

FIGURE 9.3. Construction of Lateral 2-1-4 in Casa Blanca, ca. 1915. (Reproduced courtesy of the National Archives and Records Administration)

Pima Agency Superintendent Ralph Ward was enthused by the rapid development of irrigation works on the reservation. But while much of the new irrigation system was in place, at a cost of $932,911, water resources remained inadequate.[41] The Indian Service recognized it was in a race with off-reservation farmers to see who would first beneficially put the water to use. Reed recognized water resources in the West in general and on the Pima Reservation in particular were rapidly being depleted. Despite nearly a million-dollar investment, the Indian Service's beneficial-use approach was tenable at best, as it could not divert a large enough flow of water to put the Pima back on a stable economic foundation. While there were 18,500 acres under ditch, in 1916, just 7,693 acres were irrigated.[42]

Despite lack of irrigation water, flooding along the Gila River added to the concerns of the Pima. During the winter of 1916 another flood devastated the Gila River valley, and this after flooding in the fall left the soil saturated with moisture. Heavy snowmelt in the upper reaches of the watershed kept the river flowing until the first of June.[43] While the Pima put the water to good use in the spring, the winter flooding decimated their crops and damaged their villages. Thackery telegraphed Hayden that reservation damage surpassed $100,000, with an additional $40,000 damage off reservation. Canals were destroyed; head gates, check structures, and brush dams were washed out; and incising erosion occurred throughout the newly constructed irrigation facilities on the reservation. Some three thousand Pima, Mexican, and American farmers stood to lose their crops.[44]

In the spring of 1916, the House of Representatives Committee on Indian Affairs again took up debate on the FCGP bill, believing Pima water rights had been adequately protected. While Representative William Borland (D-MO) feared construction of the project would commit the government to the larger and more costly San Carlos dam, Senator Charles Curtis (R-KS) remained skeptical the Pima would receive "all the water they need." Ashurst assured Curtis the Pima would be first in line for water and then added, "Any remaining [water] may be sold to the whites, [with] the . . . proceeds of the sale to be used for paying for this appropriation." To ensure his vote, Curtis, a Kaw Indian, demanded the water be protected "for the use of the Indians," even if they needed it all.[45]

Merritt did not wish to be bound by such restrictions and, in a personal letter to the senator, argued Pima priorities were "thoroughly safeguarded and conserved," with the secretary given "latitude" to negotiate with property owners off-reservation.[46] The bill (HR 10385) included an ambiguous provision that water would be distributed to Indian and non-Indian landowners "in accordance with the[ir] respective rights and priorities" as "determined by agreement of the owners thereof."[47] When Judge Lockwood issued his ruling in *Lobb v. Avenente*, Congress believed the decree prioritized Pima water rights to 35,000 acres of land and approved of the FCGP bill. On May 18, 1916, President Woodrow Wilson signed the bill into law, authorizing $75,000 to begin construction of a lower dam and bridge (Olberg Bridge and Sacaton Diversion Dam) and another $75,000 to begin construction of an upper diversion dam (Ashurst-Hayden Diversion Dam).[48] While the Pima were skeptical, Congress saw the bill as the first step in restoring Pima prosperity.[49]

The FCGP was a joint-use irrigation system to serve both Indian and non-Indian farmers. This project demonstrated that Congress intended to restore the reservation economy at least on par with the local economy. At the same time, the project was first and foremost for the benefit of the Pima, harnessing both the floodwaters and the remaining natural flow of the river and making them available to the Indians. But while the Senate debate indicated a desire to provide the Pima with "all the water they needed," the actual bill gave the secretary of the interior authority to negotiate a water division agreement between the Pima and their neighbors in the Florence–Casa Grande Valley.[50] The project was conditioned on the ability of the secretary to make "satisfactory adjustments" in "accordance with the respective rights and priorities" of both parties, as "determined by agreement of the owners thereof with the Secretary of the Interior."[51] Without a landowner's agreement, there would be no Florence–Casa Grande Project.

The FCGP was to irrigate 62,000 acres of land in the Gila River and Florence–Casa Grande valleys. While Olberg sought to include 50,000 acres of reservation land, with rights to 175,000 acre-feet of water, within the project (based on a population of five thousand Pima and Maricopa, each of whom would receive a ten-acre irrigable allotment), the secretary included just 35,000 acres of Indian land and 27,000 acres of non-Indian land.[52] To irrigate Pima farmland, water would continue down the Gila River to be diverted by a diversion dam east of Sacaton into the Santan Floodwater and Little Gila (i.e., Casa Blanca) canals. In times of low flow, water for the Pima would be diverted through the government-purchased and newly renamed Florence–Casa Grande Canal and carried through the proposed Pima Lateral to the reservation.

Secretary of the Interior John Barton Payne was given statutory authority to designate which lands would be made part of the FCGP. Negotiations between the secretary and off-reservation landowners began immediately. In March 1917, Florence landowners announced an agreement with Payne, only to rescind it in June. Work on the project came to a standstill. By summer, some landowners in Florence incorporated under state law for the purpose of developing their own water source using groundwater. More than 5,000 acres were signed up by 1918, placing the FCGP in jeopardy. With the project at risk, off-reservation landowners "insisted on a division of the available waters." Payne, wanting to consummate an agreement, skirted the original congressional intent of providing the Pima with all the water they might need and acquiesced to off-reservation demands. He then placed 3,500 ten-acre Pima irrigable "A" allotments on the eastern end of the reservation under the project.[53]

Hayden, understanding the needs and desires of the farmers above the reservation and aware that his political future was at stake, resisted legislative limitations for just this reason. Recognizing off-reservation landowners would not consent to government acquisition of the Florence Canal if their rights and interests were not protected, Hayden used his influence to keep the FCGP bill free of encumbrances. Acknowledging the project could have been built similar to Reclamation Service projects, with the entire expense charged to the Indian lands and any surplus water furnished to private landowners "on a rental basis," Hayden did not regard this as feasible. The only option was to grant the secretary discretionary authority to fashion an agreement with private landowners to bring them under the project and pay their share. This would protect their rights and those prioritized by the Lockwood Decree.[54]

Payne sent Indian Service Superintendent of Irrigation John R. T. Reeves to reach an agreement with off-reservation landowners, who had to convince the secretary as to the merit of their land and priority of their water rights. By May 1919, Reeves had contracts for more than 80,000 acres of land, with parcels ranging in size from 5 to 4,145 acres. By late summer, Reeves hammered out an agreement between the landowners and the Department of the Interior, with more than 85 percent of the eligible land under contract. In determining eligibility, Reeves gave priority to previously irrigated and cultivated land, as well as irrigated lands protected under the Lockwood Decree.

The Florence–Casa Grande landowners' agreement included the owners of "practically all of the said lands to which water rights in the Gila River" were appurtenant. These landowners, and the secretary on behalf of the Pima, placed their lands under burden of "a first lien" with the federal government. Deeds from "canal companies . . . and partly constructed canals and other property" were attached to the agreement, which included the statement that "a satisfactory accomplishment of the purpose of the [Florence–Casa Grande Project Act] as pertaining to providing irrigation for Indian lands in the Gila River Indian Reservation" had been met. Payne accepted the agreement, with 357 landowners encompassing 26,994.26 acres of land. He approved the agreement on April 22, 1920, declaring the Florence–Casa Grande Project feasible.[55]

When the new agreement was negotiated, it included language that was not found in the authorizing legislation. The agreement, a result of political dialogue and realities that did not include mention of Pima reserved water rights, divided the natural flow of the river between Pima farmers on the reservation and farmers in the Florence–Casa Grande Valley. Of the first 300 cubic feet per second (cfs) of water, the Indian share would be 60.6 percent, with non-Indians receiving 39.4 percent. The Indians would receive 51.7 percent of the flow between 301–600 cfs, with off-reservation lands receiving 48.3 percent. The Pima received 56.1 percent of any flow above 600 cfs. The cost of the project was to be apportioned according to division of the water. Pima farmers would be responsible for 35/62 of the project costs, with off-reservation farmers assessed 27/62 of the cost.[56]

The agreement also included a provision that denied the Pima water during times of insufficient flow, raising old arguments dating from the nineteenth century that even if Florence farmers turned back the natural flow of the river it would not reach the reservation due to its absorption into the broad, alluvial riverbed. In times of diminished flow, when the Pima share was "too small to reach the Indian reservation," the secretary could allow "all of the said water to be applied to the irrigation of privately owned lands in accordance with their priorities." By so dividing the water, the priority rights of the Pima to the waters of the Gila River were denied, weakening the foundation of the agreement from the beginning.[57]

To ensure completion of the project, construction on the Florence diversion dam had to commence within one year of May 1, 1920. On May 7, the *Casa Grande Valley Dispatch* confidently assured its readers that work would "start as soon as arrangements can be made to get same under way."[58] Olberg, in charge of designing the diversion dam, selected a site twelve miles east of Florence at Price Station on the Arizona Eastern Railroad. Here, the Gila River flowed between two granitic outcroppings 400' apart. The riverbed, however, was a deep alluvial canyon, with boring tests indicating alluvium to a depth of more than 100'. To avoid constructing a more costly dam anchored to bedrock, Olberg chose to construct an East Indian weir designed to withstand a 150,000 cfs flood.[59]

FIGURE 9.4. The Florence diversion dam was dedicated on May 10, 1922, and christened Ashurst-Hayden Diversion Dam. (Photograph by author, 2003)

On May 10, 1922, Commissioner of Indian Affairs Charles Burke dedicated the Florence diversion dam, christening it Ashurst-Hayden Diversion Dam after its two primary sponsors.[60] President Warren Harding congratulated Olberg on completion of the dam, which the president saw as ending "fifty years of strife and disputation between Indians and white [*sic*] regarding the distribution of the waters of the Gila River."[61]

Ashurst-Hayden Diversion Dam did little for the Pima. Water that was supposed to be delivered to the reservation went increasingly to the same water users as before. Continued Upper Gila River valley diversions left little natural flow in the river, with most of this diverted by Florence–Casa Grande farmers. To better provide for the needs of the Pima, the FCGP Act authorized a second diversion dam with a bridge superstructure.[62] Sacaton Dam, initially referred to as Santan Diversion Dam, was intended to complement Ashurst-Hayden Diversion Dam by catching additional floodwaters on the Gila River and diverting them into the

Santan Floodwater Canal, twenty miles below the latter dam.[63] Olberg believed the diversion dam was necessary to fully develop agriculture on the reservation. In 1919, just 2,783 acres of land were irrigated within the Sacaton Project, and "[b]ut little more land can be brought under cultivation on this project" unless the diversion dam was constructed.[64] Merritt was confident water could be diverted for 30,000 acres in Casa Blanca.[65]

While the Sacaton dam and bridge were architecturally similar to Ashurst-Hayden (both were designed by Olberg), at 1,250' in length it was three times as long. But while the Florence dam could be anchored to granitic rock on both ends, Sacaton dam could not. The south embankment was simply an earthen berm eight feet high. Because of the deep river alluvium, the dam was also of the East Indian type.[66] A 1,200'-long guide bank made up of riprap and extending at a right angle to the east of the dam was constructed along the south bank of the river to channel water over the weir. A canal was built south away from the dam to convey floodwater into the Little Gila Canal and thus "enable a double diversion, one on each side of the river."[67]

Postwar inflation escalated the cost of the project, and the Indian Service was forced to ask Congress for additional funds. By May 1924, $700,000 was appropriated for the dam and bridge.[68] As the state highway from Chandler to Casa Grande neared completion in 1925, the Arizona Highway Department constructed a small concrete bridge to span the Santan Floodwater Canal on the north bank of the river to connect the highway with the bridge.[69] The dam and bridge were completed on June 30, 1925, absent any public dedication.[70] Burke christened the structure Sacaton Diversion Dam. Estimated to cost $173,599, the dam and bridge totaled $719,793, with more than $346,000 spent on the bridge.[71] The first diversion of water occurred on April 3, 1926.

Congress authorized two diversion dams with the Florence–Casa Grande Project. While both were constructed, neither fulfilled the purpose for which they were authorized. While the annual diversion of water at Ashurst-Hayden averaged 84,434 acre-feet, at Sacaton Dam it was just 1,639 acre-feet.[72] Additional groundwater was available to the Pima, although they received far less than they expected and to which they had a statutory right. Groundwater was neither as good quality nor culturally compatible to the Pima, who retained a deep attachment to the waters of the Keli Akimel, or the Gila River. Consequently, the FCGP benefited off-reservation farmers to the further detriment of the Pima. Pima Agency Superintendent Albert Kneale later described the project, Sacaton Dam in particular, as "a failure so far as diverting water from the Gila River for irrigation purposes." While "a most excellent dam[,] had there been any water to divert [it] would have demonstrated its serviceableness."[73] With Ashurst-Hayden Diversion Dam (and especially after the 1929 completion of Coolidge Dam one hundred miles upstream), there was little water to divert at Sacaton Dam. Within a few years the dam silted over and lost its effectiveness.[74]

The FCGP circumvented the intent of Congress and did little to restore the Pima economy, let alone protect their rights to water. Having water rights for 35,000 acres, the Pima struggled to farm one-fifth of the land. H. A. Brett, assistant engineer for the reservation, noted a 48 percent decrease in acreage due to "repeated crop failure."[75] Sells admitted the division of water was "manifestly unfair to the Indians." The IRA argued that "settlers control[led] the only canal available to carry water so that, during the past two years, very little water has been allowed to reach the Pima land."[76] The sinking of new wells off-reservation compounded matters and further deprived the Pima.[77]

When Representative Homer Snyder (R-NY), chairman of the House of Representatives Committee on Indian Affairs, inquired of Reed in what state of completion the irrigation project was on the reservation, Reed could only remark that it was "a long ways from being completed."[78] Despite the diversion dams, water remained insufficient, and Pima rights to the use of the water were tenuous at best. Crops planted early in 1925 died from lack of water later in the year. The following year, Pima farmers in Casa Blanca, Sacaton Flats, and Progressive Colony were "forced to give up farming operations to a large extent because of lack of water." Indian farmers in Blackwater had water "for only about 150 acres."[79] A five-year program to restore agriculture on the reservation failed, with many Pima "divorced from field and home" looking for work. By 1930, nearly $1,500,000 had been expended on the on-reservation FCGP.[80] While some officials boasted the Pima had been "generously provided for," the reality was the irrigation works were "idle gestures."[81]

Twelve years after its 1916 inception, the FCGP was merged into the San Carlos Irrigation Project (SCIP). In the years that followed, farmers above the reservation retained de facto rights of possession to a majority of the water, leaving the Pima without a full measure of the water to which they had a moral and legal entitlement. By the end of the 1920s, the number of farms in Pinal County more than tripled to 1,008, and those in Maricopa County increased to 4,597, placing greater demands on water resources.[82] For the Pima, insufficient water, lack of financing, bureaucratic restrictions, land fractionation resulting from land severalty, and a piecemeal irrigation system resulted in much of the irrigable land on the reservation lying idle or being leased to non-Indian farmers.[83] In the coming years, the Pima received an average of 35 percent of all water passing Ashurst-Hayden Diversion Dam (54,657 acre-feet per year). Their neighbors in the Florence–Casa Grande Valley, meanwhile, received an average of 65 percent of the water (99,437 acre-feet per year). While the Pima pumped an additional 62,336 acre-feet of groundwater annually (59 percent of all groundwater), they failed to receive the quantity of natural-flow water guaranteed them under the FCGP. Even after the SCIP, and the federal courts in 1935, further divided the water on project lands, the Pima received a lesser quantity (44 percent of the total water supply available within the SCIP area) than that to which they were entitled.[84]

The Florence–Casa Grande Project, while successful in gaining support for Coolidge Dam and the San Carlos Project, failed to alleviate the need for water on the reservation and did not restore the Pima economy. By disregarding the issue of Pima reserved rights to the water in the first decades of the twentieth century, Congress delayed dealing with the matter. By abdicating its fiduciary role in protecting Pima water rights, Congress confirmed the prophetic statement of Assistant Commissioner of Indian Affairs Edgar Merritt, who warned that by ignoring the issue of Indian water rights, the United States would one day see Indian tribes take their claims to the federal courts for action.

CHAPTER 10

The Pima Economy, Water, and Federal Policy

WHILE THE FEDERAL GOVERNMENT has always been involved in encouraging the settlement and development of the territories acquired by the United States, in the mid-nineteenth century a new definition of governance was evident. Vigorous federal policies governing land and resources in the West represented a distinct federal footprint of social action. This intransigent shift in social thought influenced American action in ways that proved prejudicial to the Pima. This shift included the perception that the resources of the West were bountiful and endless, giving rise to a social attitude of improvidence that was demonstrated by emigrant and settler alike. Furthermore, the popular belief that settlement of the West awaited only the requisite American spirit and determination pervaded emigrant thought. It was, moreover, the national destiny to subdue, subjugate, and settle the land and develop its resources. Consequently, it was federal activity that facilitated settlement and shaped social thought, with federal policies encouraging the seizure, development, and exploitation of resources (i.e., water) to favor the aggressive non-Indian few.

Federal action, including the pre-emption acts that Congress periodically enacted to validate settler land titles, included the 1862 Homestead Act and the corollary 1877 Desert Land Act, both of which provided settlers with federally sanctioned rights in acquiring title to the land and making use of the water. When the National Reclamation Act of 1902 is factored in, it is clear that federal policy, not laissez-faire governance, enabled settlement of the land and provided settlers with the means of putting scarce water resources to beneficial use under local prior appropriation laws. This coup de grace was facilitated with a disregard of Indian priority rights. As a result, American Indians, including the Pima, were displaced from the land and denied their right to the use of western streams.

These federal actions represent direct intervention in populating the West and encouraging yeoman farming. At the same time, these policies served to discourage yeoman Indian agriculture. The 1887 General Allotment Act limited Indian agriculture by fractionating reservation land holdings and providing for the leasing of Indian land. The practical result of these federal activities was that tribal nations faced a juggernaut of continental imperialism.

The present study not only illustrates the economic adaptations the Pima made in the nineteenth century but also demonstrates that convenient scholarly assumptions that American Indians were inherently unfit for, or unfamiliar with, western economies are specious. It was not the triumph of western civilization that displaced the Pima from the national, and their traditional, agricultural economy, but federal policies.

The Pima quickly recognized the advantages of joining the national economy, but they did not give up their sovereignty in doing so. In fact, they repeatedly asserted sovereignty over their land, water, and people. This was further demonstrated by Pima participation in the territorial militia, as they understood that their protection of national transportation routes through central Arizona also protected their own economic interests in the growing territorial economy. While not altruistic, the Pima desired technology so that they might expand their economy, improve their standard of living, and gain access to new trade goods.

The establishment of the Southern Trail through their villages proved to be an economic boon to the Pima, whose economy rapidly expanded after 1848. Tens of thousands of emigrants passed through the villages, purchasing or trading for food and forage crops. While the Pima initially accepted red flannel and white muslin as trade for their crops, by 1850 they demanded silver and gold, using the coin to purchase goods directly from merchants in Tucson. The opening of the national road through the villages in the late 1850s further expanded their economy. While the Pima sold 145,000 pounds of grain in 1858, within four years they surpassed 2,000,000 pounds in annual sales to the military alone. Pima farmers constructed new acequias upstream of the villages in 1858 and, again, in 1859. By 1860 they grew more than 11,000,000 pounds of grain.

Pima desire for technology was fueled by emigrant traffic, and after 1850, their demand for agricultural technology increased. Tools, metal ploughs, seed, and other farm implements, including the knowledge to employ them, were coveted by the Pima so that they might increase their cultivation. This is further witnessed in that the Pima sought oxen, mules, and other draft animals, indicating that their mode of agriculture was changing from manpower to animal power. As a result, the Pima were entering a market economy that might well have paralleled that of local settlers had it not been capriciously strangled. Federal policy encouraged American Indians to cultivate the soil; the Pima, already cultivators, demonstrated their commitment to this policy and repeatedly proved their responsiveness to continuing and expanding their agrarian economy.

The newfound wealth of the Pima would not last. In 1863, Charles Poston informed federal officials of the three most important considerations facing the Pima: "water, water! water!!" Should settlement above the villages occur without protecting Pima water, there would be trouble. In 1869, the crisis erupted when settlers in Florence intentionally diverted and wasted river water to deprive the Pima of the water needed to irrigate their crops. By 1872, settlers in the Upper Gila River valley added to the users above the villages. Within two decades, tens of thousands of acres of crops were irrigated above the reservation using water that legally belonged to the Pima.

These events upstream of the Pima were sanctioned by federal policies. Following the requirements of federal law, settlers were forced to apply water to their land or risk losing it and any improvements they made. As settlers gained political hegemony, they constructed the Florence Canal, which further deprived the Pima of their rights to Gila River water. At the same time, Upper Gila River valley farmers continued to expand their operations. Increasingly, what water reached the reservation came in short, ephemeral flows that, due to environmental changes in the river system, altered the course of the Gila River. By 1905, the geomorphology of the river forced the Pima to abandon most of their traditional irrigation system. To irrigate Pima fields now required a costly conveyance system that headed farther upstream. Continued diversions resulted in the Pima share of the river declining to less than 30 percent of the total flow.

As non-Indians gained control of the land and water resources, they lobbied federal officials to enact a national reclamation policy. The organization of the National Irrigation Association led to a national lobbying effort advocating federal subsidies to reclaim the remaining arable lands of the West. To support its cause and provide a strong moral argument for federal involvement, the association used the Pima as its national poster child, blanketing the country with media reports extolling Pima agricultural virtues and lamenting the current Pima crisis. The message was clear: the only solution to the reclamation needs of the West was federal legislation authorizing a storage facility on the Gila River and, by implication, storage facilities on rivers across the West.

Congress responded with the National Reclamation Act. But there was little benefit to the Pima and American Indians, who, due to their land being held in federal trust, were not invited to participate in the act. Iron triangles, consisting of non-Indian water users, federal agencies, and congressional committees, directed, controlled, and manipulated federal water policy. This select membership disregarded Indian water needs and rights. The Pima were further disenfranchised, and with continuing crop failures, they planted less. Smaller fields resulted in reduced yields, which further lowered expectations. In the end, the Pima scaled down their expectations and standard of living, and found themselves enduring famine and poverty, having been reduced to a subsistence economy.

To provide for their families, Pima men cut firewood from the once-vast mesquite *bosques* that grew on the reservation. Between 1899 and 1905, the Pima cut an annual average of 11,000 cords to sell. At the same time, they grew less than half the grain needed to subsist. Facing desperate conditions and severe deprivation, the Pima petitioned the American people and members of the U.S. Congress in an effort to restore their rights to the waters of the Gila River and reinvigorate their agricultural economy.

Protection of their water was the one area over which the Pima lacked meaningful control. For this, they were reliant on the U.S. government. The protection of their water and the maintenance of their hydraulic-based economy were of great importance to the Pima. Less apparent was the significance to the United States. Beyond their role of protecting travelers and providing them with food and forage crops, enabling the United States to control and root settlement in the West, the Pima served the United States well. Congress established, and the Indian Service implemented, a policy of encouraging all American Indians to become yeoman Jeffersonian farmers, with the Pima a dynamic example of what tribes might do. Many tribes attempted to make this cultural and economic adaptation. Yet, the success of American Indian hydraulic-based economies rarely matched the rhetoric of policy makers. Water, or lack thereof, was the deciding factor in the success of the Pima economy. By failing to protect Pima water and involvement in the national economy, the United States undermined its own policy of pastoralizing the Indians and missed the opportunity to demonstrate its commitment to the policies defined by Congress.

Moreover, federal policy was inconsistent, failing entirely to protect the cornerstone of federal Indian policy: the water upon which agriculture depended. While some tribes struggled in adapting to market forces, the Pima did not, readily adjusting, only to be systematically squeezed out of the market by federal action. In all of this, the United States failed to grasp the opportunity to demonstrate its commitment to tribal nations that the government was sincere in its efforts to assist in their transition to an agrarian economy. To tribal nations willing to adopt an agrarian economy, the Pima might well have served as the model upon which they could look to find success.

The United States had ample opportunity to amend its policy deficiencies. The Pima repeatedly sought federal protection of their water and, at the same time, demonstrated their fidelity to the United States. Already industrious cultivators, the Pima sought inclusion in the national economy. Yet, rather than protect their rights to the water supporting the Pima economy, the United States instead attempted to relocate and pacify the Indians, turning friendship into cynicism and distrust. Not willing to make the necessary moral and legal adjustments incumbent upon the U.S. government, federal officials instead watched as Pima agricultural production declined to subsistence levels, eventually resulting in widespread starvation and famine.

Ironically, Pima hospitality, economic success, and friendliness stimulated the very settlement above and around the reservation that led to the collapse of their economy. Explorer and emigrant trails served as the commercial corridors through which missionaries, trappers, miners, soldiers, and settlers entered and eventually settled near the Pima villages. These highways encouraged commercialization of the Pima economy, but they also brought settlement that competed with the Pima for the limited water resources in the Gila River. Following the dictates of federal land and resource laws, these settlers repaid Pima kindness by appropriating the land and water for their own benefit.

The Pima initially requested federal support for their water rights in 1871, and the owners of the Florence Canal Company prepared for such litigation in 1886, although in neither instance did the U.S. government prosecute Pima water rights. In 1904, the Indian Service again rejected federal action, believing the cost of protecting Pima water rights unworthy of the expense. Not until 1913 did the Indian Service initiate action, recognizing that if federal action were not taken, Pima rights to water might be irretrievably lost.

The 1914 adjudication survey compellingly demonstrated that Pima agriculture and the Pima economy had been decimated. Compared to land once irrigated by the Pima, fields cultivated in 1914 were 21 percent smaller. With land severalty predicated on the premise that the Pima had an equal chance to participate in the national and local economy, the survey illustrated startling results. While 31 percent of Arizona acres were sown to grain, more than 82 percent of Pima acres were in grain, suggesting that the Pima economy was based on subsistence agriculture. By the 1920s, most of the surrounding land off-reservation was sown to cotton, which was an attractive market crop. The Pima did not have the luxury of growing what could be sold, cultivating crops upon which to subsist. Furthermore, water deprivation resulted in significantly smaller agricultural fields, with mean Pima field sizes more than 40 percent smaller than the older and traditionally farmed Pima fields. While the adjudication survey aided in the passage of the Florence–Casa Grande Project, it did little to restore water to the Pima. Upstream users continued to draw their water out of the river above the villages before it reached the Pima fields below.

Federal action in the West had several effects on the Pima. Initially, it fostered an economic boon among the Pima (1848–1868) that resulted in great material prosperity, expansion of the Pima economy, and an increase in acreage under irrigation. New ditches were extended above the villages and away from the river, resulting in an era of unprecedented economic growth among the Pima. This era represents the golden age of the Pima economy. But as settlement above the reservation rooted and expanded after 1864, a second stage of water deprivation (1869–1891) appeared. During this era, the Pima share of the river water declined year-by-year until it resulted in widespread famine throughout the villages. The final stage of federal activity culminated in the complete economic privation of the Pima (1891–1921). Within this timeframe the Pima faced starvation, near-complete water deprivation, and extreme poverty. Moreover, changes in the Gila River rendered the traditional Pima irrigation system unworkable. Short, ephemeral flows in the Gila River no longer reached Pima fields.

Despite deprivation, the Pima retained reserved rights to the water necessary to make their reservation a homeland. Enfranchised and politically involved, non-Indian irrigators used the water to the detriment of the Pima. It was this use that ruined the Pima economy. If not for discriminatory federal policies, the Pima might well have equaled and, perhaps, even exceeded their neighbors in agricultural output and remained part of the national economy. While the goal of yeoman Jeffersonian farmers in Indian Country made for good policy, for the Pima it was simply rhetoric that facilitated economic devastation.

The success of off-reservation irrigated agriculture in south-central Arizona placed a long-lasting strain on the Pima that deprived them of the means of earning a living. This leads to several important final thoughts. First, the Pima were not passive participants in these events. In fact, they were most versatile in dealing with this water crisis. To the extent possible, they adapted to water shortages in creative ways. For one, they reduced the amount of land they cultivated, demonstrating their commitment to an agricultural economy. They also eliminated the least-productive lands from their crop rotation, a measure that resulted in further crop reductions. In a number of instances, they abandoned villages most impacted by water losses and relocated them downstream in order to maintain a shadow of their former economy. Perhaps most telling was the shifting of their agrarian practices from water-intensive crops to those less water intensive. The practical result of these shifts demonstrates the Pima desired to remain farmers, even though their economy had been reduced to mere subsistence by 1900.

Second, it was not Pima ineptness or inability to adapt to a Western-style economy that resulted in their displacement from the national market. Federal resource policies, including the improvidence they engendered, the political schemes they fostered, and the land severalty policies they encouraged, created challenges that the Pima were powerless to combat. If the Pima were unable to adjust, popular sentiment reasoned, then it was the Indians, not federal law, who were responsible. Ignored completely is the fact that the Pima were afforded no protection of their water resources, without which their economy could not be sustained.

In the final analysis, had Pima farmers not been deprived of their rights and access to the waters of the Gila River, they might have continued their successful adaptation to a market economy. As it was, the Pima realized an adaptation to the American market economy that was ultimately frustrated by federal actions that promoted the interests of non-Indian settlers over those of the Pima. The tragic result was that the reservation economy was reduced to a subsistence status.

Notes

Introduction

1. Limerick, *Something in the Soil*. Limerick, *The Legacy of Conquest*.

2. Williams, *The American Indian in Western Legal Thought*, 308–325.

3. *Johnson v. M'Intosh* 21 *U.S. Reporter* 543 (1823).

4. Reisner, *Cadillac Desert*, 43.

5. Stegner, *Beyond the Hundredth Meridian*, 211; Reisner, *Cadillac Desert*, 45–47.

6. Powell, *Report on the Lands of the Arid West*.

7. Pisani, *To Reclaim a Divided West*, 251–266. Arizona accepted the provisions of the Carey Act in 1912 after statehood, but received no benefits from the law.

8. Hays, *Conservation and the Gospel of Efficiency*, 6–8.

9. *United States v. Rio Grande Dam and Irrigation Company*, 174 *U.S. Reporter*, 690 (1899). Dunbar, *Forging New Rights in Western Water*, 61–81.

10. *An Act to Provide for the Sale of Desert Lands in Certain Territories*, March 3, 1877. 19 Stat. 377.

11. Pisani, *Water and American Government*, 35.

12. McCool, *Command of the Waters*. Smith, "The Campaign for Water in Central Arizona."

13. McCool, *Command of the Waters*, 66–110. Pisani, *Water and American Government*, 275–276. Worster, *Rivers of Empire*, 171–172. Espeland, *Struggle for Water*.

14. Nash, *Federal Landscape*, 21–39. Pisani, *Water and American Government*, xi–xvii.

15. Article 1, Section 8 of the United States Constitution.

16. Prucha, *American Indian Policy in the Formative Years*, 32.

17. Trennert, *Alternative to Extinction*.

18. Hurt, *Indian Agriculture in America*, 106–110.

19. *Lone Wolf v. Hitchcock* 187 *U.S. Reporter* 553 (1903).

20. *United States v. Winans* 198 *U.S. Reporter* 371 (1905). *Winters v. United States* 207 *U.S. Reporter* 564 (1908).

21. Espeland, *Struggle for Water*.

22. McDonnell, *Dispossession of the American Indians, 1887–1934*, 121. Otis, *Dawes Act and the Allotment of Indian Lands*, 17.

23. Lewis, *Neither Wolf nor Dog*.

24. Pisani, *Water and American Government*, 154.

25. Hoxie, *A Final Promise*, 83–115.

Chapter 1. The Prelude

This chapter was adapted from the article "None Excel Them in Virtue and Honesty: Ecclesiastical and Military Descriptions of the Gila River Pima, 1694–1848," appearing in the *American Indian Quarterly*, volume 29, number 1, by permission of the University of Nebraska Press.

1. The term Pima villages refers to the villages along the middle Gila River inhabited by the Pima. The term *Pima* refers to the Gila River Pima, not to the Piman peoples to the south.

2. Kino, *Kino's Historical Memoir of Pimeria Alta*, 1:230, 249. Bolton, *Rim of Christendom*, 284. Bolton, *Opening a Land Route to California*, 119. Manje, *Unknown Arizona and Sonora*, 121. Corle, *Gila River of the Southwest*, 10. McNamee, *Gila*, 16.

3. Bolton, *Font's Complete Diary*, 44.

4. More than fifty edible desert plants and nearly two dozen animals—excluding nine native fish—rounded out the Pima diet. Castetter and Bell, *Pima and Papago Indian Agriculture*, 56–57. Russell, *Pima Indians*, 69–78.

5. Spicer, *Cycles of Conquest*, 119.

6. Rea, *At the Desert's Green Edge*, 9.

7. Allison, *White Man's Friend*, 9–15. Webb, *A Pima Remembers*, 64–67. Ezell, "The Hispanic Acculturation of the Gila River Pimas," 22.

8. Nathaniel Michler, "From the 111th Meridian of Longitude to the Pacific Ocean," in Emory, *Report on the United States and Mexican Boundary Survey*, 117.

9. Kino, *Kino's Historical Memoir*, 1:195–197; Bolton, *Opening a Land Route to California*, 389; Bartlett, *Personal Narrative*, 2:241–242. While the Maricopa resided downstream of the Pima and eventually confederated with them, this study focuses on the Pima experience. For the Maricopa, see Spier, *Yuman Tribes of the Gila River*.

10. Bolton, *Opening a Land Route to California*, 124.

11. Castetter and Bell, *Pima and Papago Agriculture*, 80–82. *Kino's Historical Memoir*, 1:195.

12. Bolton, *Outpost of Empire*, 263. *Rim of Christendom*, 248. Sedelmayr, *Jacobo Sedelmayr*, 23, 28. La Encarnacion del Sutaquison (Sudaccson) is between the modern communities of Sweetwater and Casa Blanca.

13. Manje, *Unknown Arizona and Sonora*, 121.

14. The practice of the Papago harvesting crops on share apparently predates contact, as Jose Augustin de Campos found the Papago visiting the Rio San Ignacio in 1693 performing such labor. Sedelmayr, *Jacobo Sedelmayr*, 23. Guiteras, *Rudo Ensayo*, 15.

15. Sedelmayr, *Jacobo Sedelmayr*, 29, 31. Manje, *Unknown Arizona and Sonora*, 88, 89, 122. Bolton, *Opening a Land Route to California*, 304.

16. Bolton, *Opening a Land Route to California*, 124, 126, 304. One *fanega*, a unit of dry measure used in Latin American countries, equals 1.58 U.S. bushels.

17. Bolton, *Font's Complete Diary*, 34, 45. Garcés, *On the Trail of a Spanish Pioneer*, 107–108. Bolton, *The San Francisco Colony*, 19.

18. Hackenberg, "Pima and Papago Ecological Adaptations," 169–170. Bolton, *Outpost*

of Empire, 263. Bolton, *Font's Complete Diary*, 44. Emory, *Notes of a Military Reconnaissance*, 85. Russell, *Pima Indians*, 87.

19. Bolton, *Opening a Land Route to California*, 390. Bolton, *Font's Complete Diary*, 43. Ezell, "The Hispanic Acculturation of the Gila River Pimas," 39, 104. Emory, *Notes of a Military Reconnaissance*, 83.

20. Venegas, *Natural and Civil History of California*, 2:184. Pfefferkorn, *Pfefferkorn's Description of the Province of Sonora*, 28–29.

21. Manje, *Unknown Arizona and Sonora*, 196.

22. Bolton, *Spanish Exploration in the Southwest*, 453.

23. Kino, *Kino's Historical Memoir*, 1:186, 206. Ezell, "The Hispanic Acculturation of the Gila River Pimas," 17. Manje, *Unknown Arizona and Sonora*, 273.

24. Russell, *Pima Indians*, 186–187. Rea, *At the Desert's Green Edge*, 49. Bolton, *Rim of Christendom*, 247. Officer, *Hispanic Arizona*, 40.

25. Underhill, "Pima Government," University of New Mexico Center for Southwest Research.

26. Ezell with Fontana, "Plants without Water," 324.

27. Bartlett, *Personal Narrative*, 2:249.

28. Bolton, *Font's Complete Diary*, 46.

29. Bolton, *Spanish Exploration in the Southwest*, 451, 453. Manje, *Unknown Arizona and Sonora*, 2. Sedelmayr, *Jacobo Sedelmayr*, 27, 32, 34–35.

30. Bolton, *Spanish Exploration in the Southwest*, 454. Sedelmayr, *Jacobo Sedelmayr*, 34–35.

31. Sedelmayr, *Jacobo Sedelmayr*, 35, 37, 41.

32. Bringas de Manzaneda y Encinas, *Friar Bringas Reports to the King*, 90.

33. Some priests in the Pimería Alta grew increasingly cynical of the military. In 1799, the priest at Hermosillo accused the military of inciting Apache uprisings to "increase the dependency of the settlers and sedentary Indians" on the military and to deny the opportunity of "carrying the gospel" to the Pima. Ibid., 74. Von Humboldt, *Political Essay on the Kingdom of New Spain*, 206–207.

34. Weber, *The Taos Trappers*, 121.

35. Russell, *Pima Indians*, 39. Emory, *Notes of a Military Reconnaissance*, 86. Officer, *Hispanic Arizona*, 120.

36. H. Turner, *Original Journals*, 107–108.

37. Emory, *Notes of a Military Reconnaissance*, 82. "Report of A. R. Johnston, aide-de-camp to S. W. Kearny," in ibid., 598.

38. "Report of A. R. Johnston," in ibid., 599. H. Turner, *Original Journals*, 108. Emory, *Notes of a Military Reconnaissance*, 84.

39. Emory, *Notes of a Military Reconnaissance*, 85.

40. Emory, *Notes of a Military Reconnaissance*, 87. "Report of A. R. Johnston," in ibid., 602.

41. Emory, *Notes of a Military Reconnaissance*, 82, 84–85. "Report of A. R. Johnston," in ibid., 600–601.

42. H. Turner, *Original Journals*, 109. Emory, *Notes of a Military Reconnaissance*, 84.

43. U.S. Department of War, *Report from the Secretary of War*, 49. Golder, *The March of the Mormon Battalion Taken from the Journal of Henry Standage*, 198. Philip St. George Cooke, "Report of Lieutenant Colonel St. George Cooke of His March from Santa Fe, New Mexico, to San Diego, Upper California," in Emory, *Notes of a Military Reconnaissance*, 254–255.

44. Cooke, *The Conquest of New Mexico and California*, 159–165. Clark, "The Pima Indians and Western Development," 28. Cannon, *The Autobiography of Christopher Layton*, 83–84. H. Turner, *Original Journals*, 108. U.S. Department of War, *Report from the Secretary of War*, 50.

Chapter 2. The Pima Villages and California Emigrants

Portions of this chapter were originally published in "Good Samaritans of the Desert: The Pima and Maricopa Villages and the California Emigrants, 1846-1852," *Journal of the Southwest* 47, no. 3 (2005): 457–496.

1. Etter, *To California on the Southern Route 1849*, 13–14. Howe, *Argonauts of Forty-Nine*, 38. Green, *Journal*, 51. Strentzel, "Letter from California," 259.

2. Ezell with Fontana, "Plants without Water," 320.

3. Portions of Emory and Cooke's journals were published as guides to California. One of the more famous guides was Creuzbaur's *Guide to California and the Pacific Ocean*. It noted daily camp sites used by both Kearny and Cooke and included seven detailed maps.

4. Foreman, *Marcy and the Gold Seekers*, 298. Ames, "A Doctor Comes to California," 209.

5. Hunter, *Missouri 49er*, 161.

6. Durivage, "Letters and Journals of John E. Durivage," 212.

7. Harris, *Gila Trail*, 80–81.

8. Miles, *Journal*, 23.

9. Durivage, "Letters and Journals of John E. Durivage," 216.

10. Green, *Journal*, 56, 66–67.

11. Eccleston, *Diary*, 207. Evans, *Mexican Gold Trail*, 153. Cox, "From Texas to California in 1850," 143. Miles, *Journal*, 24.

12. Audubon, *Audubon's Western Journal 1849–1850*, 157, 159.

13. Clarke, *Travels in Mexico and California*, 79.

14. Couts, *Hepah, California!* 66, 68.

15. Clarke, *Travels in Mexico and California*, 71–73.

16. Cozzens, *Marvelous Country*, 100.

17. Hayes, *Pioneer Notes*, 45.

18. Allison, *White Man's Friend*, 9–10. Evans, *Mexican Gold Trail*, 153.

19. Thomas Antisell, "Geological Report" in "Report of Lieutenant John G. Parke, Corps of Topographic Engineers, upon the routes . . . and upon that portion of the route near the thirty-second parallel lying between the Rio Grande and the Pima Villages of the Gila," in U.S. Congress, Senate, *Report of Explorations and Surveys*, 137.

20. Emory, *Notes of a Military Reconnaissance*, 83. Miles, *Journal*, 24. Pancoast, *Adventures*, 244.

21. Tyler, *Concise History of the Mormon Battalion in the Mexican War*, 236.

22. Clarke, *Travels in Mexico and California*, 72. Pancoast, *Adventures*, 244–245. Couts, *Hepah, California!* 66–67. Chamberlin, "From Lewisburg to California in 1849," 173.

23. Chamberlin, "From Lewisburg to California in 1849," 172. Hunter, *Missouri 49er*, 164.

24. Hayes, "Diary of Judge Benjamin Hayes' Journey Overland," Arizona Historical Society/Tucson. Bartlett, *Personal Narrative*, 2:237.

25. Hunter, *Missouri 49er*, 164.

26. Hayes, "Diary of Judge Benjamin Hayes' Journey Overland," Arizona Historical Society/Tucson.

27. Goulding, *Diary*. Bartlett, *Personal Narrative*, 2:237.

28. Couts, *Hepah, California!* 66–67.

29. Durivage, "Letters and Journals of John E. Durivage," 218. Emory, *Notes of a Military Reconnaissance*, 82–84. Pancoast, *Adventures*, 218.

30. Harris, *Gila Trail*, 80. Noel, "W. Wilberforce Alexander Ramsey, Esq., of Tennessee," 569.

31. Conard, *Uncle Dick Wootton*, 262. Bigler, *Bigler's Chronicle*, 36. Clarke, *Travels in Mexico and California*, 72.

32. Chamberlin, "From Lewisburg to California in 1849," 171.

33. Harris, *Gila Trail*, 80.

34. Powell, *Santa Fe Trail to California*, 155. When the horse was recovered and returned, Azul encouraged the emigrant to pay $2.00 to the young man for his services. Having only $1.50 on his person, Powell—accompanied by Azul—rode fifteen miles to the emigrant camp to collect the remainder of the fee.

35. Quoted in Foreman, *Marcy and the Gold Seekers*, 327. Dillon, *Texas Argonauts*, 106, 142.

36. "Sylvester Mowry, Lieutenant United States Army, to the Honorable J. W. Denver, Commissioner of Indian Affairs, Fort Yuma, September 16, 1857," in U.S. Bureau of Indian Affairs, *Annual Report of the Commissioner of Indian Affairs*, 1858, 300.

37. Couts, *Hepah, California!* 64. Hayes, *Pioneer Notes*, 44. Audubon, *Audubon's Western Journal*, 155–156. Harris, *Gila Trail*, 81. Not all testimonials were noteworthy. One, apparently written by Philip St. George Cooke (referenced in Pancoast, *Adventures*, 246) regarding an unnamed Pima man, stated, "This fellow is a d———d Rascal. Look out for him. Lt. Cook, USA."

38. Powell, *Santa Fe Trail to California*, 152–153. Pancoast, *Adventures*, 246. Turner wrote, "Never did I look upon a more benevolent face than that of the old chief" (H. Turner, *Original Journals*, 109). Durivage observed Azul was "a very dignified-looking old fellow"; Durivage, "Letters and Journals of John E. Durivage," 219. Harris called Azul "statesmanlike" and "handsome" (Harris, *Gila Trail*, 80).

39. Eccleston, *Diary*, 207–208.

40. Foreman, *Marcy and the Gold Seekers*, 312.

41. H. Turner, *Original Journals*, 108.

42. Ames, "A Doctor Comes to California," 211–212.

43. Audubon, *Audubon's Western Journal*, 156.

44. Emory, *Notes of a Military Reconnaissance*, 135.

45. Cozzens, *Marvelous Country*, 100.

46. U.S. Department of War, *Report from the Secretary of War*, 50.

47. "Report of A. R. Johnston," in Emory, *Notes of a Military Reconnaissance*, 598. Tyler, *A Concise History of the Mormon Battalion in the Mexican War*, 232.

48. Powell, *Santa Fe Trail to California*, 153. Green, *Journal*, 68. Strentzel, "Letter from California," 256. Philip St. George Cooke purchased more than one hundred bushels of corn for the Mormon Battalion in 1846. He also purchased over six hundred pounds of wheat flour. Bigler, *Bigler's Chronicle*, 36. U.S. Department of War, *Report from the Secretary of War*, 50–54.

49. Ames, "A Doctor Comes to California," 212. Van Nostrand, "Audubon's Ill-Fated Western Journal Recalled by the Diary of J. H. Bachman," 298. Aldrich, *Journal*, 53. Pancoast, *Adventures*, 244. Hayes, *Pioneer Notes*, 45. H. Turner, *Original Journals*, 108. Clarke, *Travels in Mexico and California*, 71. Evans, *Mexican Gold Trail*, 153. "Journal of Samuel Hollister Rogers," 77. U.S. Department of War, *Report from the Secretary of War*, 52. Bigler, *Bigler's Chronicle*, 37.

50. Wood, *Personal Recollections*, 12. Aldrich, *Journal*, 54. U.S. Department of War, *Report from the Secretary of War*, 49. Clarke, *Travels in Mexico and California*, 71. Durivage, "Letters and Journals of John E. Durivage," 218. Pancoast, *Adventures*, 246.

51. Audubon, *Audubon's Western Journal*, 156. Brownlee, *An American Odyssey*, 67. Cox, "From Texas to California in 1850," 145.

52. Miles, *Journal*, 23–24.

53. Hunter, *Missouri 49er*, 161.

54. Eccleston, *Diary*, 209, 211. Cox, "From Texas to California in 1850," 145.

55. Ames, "A Doctor Comes to California," 212. Couts, *Hepah, California!* 66. Durivage, "Letters and Journals of John E. Durivage," p. 218.

56. Eccleston, *Diary*, 206, 210, 213. Hayes, *Pioneer Notes*, 45. Wood, *Personal Recollections*, 12. Hayes, "Diary of Judge Benjamin Hayes' Journey Overland," Arizona Historical Society/Tucson.

57. Couts, *Hepah, California!* 66. Powell, *Santa Fe Trail to California*, 153. Hayes, *Pioneer Notes*, 43.

58. Lieutenant A. B. Chapman estimated the population at 4,117 in 1858. See Goddard Bailey to Charles E. Mix, November 4, 1858, RG 75, M234, New Mexico Superintendency, 1858–1859, roll 549, 207–208. Couts, *Hepah, California!* 67. Harris, *Gila Trail*, 82. Charles Olberg, "Report on the San Carlos Irrigation Project and the History of Irrigation along the Gila River, Appendix A," in U.S. Congress, House, Committee on Indian Affairs, *Indians of the United States*, Volume 2–Appendixes, 59–60, estimated the number of acres farmed by the Pima and Maricopa in 1850 at 12,450. Assuming that each of the five thousand Pima and Maricopa consumed five bushels of wheat and five bushels of corn per year (Castetter and Bell, *Pima and Papago Indian Agriculture*, 55) the Indians would

have cultivated about 2,500 acres of wheat and 2,083 acres of corn in 1849. This totals 4,583 acres. Considering smaller amounts of cotton, melons, pumpkins and squash were grown—say 1,500 acres total—then the Indians would have farmed around 6,000 acres for their own use, meaning they doubled their production to provide for the emigrant demand.

59. Harris, *Gila Trail*, 82.

60. Couts, *Hepah, California!* 67.

61. Green, *Journal*, 67. See quote of Alden Woodruff in Foreman, *Marcy and the Gold Seekers*, 282.

62. Eccleston, *Diary*, 211, 213.

63. Audubon, *Audubon's Western Journal*, 156.

64. Strentzel, "Letters from California," 256. Green, *Journal*, 68. Eccleston, *Diary*, 215. Chamberlain, *My Confession*, 287. Hunter, *Missouri 49er*, 166.

65. Hayes, "Diary of Judge Benjamin Hayes' Journey Overland," Arizona Historical Society/Tucson.

66. Noted by Dr. J. G. Candee in Foreman, *Marcy and the Gold Seekers*, 328.

67. Bartlett, *Personal Narrative*, 2:226, 2:259.

68. Powell, *Santa Fe Trail to California*, 153. Eccleston, *Diary*, 209.

69. Wood, *Personal Recollections*, 12.

70. Chamberlin, "From Lewisburg to California in 1849," 173–174.

71. Green, *Journal*, 67–68. Evans, *Mexican Gold Trail*, 153.

72. Durivage, "Letters and Journals of John E. Durivage," 218, 221.

73. Hunter, *Missouri 49er*, 169.

74. Aldrich, *Journal*, 54.

75. Pancoast, *Adventures*, 243, 245–256.

Chapter 3. Establishment of the Pima Reservation

Portions of this chapter were originally published in *Journal of the West* 45:3 (Summer 2006). Copyright © 2006 by ABC-CLIO, Inc. Reprinted with permission of ABC-CLIO.

1. Wilson, "How the Settlers Farmed," 346–348.

2. John Walker to Honorable Charles Mix, October 31, 1858, Tucson, New Mexico, RG 75, M234, New Mexico Superintendency, 1858–1859, roll 549. John Walker to James L. Collins, December 31, 1860, Tucson Agency, New Mexico, RG 75, T21, Letters Received from the Agencies, roll 4.

3. Bartlett, *Personal Narrative*, 2:233.

4. Emory, *Report on the United States and Mexican Boundary Survey*, 24.

5. William H. Emory, U.S. Commissioner, to Brigadier General John Garland, August 11, 1855, RG 393, M1120, Records of the U.S. Army Continental Commands, 1821–1920, roll 4.

6. Emory, *Report on the United States and Mexican Boundary Survey*, 96.

7. Emory, *Report on the United States and Mexican Boundary Survey*, 95–96.

8. Nathaniel Michler, "From the 111th Meridian of Longitude to the Pacific Ocean" in Emory, *Report on the United States and Mexican Boundary Survey*, 117.

9. "Report of Lieutenant John G. Parke, Corps of Topographic Engineers, upon the routes . . . and upon that portion of the route near the thirty-second parallel lying between the Rio Grande and the Pima Villages of the Gila," in U.S. Congress, Senate, *Report of Explorations and Surveys*, 3–5.

10. Gray, *Southern Pacific Railroad*.

11. U.S. Congress, *Congressional Globe*, 34th Cong., 1st sess., 1856, vol. 25, pt. 2:1298.

12. A. Anderson, Report to the Honorable Thomas L. Rusk, U.S. Senate, Washington City, March 10, 1857, RG 48, M95, roll 3.

13. The mail line made just forty trips across the desert before it abandoned its Arizona route in December 1858.

14. Conkling and Conkling, *Butterfield Overland Mail*, 2:166–170.

15. John Walker to James L. Collins, May 31, 1859, Tucson, New Mexico, RG 75, T21, Letters Received from the Agencies, 1859–1860, roll 4.

16. Woods, *Journal of I. C. Woods*, 111–112.

17. Sylvester Mowry to the Honorable Charles Mix, Tubac, Arizona, September 24, 1858, RG 75, M234, New Mexico Superintendency, 1858–1859, roll 549.

18. John Walker to James W. Denver, Commissioner of Indian Affairs, January 16, 1858, RG 75, M234, New Mexico Superintendency, 1858–1859, roll 549.

19. John Walker to the Honorable Commissioner of Indian Affairs, Charles Mix, Tucson Agency, Gadsden Purchase, New Mexico, March 1, 1858, RG 75, M234, New Mexico Superintendency, 1858–1859, roll 549.

20. John Walker to the Honorable Commissioner of Indian Affairs, Charles Mix, Gadsden Purchase, New Mexico, April 4, 1858, RG 75, M234, New Mexico Superintendency, 1858–1859, roll 549. Superintendent J. L. Collins to John Walker, May 22, 1858, RG 75, T21, Letters Sent, March 29, 1856 to December 11, 1859, roll 26. John Walker to James L. Collins, Superintendent, August 31, 1858, RG 75, M234, roll 549.

21. Goddard Bailey to Charles E. Mix, November 4, 1858, RG 75, M234, New Mexico Superintendency, 1858–1859, roll 549. U.S. Bureau of Indian Affairs, *Annual Report of the Commissioner of Indian Affairs*, 1858, 204. "Report of Sylvester Mowry to A. B. Greenwood, Commissioner of Indian Affairs, Washington, DC, November 21, 1859," in U.S. Bureau of Indian Affairs, *Annual Report of the Commissioner of Indian Affairs*, 1859, 354.

22. John Walker to James L. Collins, Superintendent, November 30, 1858, RG 75, T21, Letters Received from the Agencies, 1858–1859, roll 3.

23. John Walker to James L. Collins, Superintendent, January 1, 1859, RG 75, T21, Letters Received from the Agencies, 1859–1860, roll 4.

24. John Walker to James L. Collins, Superintendent, February 4, 1859, RG 75, T21, Letters Received from the Agencies, 1859–1860, roll 4.

25. James Denver to Silas St. John, February 18, 1859, Department of the Interior, Office of Indian Affairs, RG 75, T21, Letters Received from the Agencies, 1859–1860, roll 4. John Walker to James L. Collins, Superintendent, March 31, 1859, RG 75, T21, Letters Received from the Agencies, 1859–1860, roll 4. Walker arranged with the Overland Mail Company blacksmith to repair the Indians' tools. The goods were transported to Maricopa Wells by Major Samuel Heintzelman.

26. John Walker to James Collins, May 9, 1859, Tucson, New Mexico, RG 75, T21, Letters Received from the Agencies, 1859–1860, roll 4.

27. John Walker to James L. Collins, Superintendent, February 4, 1859, RG 75, T21, Letters Received from the Agencies, 1859–1860, roll 4. *Daily Alta California*, San Francisco, California, July 1, 1860, 1.

28. John Walker to James Collins, May 9, 1859, Tucson, New Mexico, RG 75, T21, Letters Received from the Agencies, 1859–1860, roll 4.

29. "Sylvester Mowry to J. W. Denver, Commissioner of Indian Affairs, November 10, 1857," in U.S. Bureau of Indian Affairs, *Annual Report of the Commissioner of Indian Affairs*, 1857, 298, 303, and "Report of Sylvester Mowry to A. B. Greenwood, Commissioner of Indian Affairs, Washington, D.C., November 21, 1859," in U.S. Bureau of Indian Affairs, *Annual Report of the Commissioner of Indian Affairs*, 1859, 354.

30. "Sylvester Mowry to J. W. Denver, Commissioner of Indian Affairs, November 10, 1857," in U.S. Bureau of Indian Affairs, *Annual Report of the Commissioner of Indian Affairs*, 1857, 304.

31. Goddard Bailey to Charles E. Mix, November 4, 1858, RG 75, M234, New Mexico Superintendency, 1858–1859, roll 549, 203.

32. Ibid.

33. Ibid. James L. Collins to A. B. Greenwood, Santa Fe, New Mexico, August 5, 1860, RG 75, M234, New Mexico Superintendency, 1860–1861, roll 550. Cyrus Lennan to the Honorable Caleb B. Smith, Secretary of the Interior, Pimo Villages, July 11, 1861, RG 75, M234, New Mexico Superintendency, 1860–1861, roll 550.

34. Goddard Bailey to Charles E. Mix, November 4, 1858, RG 75, M234, New Mexico Superintendency, 1858–1859, roll 549, 203.

35. Cyrus Lennan, Post Master, Pimo Villages, to C. S. Collins, Tucson, Arizona, July 22, 1860, RG 75, M234, New Mexico Superintendency 1860–1861, roll 550. "John Walker to James L. Collins, Superintendent, September 28, 1859," in U.S. Bureau of Indian Affairs, *Annual Report of the Commissioner of Indian Affairs*, 1859, 351.

36. John Walker to A. B. Greenwood, Santa Fe, New Mexico, August 6, 1859, RG 75, M234, New Mexico Superintendency, 1858–1859, roll 549. John Walker to James L. Collins, May 31, 1859, Tucson, New Mexico, RG 75, T21, Letters Received from the Agencies, 1859–1860, roll 4.

37. Silas St. John, Pimo Villages, to A. B. Greenwood, Commissioner of Indian Affairs, September 16, 1859, RG 75, M234, New Mexico Superintendency, 1858–1859, roll 549.

38. "John Walker to James L. Collins, Tucson, New Mexico, September 23, 1859," 351; "Sylvester Mowry to A. B. Greenwood, Commissioner of Indian Affairs, Los Pimos, October 6, 1859," 360, both in U.S. Bureau of Indian Affairs, *Annual Report of the Commissioner of Indian Affairs*, 1859.

39. Goddard Bailey to Charles E. Mix, November 4, 1858, RG 75, M234, New Mexico Superintendency, 1858–1859, roll 549, 203.

40. "Charles E. Mix to Jacob Thompson, Office of Indian Affairs, November 6, 1858," in U.S. Congress, *Congressional Globe, Appendix*, 35th Cong., 2nd sess., 1859, 40–41.

41. A. B. Greenwood to Special Agent Sylvester Mowry, June 13, 1859, RG 75, M234, New Mexico Superintendency, 1858–1859, roll 549.

42. "Charles E. Mix to Jacob Thompson, Office of Indian Affairs, November 6, 1858," in U.S. Congress, *Congressional Globe, Appendix*, 35th Cong., 2nd sess., 1859, 40–41.

43. U.S. Congress, *Congressional Globe*, 35th Cong., 2nd sess., February 2, 1859, 735.

44. U.S. Congress, *Congressional Globe*, 35th Cong., 2nd sess., February 26, 1859, 1407. *Congressional Globe, Appendix*, November 6, 1858, 1406–1407.

45. U.S. Congress, *Congressional Globe*, 35th Cong., 2nd sess., February 3, 1859, 734–736.

46. Indian Appropriation Act for 1859, 11 Stat. 401, February 28, 1859. Antonio Azul claimed 5,200 square miles (3,322,000 acres), and the Indian Claims Commission recognized Pima aboriginal rights to 3,300,00 acres. The 1859 reservation was 1.9 percent of this total.

47. A. B. Greenwood to Special Agent Sylvester Mowry, June 13, 1859, RG 75, M234, New Mexico Superintendency, 1858–1859, roll 549.

48. James L. Collins to A. B. Greenwood, Santa Fe, New Mexico, June 26, 1859, RG 75, M234, New Mexico Superintendency, 1858–1859, roll 549. John Walker to A. B. Greenwood, Santa Fe, New Mexico, August 6, 1859, RG 75, M234, New Mexico Superintendency, 1858–1859, roll 549. John Walker to James Collins, October 21, 1859, Tucson, New Mexico, RG 75, T21, Letters Received from the Agencies, 1859–1860, roll 4.

49. "Report of Sylvester Mowry to A. B. Greenwood, Commissioner of Indian Affairs, Washington, DC, November 21, 1859," in U.S. Bureau of Indian Affairs, *Annual Report of the Commissioner of Indian Affairs*, 1859, 354.

50. Ibid.

51. Ibid.

52. Walker to Collins, September 14, 1859, RG 75, M234, New Mexico Superintendency, 1858–1859, roll 549. Mowry distributed the following: 444 axes; 618 shovels; 31 handsaws; 706 butcher knives; 516 hoes; 240 sickles; 48 files; 270 harrow teeth; 48 mattocks; 72 whetstones; 15 grindstones and fixtures; 36 hay forks; 36 hammers; 48 iron rakes; 48 trowels; 12 screw drivers; 1 carpenter's shop, complete set of tools; 15 plows; 15 sets of plow harnesses; 1 forge, 1 anvil and 1 vice; 1 set of sledges; 1 cast-steel hand-hammer; 3 pair tongs; 1 set of files; 12 file handles; 36 hatchets; 120 picks and handles; 7 kegs of nails; 9 gross of screws; 1,400 needles; and 1 box sheet tin (for repairing implements). Goods for women included the following: 2,500 yards of manta (cotton cloth); 2,500 yards of blue drill; 125 yards of scarlet flannel; 108 yards of red flannel; 1,000 yards of calico; 180 check shirts; 120 fancy shirts; 180 hickory shirts; 50 yards Turkey red cloth for chiefs; 3 gross gilt buttons; 2 fancy bowie knives; 48 straw hats; 60 pairs shoes for chiefs and wives; 600 pounds smoking tobacco; 280 pounds white beads; 24 regatta shirts for chiefs of pueblos; 144 pipes, with stems. Seed was distributed as follows: 4,000 pounds of barley; 1 pint turnip seed. For the chiefs, Mowry purchased 1 American flag for head chief; 1 suit of uniform, complete; 1 suit of uniform, complete for son; 1 uniform jacket for Maricopa chief. U.S. Bureau of Indian Affairs, *Annual Report of the Commissioner of Indian Affairs*, 1859, 355–356.

53. Silas St. John, Pimo Villages, New Mexico, to Sylvester Mowry, November 9, 1859, University of Arizona Library, Special Collections.

54. Walker to M. Steck, Tucson, Arizona, November 13, 1859, RG 75, M234, New Mexico Superintendency, 1858–1859, roll 549. John Walker to James Collins, November 14, 1859, Tucson, New Mexico, RG 75, T21, Letters Received from the Agencies, 1859–1860, roll 4.

55. John Walker to James L. Collins, Superintendent, March 31, 1859, RG 75, T21, Letters Received from the Agencies, 1859–1860, roll 4.

56. "Report of Sylvester Mowry to A. B. Greenwood, Commissioner of Indian Affairs, Washington, DC, November 21, 1859," in U.S. Bureau of Indian Affairs, *Annual Report of the Commissioner of Indian Affairs*, 1859, 358.

57. Ibid., 357.

58. "Sylvester Mowry to A. B. Greenwood, Commissioner of Indian Affairs, Los Pimos, October 6, 1859," in U.S. Bureau of Indian Affairs, *Annual Report of the Commissioner of Indian Affairs*, 1859, 360. Silas St. John to Sylvester Mowry, October 6, 1859, University of Arizona Library, Special Collections. RG 75, M234, Pima Agency, 1859–1861, roll 669. "A. B. Gray to Sylvester Mowry, Pimo Villages, October 17, 1859," in U.S. Bureau of Indian Affairs, *Annual Report of the Commissioner of Indian Affairs*, 1859, 358. John A. Clark, Surveyor General, to J. M. Edwards, Commissioner of the General Land Office, Santa Fe, New Mexico, November 30, 1861, RG 75, M234, New Mexico Superintendency, 1860–1861, roll 550.

59. "Report of Sylvester Mowry to A. B. Greenwood, Commissioner of Indian Affairs, Washington, DC, November 21, 1859," in U.S. Bureau of Indian Affairs, *Annual Report of the Commissioner of Indian Affairs*, 1859, 359.

60. Walker to Collins, September 14, 1859, RG 75, M234, New Mexico Superintendency, 1858–1859, roll 549.

61. Silas St. John to A. B. Greenwood, January 18, 1860, Pimo villages, RG 75, M234, Pima Agency, 1859–1861, roll 669.

62. A treaty was made April 9, 1863, at Fort Yuma among the southern Arizona tribes, including representatives of the Mohave, Pima, Papago, Maricopa, Quechan, Chemehuevi, and Hualapai. The purpose of the treaty was to bring peace to the area, which would then allow mineral exploration to increase. RG 75, M734, roll 8.

63. Walker to Collins, December 2, 1859, Tucson, New Mexico; see also Walker to Collins, June 8, 1860, Tucson, New Mexico, both RG 75, T21, Letters Received from the Agencies, 1859–1860, roll 4.

64. "Report of Sylvester Mowry to A. B. Greenwood, Commissioner of Indian Affairs, Washington, DC, November 21, 1859," in U.S. Bureau of Indian Affairs, *Annual Report of the Commissioner of Indian Affairs*, 1859, 359.

Chapter 4. Civil War, Settlers, and Pima Agriculture

This chapter was adapted from "The Granary of Arizona: Civil War, Settlers and Pima-Maricopa Agriculture: 1860-1869," *Journal of Arizona History* 48, no. 3 (2007): 221–256.

1. Walker to Collins, January 4, 1860, RG 75, T21, Letters Received from the Agencies, 1859–1860, roll 4.

2. Charles D. Poston to William Dole, April 15, 1863, Charles D. Poston Letterbook, RG 75, M734, roll 8.

3. Walker to Collins, Tucson, New Mexico, June 8, 1860, RG 75, T21, Letters Received from the Agencies, 1859–1860, roll 4.

4. *Daily Alta California*, December 14, 1860, 1. Browne, *Adventures in Apache Country*, 110–111.

5. Superintendent James L. Collins to William Dole, Commissioner of Indian Affairs, Santa Fe, New Mexico, May 25, 1861, RG 75, M234, roll 550. "James A. Lucas to Dr. Lorenzo Labadi, Mesilla, 14 de Junio de 1861," in *War of the Rebellion*, ser. 1, vol. 4, 39.

6. Altshuler, "Military Administration in Arizona," 220.

7. Captain George Andrews, Fort Yuma, to Ebenezer Noyes and Ammi White, August 9, 1861, RG 109, M323, roll 182. A. M. White to Lieutenant Colonel George Andrews, Pima Villages, August 23, 1861, in *War of the Rebellion*, ser. 1, vol. 50, pt. 1, 588.

8. *Mesilla Times*, August 24, 1861, 2.

9. Ammi White to General James Carleton, Pima Villages, January 16, 1862, RG 393, M1120, Miscellaneous Records of the Column from California, 1862.

10. "Report of John R. Baylor, Fort Bliss, September 24, 1861," in *War of the Rebellion*, ser. 1, vol. 4, 109. Finch, "Sherod Hunter and the Confederates in Arizona," 202. "Letter from Thomas Robinson," in "George Wright to Brigadier General Lorenzo Thomas," San Francisco, January 29, 1862, in *War of the Rebellion*, ser. 1, vol. 9, 628.

11. See Finch, "Sherod Hunter and the Confederates in Arizona," 146. Poston, *Building a State in Apache Land*, 104.

12. "Rigg to Carleton," Fort Yuma, January 17, 1862, in *War of the Rebellion*, ser. 1, vol. 50, pt. 1, 809.

13. "Statement of Walker," in *War of the Rebellion*, ser. 1, vol. 50, pt. I, 898–900.

14. *War of the Rebellion*, ser. 1, vol. 50, pt. 1, 136–137. Colton, *Civil War in the Western Territories*, 101.

15. "Edwin A. Rigg to Colonel J.H. Carleton, January 17, 1862," in *War of the Rebellion*, ser. 1, vol. 50, pt. 1, 809. "Edwin A. Rigg to Colonel James H. Carleton, Fort Yuma, January 19, 1862," in *War of the Rebellion*, ser. 1, vol. 50, pt. 1, 825.

16. "Report of Surgeon James M. McNulty, U.S. Army, Acting Medical Inspector, October 1863," in *War of the Rebellion*, ser. 1, vol. 50, pt. 1, 139.

17. "Brigadier General George Wright, Headquarters, District of Southern California, to Major R. C. Drum, Assistant Adjutant General, San Francisco, Los Angeles, California, February 18, 1862," in *War of the Rebellion*, ser. 1, vol. 50, pt. 1, 873.

18. "Edwin Rigg to Lieutenant B. C. Cutler, Fort Yuma, March 1, 1862," enclosure No. 1 (statement of Walker) and enclosure No. 3 (letter of Ammi White) in *War of the Rebellion*, ser. 1, vol. L, pt. 1, 898–900.

19. "Sherod Hunter to Colonel John Baylor, Tucson, Arizona, April 5, 1862," in *War of the Rebellion*, ser. 1, vol. IX, pt. 1, 708.

20. "Edwin Rigg to James Carleton, Fort Yuma, March 30, 1862," in *War of the Rebellion*, ser. 1, vol. 50, pt. 1, 966.

21. "Benjamin C. Cutler to Lieutenant Colonel J. R. West, Los Angeles, California, March 31, 1862," in *War of the Rebellion*, ser. 1, vol. 50, pt. 1, 969–970. "Edwin Rigg to James Carleton, Fort Yuma, California, March 25, 1862," in *War of the Rebellion*, ser. 1, vol. 50, pt. 1, 952.

22. "Benjamin C. Cutler—General Order #8, Fort Yuma, May 10, 1862," in *War of the Rebellion*, ser. 1, vol. 50, pt. 1, 1061. "William Calloway to Edwin Rigg, Sacaton Station, April 18, 1862," in Finch, "Sherod Hunter and the Confederates in Arizona," 205–206.

23. Barnes, *Arizona Place Names*, 38, described the post as "only an earthwork thrown around a trading post." "Benjamin C. Cutler—General Order #8, Fort Yuma, May 10, 1862," in *War of the Rebellion*, ser. 1, vol. 50, pt. 1, 1061.

24. "James H. Carleton to Señor Gobernador Don Ignacio Pesqueira, Fort Yuma, California, May 2, 1862," in *War of the Rebellion*, ser. 1, vol. 50, pt. 1, 1044. Carleton offered to purchase from Sonora Governor Don Ignacio Pesqueria flour, pork, mutton, sugar, coffee, wheat, barley, fruit, vegetables, and any other supplies the Mexicans might be willing to sell and transport to the Pima villages (later Tucson).

25. "J. R. West to B. C. Cutler, Pima Villages, May 4, 1862," in *War of the Rebellion*, ser. 1, vol. 50, pt. 1, 1050.

26. "J. R. West to Lieutenant Benjamin Cutler, Pima Villages, May 5, 1862," in *War of the Rebellion*, ser. 1, vol. 50, pt. 1, 1052. "James H. Carleton to Major R. C. Drum, May 10, 1862," in *War of the Rebellion*, ser. 1, vol. 50, pt. 1, 1060.

27. "J. R. West to Lieutenant Benjamin Cutler, Fort Barrett, Pima Villages, May 13, 1862," in *War of the Rebellion*, ser. 1, vol. 50, pt. 1, 1070. "James H. Carleton to Major R. C. Drum, Gila City, New Mexico (Fort Yuma), May 17, 1862," in *War of the Rebellion*, ser. 1, vol. 50, pt. 1, 1078.

28. "James H. Carleton to Major Richard C. Drum, Fort Barrett, Pima Villages, Arizona Territory, May 24, 1862," in *War of the Rebellion*, ser. 1, vol. 50, pt. 1, 1095.

29. "J. R. West to B. C. Cutler, Tucson, Arizona Territory, May 26, 1862," in *War of the Rebellion*, ser. 1, vol. 50, pt. 1, 1100.

30. "James H. Carleton to Major Theodore A. Coult, Fort Barrett, Arizona Territory, June 21, 1862," in *War of the Rebellion*, ser. 1, vol. 50, pt. 1, 1152.

31. "D. Fergusson to Lieutenant C. Nichols, Tucson, Arizona Territory, August 17, 1862," in *War of the Rebellion*, ser. 1, vol. 50, pt. 2, 74–75.

32. "J. R. West to Lieutenant B. C. Cutler, Pima Villages, May 4, 1862," in *War of the Rebellion*, ser. 1, vol. 50, pt. 2, 1050.

33. "D. Fergusson to Lieutenant B. C. Cutler, Tucson, Arizona Territory, September 21, 1862," in *War of the Rebellion*, ser. 1, vol. 50, pt. 2, 129.

34. "Theodore A. Coult to Lieutenant W. A. Thompson, Tucson, Arizona Territory, October 14, 1862," in *War of the Rebellion*, ser. 1, vol. 50, pt. 2, 172.

35. Browne, *Adventures in Apache Country*, 111. *Daily Alta California*, June 29, 1862, 1.

36. "James H. Whitlock to J. F. Bennett, Tucson, Arizona Territory, March 15, 1863," in *War of the Rebellion*, ser. 1, vol. 50, pt. 2, 353.

37. Browne, *Adventures in Apache Country*, 111. "William Ffrench to Lieutenant Colonel T. A. Coult, Tucson, Arizona Territory, October 28, 1863," in *War of the Rebellion*, ser. 1, vol. 50, pt. 2, 660.

38. Miller, *Soldiers and Settlers*, 27.

39. "Charles Poston to William Dole," in U.S. Bureau of Indian Affairs, *Annual Report of the Commissioner of Indian Affairs*, 1864, 153.

40. *The Weekly Arizona Miner*, March 23, 1867, 3; April 6, 1867, 3; and May 4, 1867, 3. M. O. Davidson to D. N. Cooley, Enriquilla, January 12, 1866, RG 75, M234, roll 3. Altshuler, "Poston and the Pimas," 31. Poston to Honorable Wm. Dole, Pima Villages, Arizona, March 10, 1864; and Charles Poston to Abraham Lyons, Pimo Villages, January 10, 1864, both RG 75, M234, roll 3.

41. Coult to Walker, March 8, 1864; and Coult to Davis, March 10, 1864, both RG 393, M1120, Records of the U.S. Army Continental Commands, 1821–1920, roll 23.

42. Altshuler, "Poston and the Pimas," 32–40, provides the details of the complaint and the subsequent investigation. By the time a military board found Poston guilty of defrauding the government, the superintendent was en route to Washington, D.C., where he prepared to take his seat as a territorial delegate.

43. "J. R. West to Lieutenant Benjamin Cutler, Fort Barrett, Pima Villages, May 13, 1862," in *War of the Rebellion*, ser. 1, vol. 50, pt. 1, 1070. "James H. Carleton to Major Richard C. Drum, Fort Barrett, Pima Villages, Arizona Territory, May 24, 1862," in *War of the Rebellion*, ser. 1, vol. 50, pt. 1, 1095.

44. "Theodore A. Coult to Lieutenant W. L. Rynerson, Tucson, December 30, 1862," in *War of the Rebellion*, ser. 1, vol. 50, pt. 2, 269.

45. "D. Fergusson to Lieutenant J. F. Bennett, Tucson, Arizona Territory, April 14, 1863," in *War of the Rebellion*, ser. 1, vol. 50, pt. 2, 395.

46. Charles Poston to William Dole, New York, April 16, 1863, RG 75, M234, roll 3. When arms were distributed, Poston complained it occurred without "consulting their legal guardian on the subject or even inviting his presence." Poston to Brigadier General James Carleton, Pima Villages, March 10, 1864, RG 75, M234, roll 3.

47. "D. Fergusson to Lieutenant George A. Burkett, Tucson, Arizona Territory, April 17, 1863," in *War of the Rebellion*, ser. 1, vol. 50, pt. 2, 405.

48. Allyn, *Arizona of Joseph Pratt Allyn*, 162.

49. Underwood, *First Arizona Volunteer Infantry*, 11.

50. Miller, *Soldiers and Settlers*, 50.

51. Wagoner, *Early Arizona*, 408–412 and 425–434.

52. "Brigadier Jonathan S. Mason to Colonel R. C. Drum, Maricopa Wells, Arizona, May 30, 1865," in *War of the Rebellion*, ser. 1, vol. 50, pt. 1, 1247. Juan Cheveria requested a trip to San Francisco as his payment. The trip was approved in May 1865. "Jonathan S. Mason to Colonel R. C. Drum, Maricopa Wells, May 31, 1865," in *War of the Rebellion*, ser. 1, vol. 50, pt. 2, 1251.

53. Underwood, *First Arizona Volunteer Infantry*, 18–23. The three remaining companies (mostly Mexican) were mustered into service in October and November.

54. M. O. Davidson to R. B. Valkenburgh, U.S. Indian Agency, Tucson, September 30, 1865, RG 75, M234, roll 3.

55. Altshuler, *Cavalry Yellow and Infantry Blue*, 223.

56. U.S. Bureau of Indian Affairs, *Annual Report of the Commissioner of Indian Affairs*, 1867, 163. Altshuler, "Men and Brothers," 315–322.

57. Browne, *Adventures in Apache Country*, 107.

58. Ammi White to Charles Poston, Agency of Pima and Maricopa Indians, Pimo Villages, June 30, 1864, RG 75, M234, roll 3.

59. Allyn, *Arizona of Joseph Pratt Allyn*, 109.

60. *The Arizona Miner*, August 24, 1864, 3.

61. Davidson to Cooley, January 12, 1866.

62. "C. H. Lord to D. N. Cooley, Tucson, Arizona, June 4, 1866," in U.S. Bureau of Indian Affairs, *Annual Report of the Commissioner of Indian Affairs*, 1866, 112.

63. Levi Ruggles to George Dent, Pima Villages, March 4, 1867, RG 75, M234, roll 3.

64. George Hooper to Commissioner of Indian Affairs, San Francisco, March 23, 1865, RG 75, M234, roll 3. George Hooper to Charles Poston, San Francisco, April 12, 1865, RG 75, M234, roll 3.

65. *The Weekly Arizona Miner*, March 23, 1867, 3; April 6, 1867, 3; and May 4, 1867, 3. Davidson to Cooley, January 12, 1866. Constance Wynn Altshuler, "Poston and the Pimas," 31. Poston to Honorable Wm. Dole, Pima Villages, Arizona, March 10, 1864, RG 75, M234, roll 3. Charles Poston to Abraham Lyons, Pimo Villages, January 10, 1864, RG 75, M234, roll 3.

66. *The Weekly Arizona Miner*, May 4, 1867, 3; June 1, 1867, 3. Rusling, *Across America*, 370.

67. Miller, *Soldiers and Settlers*, 73–86.

68. Lt. Colonial and Inspector General S. A. Lathroop to William Dole, Washington, D.C., October 24, 1863, RG 75, M234, roll 3.

69. Charles Poston to William Dole, New York, May 13, 1863, RG 75, M234, roll 3.

70. Charles D. Poston to William Dole, April 15, 1863, Charles D. Poston Letterbook, RG 75, M734, roll 8.

71. John N. Goodwin to D. N. Cooley, Washington, June 7, 1866, RG 75, M234, roll 3.

72. U.S. Bureau of Indian Affairs, *Annual Report of the Commissioner of Indian Affairs*, 1870, 118–119.

73. Miller, *Soldiers and Settlers*, 77.

74. Reed, *Last Bugle Call*, 43–52.

75. Nichols, "A Miniature Venice," 339–340.

76. *The Weekly Arizona Miner*, February 1, 1868, 2; February 8, 1868, 2; April 18, 1868, 2.

77. *The Weekly Arizona Miner*, April 18, 1868, 2.

78. The Department of the Interior surveyed 69,120 acres as an addition to the reservation, but never consummated the action. Consequently, while the Interior Department extended the reservation, the 69,120 acres were not officially added to the reservation until the Presidential Executive Order of 1879.

79. Thomas Devin to George Dent, Tucson, Arizona, March 14, 1865, RG 75, M234, roll 3.

80. George Andrews to Ely Parker, Office of the Superintendent of Indian Affairs, November 6, 1869, RG 75, M234, roll 3.

81. Frederick Grossman to George Andrews, Pima Villages, October 19, 1869, RG 75, M234, roll 3.

82. U.S. Bureau of Indian Affairs, *Annual Report of the Commissioner of Indian Affairs*, 1869, 219–220.

83. Talk of the Pima and Maricopa Indians by Captain Frederick Grossman at Casa Blanca, Arizona Territory, October 30, 1869, RG 75, M234, roll 3.

84. U.S. Bureau of the Census, *Ninth Census*, vol. 3: *The Statistics of the Wealth and Industry of the United States, Embracing the Tables of Wealth, Taxation, and Public Indebtedness; of Agriculture; Manufacturing; Mining; and the Fisheries, With Which Are Produced, from the Volume of Population, the Major Tables of Occupations. Compiled from the Original Returns of the Ninth Census, June 1, 1870*, 97–98.

Chapter 5. A Crisis on the River

This chapter was adapted from "See the New Country: The Removal Controversy and Pima and Maricopa Water Rights, 1869-1879," *Journal of Arizona History* 33, no. 4 (1992): 23–45.

1. Thomas C. Devin to George Dent, Headquarters, Department of Arizona, Tucson, March 14, 1869, RG 75, M734, roll 2. Major John S. Sherburne to Colonel George Andrews, RG 75, M734, roll 3.

2. George Andrews to Ely Parker, September 9, 1869, RG 75, M734, roll 8.

3. Levi Ruggles to George W. Dent, Pima Villages, December 21, 1867; and Levi Ruggles to George W. Dent, Pima Villages, November 4, 1867, both RG 75, M734, roll 2.

4. E.O.C. Ord to Thomas C. Devin, San Francisco, California, April 2, 1869, RG 75, M734, roll 3.

5. George W. Dent to Nathaniel Taylor, La Paz, Arizona Territory, April 15, 1869, RG 75, M734, roll 3.

6. Levi Ruggles to George W. Dent, Pima villages, June 20, 1867, RG 75, M734, roll 2.

7. Ely Parker to George W. Andrews, Office of Indian Affairs, Washington, D.C., August 4, 1869; and Frederick Grossman to George W. Andrews, Pima villages, Arizona Territory, October 31, 1869, both RG 75, M734, roll 3.

8. Levi Ruggles to George W. Dent, Pima villages, June 20, 1867, RG 75, M734, roll 2.

9. Milton Cogswell to Thomas C. Devin, Headquarters, Sub-District of the Verde, Camp McDowell, Arizona Territory, November 28, 1869, RG 75, M734, roll 4.

10. "Roger Jones to Randolph B. Marcy, Washington, D.C., July 21, 1869," in U.S. Department of the Interior, Inspector General, *Records of the Inspector General*, 662.

11. J. D. Cox, Secretary of the Interior, to John Rawlins, Secretary of War, Department of Interior, Washington, D.C., June 9, 1869, RG 393, M1120, Records of the U.S. Army Continental Commands, 1821–1920, Fort Mojave, Letters Sent and Received, 1859–1890, roll 6.

12. Frederick Grossman to George W. Andrews, Sacaton, Arizona Territory, November 9, 1869, RG 75, M734, roll 3. Frederick Grossman to George W. Andrews, February 15, 1870, RG 75, M734, roll 4. *The Weekly Arizona Miner*, September 26, 1868, 3.

13. Frederick Grossman to George W. Andrews, Sacaton, Arizona Territory, November 11, 1869, RG 75, M734, roll 3.

14. "John Stout to Vincent Colyer, October 25, 1871," in U.S. Bureau of Indian Affairs, *Annual Report of the Commissioner of Indian Affairs*, 1871, 475.

15. John Stout to Ely Parker, October 25, 1871, RG 75, M234, roll 2.

16. "Frederick Grossman to Herman Bendell, August 16, 1871," in U.S. Department of the Interior, *Annual Report of the Secretary of the Interior*, 1871, 776. Frederick Grossman to George W. Andrews, January 8, 1870, RG 75, M734, roll 4.

17. John A. Rawlins, Secretary of War; Major General E.O.C. Ord, Commander of the Department of California; and Brevet Brigadier General Thomas C. Devin, Commander of the Sub-District of Southern Arizona, all favored the extension of the reservation. The *Arizona Weekly Citizen* also opposed the extension. *Arizona Weekly Citizen*, October 15, 1870, 1:2; January 14, 1871, 1:14; and April 8, 1871, 1:26. McCormick traveled to Washington to personally oppose the extension in February 1871.

18. Andrews, *Survey of Pima and Maricopa Reservation*, 3. "Roger Jones to R. B. Macy, Inspector General's Office, San Francisco, Ca.," in U.S. Department of the Interior, *Annual Report of the Secretary of the Interior*, 1869, 219–220.

19. "Frederick Grossman to George W. Andrews, September 1, 1870," in U.S. Department of the Interior, *Annual Report of the Secretary of the Interior*, 1870, 584.

20. "Herman Bendell to Ely Parker, August 22, 1871," in U.S. Bureau of Indian Affairs, *Annual Report of the Commissioner of Indian Affairs*, 1871, 766.

21. U.S. Department of the Interior, *Annual Report of the Secretary of the Interior*, 1870, 472.

22. U.S. Bureau of Indian Affairs, *Annual Report of the Commissioner of Indian Affairs*, 1870, 117.

23. "Bendell to Parker," in U.S. Bureau of Indian Affairs, *Annual Report of the Commissioner of Indian Affairs*, 1871, 766. The proposed extension would add 23,120 acres on the western and 58,020 acres on the southeastern end of the Pima Reservation.

24. U.S. Bureau of Indian Affairs, *Annual Report of the Commissioner of Indian Affairs*, 1869, 19. "Report of Francis A. Walker to Columbus Delano, November 1, 1872," in U.S. Bureau of Indian Affairs, *Annual Report of the Commissioner of Indian Affairs*, 1872, 57.

25. *Arizona Weekly Citizen*, Tucson, Pima County, September 9, 1871 (1:48). On October 26, 1872, 3:3, the *Citizen* reported a similar occurrence.

26. Beadle, *Undeveloped West*, 611–612.

27. Vincent Colyer, chairman of the Board of Indian Commissioners, had been sent by Grant, in 1871, to negotiate peace with the tribes in Arizona. The War Department—as well as most territorial newspapers—opposed Colyer's efforts and succeeded in convincing Grant to dispatch Howard to the territory.

28. "Oliver O. Howard to Columbus Delano, June 1872," in U.S. Bureau of Indian Affairs, *Annual Report of the Commissioner of Indian Affairs*, 1872, 153.

29. Ibid., 154.

30. Board of Indian Commissioners, *Annual Report of the Board of Indian Commissioners*, 1870, 9.

31. U.S. Department of the Interior, *Annual Report of the Secretary of the Interior*, 1871, 6.

32. John H. Stout to Reverend J. M. Ferris, Gila River Reservation, May 9, 1872; John Stout to J. M. Ferris, Gila River Reservation, April 30, 1873; and John Stout to J. M. Ferris, May 31, 1872, all Stout Letterbook, University of Arizona Library, Special Collections.

33. Report of a Council Held by the Chiefs and Headmen of the Pima and Maricopa Indians, at the United States Indian Agency, Gila River Reservation, Arizona Territory, on the 11th of May, 1872, Stout Letterbook, University of Arizona Library, Special Collections.

34. Report of a Council of the Chiefs and Headmen of the Pima and Maricopa Indians at the Gila River Reservation, Arizona Territory, held at the Agency building August 27, 1872, Stout Letterbook, University of Arizona Library, Special Collections.

35. Herman Bendell to Frances Walker, Prescott, Arizona Territory, September 11, 1872, RG 75, M734, roll 8. Bendell told Walker that Pima water rights were "paramount to every other condition respecting the progress and well-being of the Indians." For Walker's letter to Delano, see "Report of Francis A. Walker to Columbus Delano, November 1, 1872," in U.S. Bureau of Indian Affairs, *Annual Report of the Commissioner of Indian Affairs*, 1872, 57.

36. "John Stout to Frances Walker," in U.S. Bureau of Indian Affairs, *Annual Report of the Commissioner of Indian Affairs*, 1872, 318. See also U.S. Bureau of Indian Affairs, *Annual Report of the Comissioner of Indian Affairs*, 1873, 282.

37. Russell, *Pima Indians*, 52–61.

38. "John Stout to E. Smith," in U.S. Bureau of Indian Affairs, *Annual Report of the Commissioner of Indian Affairs*, 1873, 281.

39. Undated Petition from the Settlers of Florence, Pima County, Arizona Territory, and Settlers of the Salt River Valley, Phoenix, Arizona Territory, to Commissioner Edward Smith, RG 75, M234, roll 9.

40. *Arizona Weekly Citizen*, October 26, 1872, 3:3.

41. Board of Indian Commissioners. *Annual Report of the Board of Indian Commissioners*, 1873, 57.

42. "John Stout to E. Smith," in U.S. Bureau of Indian Affairs, *Annual Report of the Commissioner of Indian Affairs*, 1873, p. 283.

43. John Stout to Oliver O. Howard, Gila River Reservation, March 17, 1873, Stout Letterbook, University of Arizona Library, Special Collections.

44. U.S. Bureau of Indian Affairs, *Annual Report of the Commissioner of Indian Affairs*, 1873, 281. *Arizona Weekly Citizen*, November 3, 1873, 4:4.

45. John Stout to E. Smith, Gila River Reservation, July 1, 1873, Stout Letterbook, University of Arizona Library, Special Collections. Stout estimated the cost of transporting fourteen delegates at $9,500, an amount rejected as much too high by Delano and Smith. The secretary approved of the trip after Smith convinced Delano that it would be

wise to take one-third of the tribe now and the remainder in a few years, at which time the reservation could be sold and the proceeds used to defray the cost of removal. E. Smith to Columbus Delano, Washington, D.C., June 4, 1873, RG 75, M348, roll 23.

46. The delegation went to the Indian Territory by way of San Francisco, meeting Kansas Superintendent of Indian Affairs Enoch Hoag in Lawrence. Hoag suggested that the delegation prospect west of the Sac and Fox Agency in the "unoccupied lands" of western Indian Territory. On the return trip, the delegation returned to Lawrence and then took the Kansas and Pacific Railroad to Denver, whereupon they commenced travel on horse back to the Pima Reservation. John Stout to E. Smith, Gila River Reservation, September 9, 1874, Stout Letterbook, University of Arizona Library, Special Collections.

47. John Stout to E. Smith, Gila River Reservation, May 12, 1874, Stout Letterbook, University of Arizona Library, Special Collections. *Arizona Weekly Citizen*, January 24, 1872, 2; February 21, 1874, 3; and February 28, 1874, 1. "John Stout to E. Smith, U.S. Indian Agency, Gila River Reservation, Arizona Territory, August 31, 1874," in U.S. Bureau of Indian Affairs, *Annual Report of the Commissioner of Indian Affairs*, 1874, 292.

48. Russell, *Pima Indians*, 206–208; Bahr, Gregorio, Lopez and Alvarez, *Piman Shamanism and Staying Sickness*, 43.

49. "John Stout to E. Smith," in U.S. Bureau of Indian Affairs, *Annual Report of the Commissioner of Indian Affairs*, 1874, 294. "John Stout to Edward P. Smith," in U.S. Bureau of Indian Affairs, *Annual Report of the Commissioner of Indian Affairs*, 1875, 214. John Stout to E. Smith, May 12, 1874, RG 75, M234, roll 9.

50. Both publications were antagonistic to the Grant administration and Peace Policy. They largely reflected the views of the Indian traders and departmental provisions contractors.

51. Reprinted in the *Arizona Weekly Citizen*, January 10, 1874, 4:14.

52. *Arizona Weekly Citizen*, January 3, 1874, 4:13. The *Citizen* exaggerated the costs of the trip by reporting the expense to be $50,000, with stops in New York and other prominent eastern cities (November 4, 1873, 3:52).

53. "E. Smith to Columbus Delano," in U.S. Bureau of Indian Affairs, *Annual Report of the Commissioner of Indian Affairs*, 1874, 12.

54. Stout to E. Smith, May 12, 1874, RG 75, M234, roll 9.

55. A.P.K. Safford to Edward Smith, Executive Department, Tucson, November 3, 1874, RG 75, M234, roll 9.

56. "E. Smith to Columbus Delano," in U.S. Bureau of Indian Affairs, *Annual Report of the Commissioner of Indian Affairs*, 1874, 60. "John Cornyn to Edward Smith," in U.S. Bureau of Indian Affairs, *Annual Report of the Commissioner of Indian Affairs*, 1875, 213.

57. "Stout to Edward Smith," in U.S. Bureau of Indian Affairs, *Annual Report of the Commissioner of Indian Affairs*, 1875, 214.

58. "Edward Smith to Columbus Delano," in ibid., 79.

59. "Charles Hudson to John Q. Smith, Pima Agency, August 31, 1876," in U.S. Bureau of Indian Affairs, *Annual Report of the Commissioner of Indian Affairs*, 1876, 7–8.

60. "John Q. Smith to Columbus Delano," in U.S. Bureau of Indian Affairs, *Annual Report of the Commissioner of Indian Affairs*, 1877, 236.

61. "John Stout to Ezra A. Hayt, August 31, 1877," in U.S. Bureau of Indian Affairs, *Annual Report of the Commissioner of Indian Affairs*, 1877, 32.

62. John Stout to Ezra Hayt, Pima Agency, December 15, 1877, RG 75, M234, roll 19.

63. John Stout to Ezra Hayt, Pima Agency, December 21, 1877, RG 75, M234, roll 19.

64. "John H. Stout to Commissioner of Indian Affairs, Pima Agency, Arizona, August 15, 1878" in U.S. Bureau of Indian Affairs, *Annual Report of the Commissioner of Indian Affairs*, 1878, p. 3.

65. John Stout to Ezra Hayt, Pima Agency, March 5, 1878, RG 75, M234, roll 19.

66. "Ezra Hayt to Carl Schurz," in U.S. Bureau of Indian Affairs, *Annual Report of the Commissioner of Indian Affairs*, 1877, 6.

67. Ibid., 1878, 4.

68. Ibid., 1878, 5.

69. "Memorial Asking for the Removal of Certain Indians," Approved February 8, 1877, in *Acts, Resolutions and Memorials*, 125–126. H. Oury to Territorial Delegate Hiram S. Stevens, January 20, 1876, RG 75, M234, roll 15; and J. A. Parker to Commissioner J. Q. Smith, April 15, 1877, RG 75, M234, roll 16.

70. In Hayt's report to Schurz, U.S. Bureau of Indian Affairs, *Annual Report of the Commissioner of Indian Affairs*, 1878, 39.

71. "John Stout to Ezra Hayt," in U.S. Bureau of Indian Affairs, *Annual Report of the Commissioner of Indian Affairs*, 1878, 3.

72. John Stout to Ezra Hayt, March 6, 1878, RG 75, M234, roll 19.

73. Hayt consented to Stout's taking of a delegation on March 25, 1878. Apparently Stout was not informed, because on May 2 he wrote a second letter seeking permission to transport the delegation.

74. "John Stout to Ezra Hayt," in U.S. Bureau of Indian Affairs, *Annual Report of the Commissioner of Indian Affairs*, 1877, 32.

75. "John Stout to Ezra Hayt," in U.S. Bureau of Indian Affairs, *Annual Report of the Commissioner of Indian Affairs*, 1878, 5. John Stout to Ezra Hayt, June 28, 1877, RG 75, M234, roll 19.

76. "John Stout to Ezra Hayt, Pima Agency, Arizona, August 15, 1878," in U.S. Bureau of Indian Affairs, *Annual Report of the Commissioner of Indian Affairs*, 1878, 3.

77. John Stout to Ezra Hayt, November 28, 1878, RG 75, M234, roll 19.

78. Irvin McDowell to Adjutant General, Department of California, San Francisco, California, June 24, 1878, RG 75, M234, roll 22.

79. William T. Sherman to Irvin McDowell, Washington, D.C., November 25, 1878, RG 75, M234, roll 20.

80. Adna R. Chaffee to the Assistant Adjutant General, Headquarters, Department of Arizona, Prescott Barracks, Camp McDowell, Arizona Territory, November 24, 1878, RG 94, M666, roll 403, 3–8.

81. Orlando B. Willcox to the Assistant Adjutant General, Military Division of the Pacific, Presidio San Francisco, Headquarters, Department of Arizona, Prescott Barracks, December 3, 1878, RG 94, M666, roll 403.

82. Irvin McDowell to General William T. Sherman, Headquarters, Military Division of the Pacific and Department of California, Presidio of San Francisco, December 4, 1878, RG 94, M666, roll 403.

83. Irvin McDowell to General William T. Sherman, Washington, DC (referring to telegram sent this morning), Headquarters, Military Division of the Pacific and Department of California, Presidio of San Francisco, December 4, 1878, RG 94, M666, roll 403.

84. Irvin McDowell to the Adjutant General of the United States Army, Headquarters, Military Division of the Pacific and Department of California, Presidio of San Francisco, California, December 26, 1878, RG 95, M666, roll 403.

85. William T. Sherman to Irvin McDowell, December 5, 1878, RG 94, M666, roll 403.

86. Irvin McDowell to General Sherman, Presidio of San Francisco, California, December 23, 1878, RG 95, M666, roll 403. Irvin McDowell to William T. Sherman, San Francisco, California, December 23, 1878, RG 75, M234, roll 20.

87. William T. Sherman to Irvin McDowell, Washington, D.C., December 26, 1878, RG 95, M666, roll 403.

88. Irvin McDowell to William T. Sherman, Headquarters, Military Division of the Pacific and Department of California, Presidio of San Francisco, California, December 26, 1878, RG 95, M666, roll 403.

89. General Land Office Commissioner J. A. Williamson wrote to Hayt that the new reservation enclosed twenty townships of patented land. Williamson pointed out that Americans had already settled on 85,602 acres, either through entry or filing. J. A. Williamson to Ezra Hayt, General Land Office, Washington, D.C., January 15, 1879; and J. A. Williamson to Carl Schurz, March 3, 1879, both RG 75, M234, roll 22.

90. John C. Frémont to Carl Schurz, Territory of Arizona, Executive Department, Prescott, February 6, 1879, RG 75, M234, roll 21.

91. Letter from Governor Frémont to Secretary Schurz, Executive Department, Prescott, January 25, 1879, RG 48, M576, roll 19.

92. *Phoenix Herald*, February 3, 1879.

93. Captain Adna Chaffee, Report to Assistant Adjutant General, Headquarters, Department of Arizona, Prescott Barracks, February 7, 1879, RG 94, M666, roll 403. The extended reservation in the Salt River valley encompassed 656,000 acres.

94. "John C. Frémont to Colonel Orlando Willcox, St. Charles Hotel, Los Angeles, California, March 1, 1879," in Irvin McDowell, *Report to the Adjutant General, U.S. Army, Headquarters, Military Division of the Pacific and Department of California, Presidio of San Francisco, California*, RG 94, M666, roll 403.

95. Irvin McDowell, *Report to the Adjutant General, U.S. Army, Headquarters, Military Division of the Pacific and Department of California, Presidio of San Francisco, California*, RG 94, M666, roll 403, 1–4.

96. William Hammond to Ezra Hayt, September 13, 1879, RG 75, M234, roll 21.

97. "House Debate on Removal of Southwest Indians," in U.S. Congress, *Congressional Record*, 45th Cong., 3rd sess. (December 19, 1878), 311–325.

98. Ibid., 311.

99. 20 Stat. 313. The bill was enacted into law on February 17, 1879.

100. In January 1886, Senator Bowen submitted a resolution to the full Senate, urging the Committee on Indian Affairs to "inquire into the expediency of removing all the Indians in the United States to the Indian Territory." No action was taken on the resolution. U.S. Congress, Senate, Senate Miscellaneous Document 32.

Chapter 6. Famine and Starvation

This chapter was adapted from "Forced to Abandon Their Farms: Water Deprivation and Starvation among the Gila River Pima, 1892–1904," *American Indian Culture and Research Journal* 28, no. 3 (2004): 29–56.

1. "Letter from John Stout, Agent, to Commissioner of Indian Affairs Ezra Hayt, Pima Agency, August 15, 1878," in U.S. Bureau of Indian Affairs, *Annual Report of the Commissioner of Indian Affairs,* 1878, 3. "Ludlam to Hayt, Pima Agency, September 5, 1880," in U.S. Bureau of Indian Affairs, *Annual Report of the Commissioner of Indian Affairs*, 1880, 4.

2. Southworth, "Statements by Pima Indians," Arizona State Museum Archives. Statement of Juan Manuel (Chir-purtke) in Southworth, "Statements by Pima Indians," 73.

3. P. McCormick, United States Indian Inspector, to Cornelius Bliss, Secretary of the Interior, Sacaton, Arizona Territory, April 4, 1897, RG 48, M1070, roll 36, 3. Statement of William Wallace in Southworth, 6, "Statements by Pima Indians," Arizona State Museum Archives. "Report of Elmer A. Howard to Commissioner J.D.C. Atkins," in U.S. Bureau of Indian Affairs, *Annual Report of the Commissioner of Indian Affairs,* 1887, 4.

4. Gardner to Teller March 3, 1885, RG 48, M1070, 2. William Junkin, United States Indian Inspector, to John Noble, Secretary of the Interior, Pima Agency, September 30, 1890, RG 48, M1070, roll 36, 2. "Report of R. Pearsons on Pima Agency Investigation of Charges against Agent Wheeler, Pima Agency, December 31, 1885," RG 48, M1070, roll 35. Indian Rights Association, *Annual Report of the Board of Directors of the Indian Rights Association*, 1912, 21–23. See also U.S. Bureau of Indian Affairs, *Annual Report of the Commissioner of Indian Affairs,* 1911, 12–18.

5. U.S. Bureau of the Census, *Thirteenth Census of the United States Taken in the Year 1910*, vol. 6: *Agriculture 1909 and 1910, Report by States, with Statistics for Counties*, 78.

6. U.S. Bureau of Indian Affairs, *Annual Report of the Commissioner of Indian Affairs*, 1888, 4–5.

7. U.S. Congress, Senate, *Survey of Conditions of the Indians, Part 17, Arizona*, 8236.

8. Board of Indian Commissioners, *Annual Report of the Board of Indian Commissioners*, 1897, 11. "Walter Graves, United States Indian Inspector, to Ethan Allen Hitchcock, Secretary of the Interior, Pima Indian Reservation, Arizona, September 8, 1900," RG 48, M1070, roll 35.

9. Robert S. Gardner, United States Indian Inspector, to H. M. Teller, Secretary of the Interior, Pima and Maricopa Agency, September 2, 1886, RG 48, M1070, roll 35, 1; and Franklin Armstrong, United States Indian Inspector, to Lucius Q. C. Lamar, Secretary of the Interior, Pima Agency, February 26, 1887, both RG 48, M1070, roll 35, 1.

10. Copy of Minutes of the Florence Canal Company Board of Directors, November First, A.D. 1887, in Report of C. C. Duncan, United States Indian Inspector, to the Honorable Secretary of the Interior Michael H. Smith, Pima Agency, November 23, 1894, RG 48, M1070, roll 36.

11. Ibid. Nicklason, "Report for the Gila River Pima and Maricopa Tribes," 657–659. The volume of water in the Gila River was not measured until 1889–1890 and then again in 1895.

12. U.S. Bureau of Indian Affairs, *Annual Report of the Commissioner of Indian Affairs*, 1904, 17–18. Graves to Hitchcock, Pima Agency, Arizona, January 19, 1899, RG 48, M1070, roll 36, 5.

13. Graves to Hitchcock, Pima Agency, Arizona, January 19, 1899, RG 48, M1070, roll 36, 5. U.S. Bureau of Indian Affairs, *Annual Report of the Commissioner of Indian Affairs*, 1904, 7. "Gila River Priority Analysis, Water Distribution Chart #3," San Carlos Irrigation Project Archives.

14. Graves to Hitchcock, Pima Agency, Arizona, January 19, 1899, RG 48, M1070, roll 36, 5.

15. Smith, "The Campaign for Water in Central Arizona, 1890–1903," 130. Smith and Dudley, "The Marriage of Law and Public Policy in the Southwest."

16. U.S. Congress, House, *Report in the Matter of the Investigation of the Salt and Gila Rivers*, 5–7.

17. *An Act Making Appropriations for Sundry Civil Expenses of the Government for the Fiscal Year ending June 30, 1895, and for Other Purposes*, 28 Stat. 422.

18. Salt River Project, *Taming of the Salt*, 59.

19. Smith, "The Campaign for Water in Central Arizona," 132. Board of Indian Commissioners, *Annual Report of the Board of Indian Commissioners*, 1896, 118.

20. Davis, *Report on the Irrigation Investigation*, 3–4, 12, 54. Davis calculated one and a half acres per Indian, and with four thousand Indians, the total was six thousand acres of land. This was multiplied by one and a half acre-feet per acre to arrive at approximately ten thousand acre-feet of water. For future growth, Davis doubled the amount. Davis, *Irrigation Near Phoenix, Arizona*, 65–66.

21. The Land Act of March 3, 1891 (26 Stat. 1096–97, section 2) provided the company with the rights to the Box Canyon site at the confluence of the Salt River and Tonto Creek. Hudson proposed to build a dam capable of storing 757,000 acre-feet of water. Salt River Project, *Taming of the Salt*, 59.

22. *Act of February 15, 1897*. U.S. Congress, *Congressional Record*, Senate, June 6, 1896, vol. 28, 54th Cong., 1st sess., 6184. The House concurred in February of 1897 (ibid., vol. 29, 1630).

23. The dam site was sold and later became the site of Roosevelt Dam. This proposal is interesting as it indicates a congressional intent to deliver Salt River water to the reservation.

24. Davis, *Report on the Irrigation Investigation*, 24.

25. Arizona, Governor, *Annual Report of the Governor of Arizona to the Secretary of the Interior*, 1894, 19.

26. "Frank C. Armstrong, Special Agent, to The Secretary of the Interior, November 23, 1901," in U.S. Congress, House, *Conditions of Reservation Indians*, 56.

27. William Junkin, United States Indian Inspector, to John Noble, Secretary of the Interior, Pima Agency, September 30, 1890, RG 48, M1070, roll 36, 2–3. Indian Appropriation Act of 1 July 1898, 30 Stat. 571.

28. U.S. Bureau of Indian Affairs, *Annual Report of the Commissioner of Indian Affairs*, 1897, 115.

29. Ibid., 1904, 11.

30. Arizona, Governor, *Annual Report of the Governor of Arizona to the Secretary of the Interior*, 1902, 27. Gardner to Michael Smith, Secretary of the Interior, Pima Agency, June 5, 1891, RG 48, M1070, roll 36, 1. Dobyns, "Who Killed the Gila?"

31. Wilson, *Peoples of the Middle Gila*, 8–12.

32. Lee, *Underground Waters of Gila Valley, Arizona*. Statement of Ho-Ke Wilson in Southworth, "Statements by Pima Indians," 45, Arizona State Museum Archives.

33. U.S. Bureau of Indian Affairs, *Annual Report of the Commissioner of Indian Affairs*, 1890, 5. Arthur Tinker, United States Indian Inspector, to John Noble, Secretary of the Interior, Pima Agency, May 29, 1890, RG 48, M1070, roll 36, 1. Statement of William Wallace in Southworth, "Statements by Pima Indians," 6, Arizona State Museum Archives.

34. "Gila River Priority Analysis, Water Distribution Chart #3," San Carlos Irrigation Project Archives.

35. "Report of George J. Fanning, Agency Physician, to Elwood Hadley, United States Indian Agent," in U.S. Bureau of Indian Affairs, *Annual Report of the Commissioner of Indian Affairs*, 1900, 197.

36. Russell, *Pima Indians*, 64–66, notes that at least five persons died of starvation in 1898–1899 alone. Ravesloot, "The Anglo American Acculturation of the Gila River Pima, Arizona," 16.

37. U.S. Bureau of Indian Affairs, *Annual Report of the Commissioner of Indian Affairs*, 1890, 5. William Junkin, United States Indian Inspector, to John Noble, Secretary of the Interior, Pima Agency, September 30, 1890, RG 48, M1070, roll 36, 3.

38. Arizona, Governor, *Annual Report of the Governor of Arizona to the Secretary of the Interior*, 1896, 22.

39. "Report of Colin Cameron, Chairman of the Territorial Livestock Sanitary Commission," in Arizona, Governor, *Annual Report of the Governor of Arizona to the Secretary of the Interior*, 1892, 9.

40. Cornelius Crouse, U.S. Indian Agent, Sacaton, Arizona Territory, to Commissioner of Indian Affairs Daniel Browning, May 10, 1893, RG 75, M234. "Report of C. C. Duncan, United States Indian Inspector, to the Honorable Secretary of the Interior Michael H. Smith, Pima Agency, November 23, 1894," RG 48, M1070, roll 36, 1.

41. In Tucson, "rivers, reservoirs, and canals contain[ed] an abundance of water for irrigation, and the fields and ranges are well moistened." Arizona, Governor, *Annual Report of the Governor of Arizona to the Secretary of the Interior*, 1894, 23.

42. U.S. Bureau of Indian Affairs, *Annual Report of the Commissioner of Indian Affairs*,

1895, 121. J. R. Young to Secretary of the Interior Michael H. Smith, December 4, 1894, RG 75, M234.

43. This includes acreage filed upon. "Report of C. C. Duncan, United States Indian Inspector, to the Honorable Secretary of the Interior Michael H. Smith, Pima Agency, November 23, 1894," RG 48, M1070, roll 36.

44. "Gila River Priority of Irrigated Acres, Chart #2, United States Indian Service, Irrigation, January 20, 1926," San Carlos Irrigation Project Archives.

45. "Young to Browning, September 1, 1894, Pima Agency, Sacaton, Arizona," in U.S. Bureau of Indian Affairs, *Annual Report of the Commissioner of Indian Affairs*, 1894, 104.

46. Reported in Arizona, Governor, *Annual Report of the Governor of Arizona to the Secretary of the Interior*, 1895, 43.

47. U.S. Bureau of Indian Affairs, *Annual Report of the Commissioner of Indian Affairs*, 1896, 115. Ibid. 1900, 196.

48. Arizona, Governor, *Annual Report of the Governor of Arizona to the Secretary of the Interior*, 1896, 14–15.

49. Board of Indian Commissioners. *Annual Report of the Board of Indian Commissioners*, 1898, 24; and Arizona, Governor, *Annual Report of the Governor of Arizona to the Secretary of the Interior*, 1901, 217. Murphy especially called the attention of the secretary to "the great injury done to the Pimas by reason of the white man's preemption of all the water."

50. U.S. Bureau of Indian Affairs, *Annual Report of the Commissioner of Indian Affairs*, 1898, 126. Ibid., 1900, 196. "Frank C. Armstrong, Special Agent, to The Secretary of the Interior, November 23, 1901," in U.S. Congress, House, *Conditions of Reservation Indians*, 57.

51. U.S. Department of the Interior, *Annual Report of the Department of the Interior for 1899, Indian Affairs*, pt. I, 161–162.

52. Arizona territorial delegate John F. Wilson introduced a bill in Congress to authorize the San Carlos Project. The preamble stated the intent was to relieve the "dependent" Indians of their destitution. Hayden, *History of the Pima Indians and the San Carlos Irrigation Project*, 53.

53. Graves to Hitchcock, Pima Agency, Arizona, January 19, 1899, RG 48, M1070, roll 36, 2–4, 8.

54. "Pimas and Papagos," *Florence Tribune*, May 19, 1900, 2. "Distress among Indians," *Phoenix Republican*, June 29, 1900, 4.

55. "Indians Starving: Six Thousands Perishing on the Gila Reservation because of Lack of Water," *Chicago Tribune*, reprinted in the *Florence Tribune*, July 14, 1900, 1.

56. "The First Irrigators, Gross Injustice to the Friendly Pima Indians of Arizona," *New York Tribune*, reprinted in the *Florence Tribune*, March 17, 1900, and again on August 5, 1900.

57. "Indians Starving: Six Thousands Perishing on the Gila Reservation because of Lack of Water," *Chicago Tribune*, reprinted in the *Florence Tribune*, July 14, 1900, 1. U.S. Bureau of Indian Affairs, *Annual Report of the Commissioner of Indian Affairs*, 1905, 175.

58. Arizona, Governor, *Annual Report of the Governor of Arizona to the Secretary of the Interior*, 1900, 133. Ibid., 1904, 33.

59. Jackson and Spinning, *Our Red Reconcentrados*.

60. "The Indian Destitution," *Florence Tribune*, July 21, 1900, 5.

61. Elwood Hadley to Commissioner William A. Jones, July 21, 1900, 1, RG 75, Office of Indian Affairs, Indian School Service, Office of Superintendent. U.S. Congress, Senate, *Irrigation for the Pima Indians*, 7.

62. Elwood Hadley to Commissioner William A. Jones, July 21, 1900, RG 75, Office of Indian Affairs, Indian School Service, Office of Superintendent, 1. The cost of the wood was $30,000. U.S. Department of the Interior, *Annual Report of the Department of the Interior for 1900, Indian Affairs*, pt. I, 196. Arthur Tinker, Indian Inspector, to Commissioner of Indian Affairs William Jones, Pima Agency, May 29, 1900, 2, RG 75, M234.

63. Southworth, "A Pima Calendar Stick," 50. Hackenberg, "Pima and Papago Ecological Adaptations," 173.

64. *Arizona Gazette*, April 16, 1900. It took a man two to three days to cut and stack a load of mesquite, which he sold for about six dollars. Hoover, "The Indian Country of Southern Arizona."

65. Hadley to Jones, and Hadley to Jones, Pima Agency, August 17, 1900, RG 75, M234. The siding was originally called Sacaton Station, but eventually became known as Sacate.

66. Dobyns, *Creation and Expansion of the Gila River Indian Reservation*, 12–19.

67. Rea, *At the Desert's Green Edge*, 54–55.

68. Board of Indian Commissioners, *Annual Report of the Board of Indian Commissioners*, 1897, 11 and ibid., 1898, 17.

69. Ibid., 1901 and 1902, 15. Emphasis is in the original.

70. Ibid., 1904, 16.

71. U.S. Congress, Senate, *Irrigation for the Pima Indians*, 1, 3.

72. Hadley to Jones, July 26, 1901, RG 75, Office of Indian Affairs, Indian School Service, Office of Superintendent.

73. Hadley to Commissioner William Jones, Sacaton, Arizona, September 13, 1902, RG 75, M234.

74. U.S. Geological Survey, *Annual Report of the United States Geological Survey*, pt. 4: *Hydrology*, 357.

75. Antonio Azul and Subchiefs to Commissioner of Indian Affairs William Jones, Sacaton, Arizona, March 29, 1902, transmitted by Hadley to Jones, September 13, 1902, RG 75, 234.

76. Statement of Juan Jose in Southworth, "Statements by Pima Indians," 67–68, Arizona State Museum Archives.

77. U.S. Congress, Senate, *Hearings on HR 11353*, 6.

78. Antonio Azul and Twelve Subchiefs Petition to President Theodore Roosevelt, Pima Agency, February 28, 1903, RG 75, M234.

79. Quoted in Hackenberg, "Pima and Papago Ecological Adaptations," 173.

80. See Spinning and Jones, *Report of Findings*.

81. Handwritten report of C. H. Southworth on the San Carlos Water Supply, n.d., "Irrigation in the Florence District," file folder, Pinal County Historical Society, 3–4. Statement of Oliver Sanderson in Southworth, "Statements by Pima Indians," 85, Arizona State Museum Archives.

Chapter 7. Allotment of the Pima Reservation

This chapter was adapted from "A Scheme to Rob Them of Their Land: Water, Allotment and the Economic Integration of the Pima Reservation, 1902–1921," *Journal of Arizona History* 44, no. 2 (2003): 99–132.

1. U.S. Bureau of the Census, *Thirteenth Census of the United States Taken in the Year 1910*, vol. 6: *Agriculture*, 70–76.

2. Ibid., 79.

3. U.S. Congress, House, *Report in the Matter of the Investigation of the Salt and Gila Rivers*.

4. Lummis, "In the Lion's Den," 754–756.

5. Hoxie, *Final Promise*, 173.

6. "Memorial of the 19th Territorial Legislature sent to the United States Congress." Reprinted in the *Florence Tribune*, December 7, 1901.

7. U.S. Congress, Senate, *Irrigation for the Pima Indians*, 2, 4–5.

8. U.S. Department of the Interior, *Annual Report of the Secretary of the Interior*, 1905, 15. U.S. Reclamation Service, *Annual Report of the United States Reclamation Service*, 1905, 50–52.

9. U.S. Congress, House, Committee on Expenditures in the Interior Department, *Hearings before the Committee on Expenditures in the Interior Department*, pt. 16, 662.

10. Cook called the Salt River valley speculators "grafters, who I am afraid have the Salt River Water User's Association and Mr. W. H. Code to aid them." U.S. Congress, House, *Memorials in RE Investigations of Pima Indians, Arizona*, 4.

11. "An Irrigation Meeting," *The Arizona Republican*, July 15, 1902. U.S. Congress, House, *Report in the Matter of the Investigation of the Salt and Gila Rivers*, 312–314. Between thirty and forty prominent settlers and speculators in the Salt River valley joined forces to pressure federal officials to select the Roosevelt site. They included A. J. Chandler, W. M. Dobson, Benjamin Fowler, Dwight B. Heard, J. T. Priest, William Christy, J. C. Adams, Frank Grummell, B. A. Fickus, S. S. Greene, J. H. Wolfe, Joseph Stewart, Joseph Kibbey, and W. J. Murphy.

12. On March 23, 1903, a contract for the construction of five wells costing $5,000 was approved. U.S. Bureau of Indian Affairs, *Annual Report of the Commissioner of Indian Affairs*, 1904, 16. Arizona, Governor, *Annual Report of the Governor of Arizona to the Secretary of the Interior*, 1904, 34.

13. "Report of J. R. Meskimons to Commissioner of Indian Affairs," February 8, 1904, in U.S. Bureau of Indian Affairs, *Annual Report of the Commissioner of Indian Affairs*, 1904, 16.

14. "Letter of William Code, Irrigation Engineer, to Commissioner of Indian Affairs,

April 14, 1904," in U.S. Bureau of Indian Affairs, *Annual Report of the Commissioner of Indian Affairs*, 1904, 16.

15. Ibid., 18.

16. *United States v. N. W. Haggard*, No. 19 (D AZ, 3rd Judicial District, June 11, 1903).

17. U.S. Congress, House, Committee on Expenditures in the Interior Department, *Hearings before the Committee on Expenditures in the Interior Department*, pt. 5, 127.

18. Ibid.

19. The Winters decision applied to the Fort Belknap Reservation and was interpreted as applying to treaty reservations only. It would not be until 1963 in the *Arizona v. California* decision that the Winters Doctrine was recognized as applying to all reservations. *United States v. Wightman*, 230 *Federal Reporter* 277 (1916).

20. U.S. Congress, House, Committee on Expenditures in the Interior Department, *Hearings before the Committee on Expenditures in the Interior Department*, pt. 16, 654–656.

21. Book A, Dr. Cook's First Record Book, Cook Collection, Cook Theological School, 103.

22. Antonio Azul and Pima Headmen to Secretary Hitchcock and Commissioner of Indian Affairs Francis E. Leupp, March 1, 1906, in ibid., 79–80. "A Storage Reservoir," *The Arizona Republican*, July 15, 1902, and July 25, 1902. The *Republican* expressed its opinion that the Highland and Consolidated canals running south from the Salt River to the northern boundary of the reservation could be extended to convey Salt River project water for "at least 15,000 acres of land on the reservation."

23. U.S. Congress, House, *Report in the Matter of the Investigation of the Salt and Gila Rivers*, 358–360.

24. Contract between the Secretary and the SRVWUA, June 3, 1907, in U.S. Congress, House, *Report in the Matter of the Investigation of the Salt and Gila Rivers*, 162–164.

25. Ibid., 363.

26. U.S. Congress, Senate, Committee on Indian Affairs, *Indian Appropriation Bill, 1906*, 56–59.

27. U.S. Bureau of Indian Affairs, *Annual Report of the Commissioner of Indian Affairs*, 1904, 20.

28. U.S. Congress, Senate, Committee on Indian Affairs, *Indian Appropriation Bill, 1906*, 58.

29. U.S. Congress, House, *Report in the Matter of the Investigation of the Salt and Gila Rivers*, 363.

30. U.S. Congress, House, Committee on Expenditures in the Interior Department, *Hearings before the Committee on Expenditures in the Interior Department*, pt. 15, 630.

31. Lee, *Underground Waters of Gila Valley, Arizona*, 48. The low calculation was based on a pressure gradient of 10 feet per mile or 1,360 feet per year. If the movement were 10,560 feet per year, the maximum flow would have been 278,256 acre-feet.

32. Book A, Dr. Cook's First Record Book, Cook Collection, Cook Theological School, 102.

33. Indian Appropriation Act of 1906, 33 Stat. 1048. In 1906, Congress appropriated another $250,000. Indian Appropriation Act of 1907, 34 Stat. 325.

34. U.S. Reclamation Service, *Annual Report of the United States Reclamation Service*, 1907–1908, 52. See also 35 Stat. 70.

35. U.S. Reclamation Service, *Annual Report of the United States Reclamation Service*, 1911, 66. Ibid., 1912, 66–67 and ibid., 1913, 49.

36. U.S. Congress, House, *Report in the Matter of the Investigation of the Salt and Gila Rivers*, 8.

37. "Report of Samuel M. Brosius" in U.S. Congress, House, *Conserving the Rights of the Pima Indians*, 32.

38. "Letter to the Honorable F. E. Leupp, Commissioner of Indian Affairs, from C. H. Cook, Washington, D.C., July 30, 1906," in Book A, Dr. Cook's First Record Book, Cook Collection, Cook Theological School, 100–101.

39. Allison, *White Man's Friend*, 12.

40. U.S. Congress, House, Committee on Expenditures in the Interior Department, *Hearings before the Committee on Expenditures in the Interior Department*, pt. 17, 671.

41. F. E. Leupp, Commissioner of Indian Affairs, to Chief Antonio Azul, through the Pima School, March 27, 1906, in Book A, Dr. Cook's First Record Book, Cook Collection, Cook Theological School, 80–81.

42. Antonio Azul to the Honorable James R. Garfield, Secretary of the Interior, November 28, 1907, in U.S. Congress, House, *Report in the Matter of the Investigation of the Salt and Gila Rivers*, 153.

43. "Letter from Antonio Azul and all the Subchiefs, written by Hugh Patten, to the Hon. Commissioner of Indian Affairs F. E. Leupp, Sacaton, July 30, 1906," in Book A, Dr. Cook's First Record Book, Cook Collection, Cook Theological School, 108.

44. "Antonio Azul to the Honorable James R. Garfield, November 29, 1907," in ibid., 109.

45. "Letter from the Hon. James Garfield to Hugh Patten and Lewis Nelson, Delegates Representing the Pima Tribe of Indians, May 6, 1908," in Book A, Dr. Cook's First Record Book, Cook Collection, Cook Theological School, 111.

46. "A Petition Addressed to the Indian Rights Association by the Chiefs of the Pima Tribe of Indians, July 31, 1911," in U.S. Congress, House, *Conserving the Rights of the Pima Indians*, 10.

47. Ibid. The petition is signed by John Hays, chief of Sacaton Flats Reservation; Antonito Azul, head chief of the Pima Nation; Chief Henry Austin; Chief James Tompson; Chief Henry Adams; Chief James Hollen; Chief Thomas; Juan Jackson; and Haveline Enas.

48. Letter of Antonito Azul, Chief of the Pimas, December 16, 1911, ibid. 8–9.

49. Ibid., 4–8.

50. Ibid., 12.

51. Ibid., 15.

52. Code told the House of Representatives Committee on Indian Affairs that only "those that desired to move" would have to relocate. See U.S. Congress, House, Committee on Indian Affairs, *Hearings before the Committee on Indian Affairs*, 674.

53. See "Letter from Special Allotting Agent Charles E. Roblin to Herbert Marten, Pima Agency Financial Clerk, June 2, 1911," in ibid., 16. Ibid. no. 2, 53.

54. Head Chief Antonio Azul, Chief Juan Jackson, Chief Vanico and 38 others who represent more than 4,500 Pimas, including some Maricopas and Papagos, to Richard Ballinger, Secretary of the Interior,Sacaton, Arizona, July 1, 1909, in U.S. Congress, House, *Report in the Matter of the Investigation of the Salt and Gila Rivers*, 158.

55. "R. G. Valentine, Commissioner, to Charles E. Roblin, Special Allotting Agent, April 29, 1911," in U.S. Congress, House, *Conserving the Rights of the Pima Indians*, 20–21.

56. "Charles H. Cook, Quarterly Report to the Home Board, April 3, 1911," in Book A, Dr. Cook's First Record Book, Cook Collection, Cook Theological School, 123–124.

57. Board of Indian Commissioners, *Annual Report of the Board of Indian Commissioners*, 1911–1912, 11.

58. U.S. Congress, House, *Report in the Matter of the Investigation of the Salt and Gila Rivers*, 35. Indian Rights Association, *Annual Report of the Board of Directors of the Indian Rights Association*, 1913, 20.

59. "Hauke telegram to Indian School, Sacaton, Arizona, July 10, 1911," and "Hauke to Pima Agency," both reprinted in U.S. Congress, House, *Conserving the Rights of the Pima Indians*, 16.

60. U.S. Congress, House, Committee on Indian Affairs, *Hearings before the Committee on Indian Affairs*, 15.

61. Book A, Dr. Cook's First Record Book, Cook Collection, Cook Theological School, 105. Cook determined losses as follows: 180,000 acres of land @ $1,000,000; pumping plants @ $600,000; Reclamation Service work to date, $50,000; running the pumps for five years, $50,000; damage to the land from well water, $1,000,000; loss to the Indians from lack of water, $1,000,000; and feeding Indians unable to support themselves, $100,000. The total was $3,800,000 over ten years, or $380,000 per year.

62. U.S. Congress, House, Committee on Indian Affairs, *Hearings before the Committee on Indian Affairs*, 9.

63. "Letter of Lewis D. Nelson, Representing the Pima Tribe of Indians, Sacaton, Arizona, to the Honorable Jno. H. Stephens, Chairman, Committee on Indian Affairs, January 4, 1912," in U.S. Congress, House, Committee on Indian Affairs, *Hearings before the Committee on Indian Affairs*, 26–27. Board of Indian Commissioners, *Annual Report of the Board of Indian Commissioners*, 1909, 10. U.S. Congress, House, *Conserving the Rights of the Pima Indians*, 3, 32.

64. *Timely Hints to Farmers*.

65. U.S. Congress, House, Committee on Indian Affairs, *Hearings before the Committee on Indian Affairs*, 21–24.

66. Ibid., 6.

67. U.S. Congress, House, Committee on Expenditures in the Interior Department, *Hearings before the Committee on Expenditures in the Interior Department*, no. 5, pt. 5, 125 and pt. 15, 628–629. U.S. Bureau of Indian Affairs, *Annual Report of the Commissioner of Indian Affairs*, 1911, 17. U.S. Reclamation Service, *Reclamation Record*, 4:7, 137.

68. "Letter of Kisto Morago, Lewis D. Nelson, Harvey Cawker, and Jackson Thomas to the Members of the Committee on Indian Affairs of the Senate and House of Representatives, December 16, 1911," in U.S. Congress, Senate, Committee on Indian Affairs,

Pima Indian Reservation, 16–17. "Petition of the Indians of the Pima Tribe of the Gila River, November 21, 1911," in ibid., 15.

69. Abbott, *Briefs on Indian Irrigation*, 43. U.S. Indian Service, U.S. Indian Irrigation Service, *Annual Report of the Indian Irrigation Service*, 1913, 4, 16–19 and 44–47.

70. U.S. Congress, House, *Report in the Matter of the Investigation of the Salt and Gila Rivers*, 171 and 174. It was reported (hearsay) that Chandler wanted floodwater to mix with the groundwater he was pumping. Outside of the delivery area of the Salt River Project, Chandler had rights only to electrical power to pump groundwater. Floodwater would dilute the alkaline-rich groundwater.

71. "Report of M.O. Leighton, February 8, 1910," in U.S. Army, *San Carlos Irrigation Project, Arizona*, 16. Leighton's estimates for irrigation were between 32,200 and 43,000 acres. The former was based on 4.355 acre-feet of water per acre, while the latter was based on a 25 percent margin of non-productive land within the project (for roads, transmission lines, corners, poor lands, etc.).

72. "Report of F. E. Herrmann," in ibid., 16. Hermann assumed 4 acre-feet at the field and 7.5 acre-feet released from the dam, the difference being lost in transit.

73. "Report of J. D. Schuyler and H. Hawgood, September 27, 1910," in U.S. Army, *San Carlos Irrigation Project, Arizona*, 17.

74. "Report of J. H. Quinton, September 11, 1909," in U.S. Army, *San Carlos Irrigation Project, Arizona*. Quinton estimated 46,000 acres could receive 3 acre-feet of water per year and that an additional 50,000 acres might receive 1.5 acre-feet per year (enough for one crop). "Report of J. H. Quinton, September 3, 1912," in ibid., 17. "Reservoir Site at San Carlos: Report of William H. Rosecrans, 1912," in ibid., 18–19.

75. William H. Rosecrans, "Irrigation of the Pima Indian Reservation, Gila River Valley, Arizona, January 4, 1912," in U.S. Army, *San Carlos Irrigation Project, Arizona*, 19.

76. J. D. Schuyler, "Water Supply and Proposed Irrigation Works of the Pinal Mutual Irrigation Company of Florence, Arizona," December 5, 1911, in U.S. Army, *San Carlos Irrigation Project, Arizona*, 19–21.

77. U.S. Army, *San Carlos Irrigation Project, Arizona*, 24–26. Secretary of War Lindley S. Garrison appointed Lt. Col. William C. Langfitt, Lt. Col. Charles H. McKinstry, and Major Harry Burgess to conduct the study. The Board of Engineers convened in Phoenix on November 12, 1912, and spent the next week visiting the Pima Reservation, Florence, Upper Gila River valley towns, and the proposed dam site.

78. Ibid., 46.

79. Irrigation engineer Charles Real Olberg and Superintendent Frank Thackery requested water for fifty thousand acres based on the projected population of five thousand Pimas and Maricopas and an allotment of ten acres per person. The U.S. Army Corps of Engineers adopted the latest (1912) population count of 3,996 in coming up with 40,000 acres. U.S. Army, *San Carlos Irrigation Project, Arizona*, 47.

80. U.S. Congress, House, *Conserving the Rights of the Pima Indians*, 17. U.S. Congress, House, Committee on Expenditures in the Interior Department, *Hearings before the Committee on Expenditures in the Interior Department*, pt. 15, 671–674.

81. Indian Rights Association, *Annual Report of the Board of Directors of the Indian Rights Association*, 1910, 26.

82. "Letter from R. G. Valentine, Commissioner of Indian Affairs, to Mr. Charles E. Roblin, Special Allotting Agent, April 29, 1911," in Indian Rights Association, *Annual Report of the Board of Directors of the Indian Rights Association*, 1911, 19–21. H. C. Russell, "Annual Statistical Report, Narrative Section, Pima Agency, Sacaton, Arizona, November 7, 1910, 24," RG 75, M1011, roll 104–105.

83. U.S. Congress, House, *Survey and Allotment Work, for the Fiscal Year Ended June 30, 1914*, 63–3; Ibid., *Fiscal Year Ended June 30, 1915*, 64–1; and Ibid., *Fiscal Year Ended June 30, 1916*; 64–2. Ibid., *Fiscal Year Ended June 30, 1918*, 65–3.

84. Allison, *White Man's Friend*, 13–14. Allotments were made at the old Olberg Trading Post. Each day the Indians came to find out where their allotment would be, although four Pima men—Joseph Moffett, Joshua Russell, Hijorshmut, and Sampson—were leaders of a resistance movement opposed to allotment. To prevent them from disrupting the process, the allotting agent had the four arrested by a U.S. marshall, who incarcerated the men in a Phoenix jail.

85. Ibid., 14.

86. Ralph Ward, *Annual Statistical Report*, RG 75, M1011, roll 104–105, 9–10.

87. Clothier, *Farm Organization*, 9.

88. Darling, *S-cuk Kavick*.

89. *United States of America v. Henry A. Wattson and Carrell A. Spicer*, in the District Court of the United States in and for the District of Arizona, National Archives and Records Service, Pacific Region.

90. "Pima Original Allotments (1914–1921)," Arizona State Museum Archives.

91. *Annual Statistical Report*, 1922, Statistical Section, RG 75, M1011, 6–7. There were actually 5,176 Pima, Papago, and Maricopa who were allotted, 282 of whom did not receive a trust patent. There were an estimated 824 members (270 children and 554 adults) that had yet to be allotted in 1922. Some of these were removed from the allotment schedule due to dual enrollment, death, or other eligibility requirements. The 1921 *Annual Report of the Commissioner of Indian Affairs* (U.S. Bureau of Indian Affairs) erroneously lists 4,869 approved allotments.

92. *Annual Statistical Report*, 1922, 42, RG 75, M1011.

93. *Annual Statistical Report*, 1920, 26; 1921, 26; 1922, 26; and 1923, 26, RG 75, M1011.

94. Preston and Engle, "Irrigation on Indian Reservations," 2440 and 2464.

95. Kneale, *Indian Agent*, 396.

96. *Annual Statistical Report*, 1934, RG 75, M1011, 6. Kneale, *Indian Agent*, 397.

97. *Annual Statistical Report*, 1923, RG 75, M1011, 2, 26.

98. *History of the Indians and Irrigation on Indian Reservations*, 13.

99. *Annual Statistical Report*, 1923, Section IV, *Industries*, RG 75, M1011, 1.

100. *Annual Statistical Report*, 1925, RG 75, M1011, 13.

101. U.S. Army, *San Carlos Irrigation Project, Arizona*, 65.

102. Indian Rights Association, *Annual Report of the Board of Directors of the Indian Rights Association*, 1922, 26.

Chapter 8. The Pima Adjudication Survey

This chapter was adapted from "Abandoned Little by Little: The 1914 Pima Indian Adjudication Survey, Water Deprivation and Farming on the Pima Reservation," *Agricultural History* 81, no. 1 (2007): 36–69.

1. Meeks, "The Tohono O'odham, Wage Labor, and Resistant Adaptation," 468–489.

2. McCool, *Command of the Waters*.

3. August, "Carl Hayden's Indian Card."

4. C. H. Southworth, "The History of Irrigation along the Gila River," in "Report of the San Carlos Irrigation Project and History of Irrigation along the Gila River, Appendix A," in U.S. Congress, House, Committee on Indian Affairs, *Indians of the United States, Appendixes*.

5. E. B. Merritt, Assistant Commissioner of Indian Affairs, to the Honorable Charles Curtis, United States Senate, Washington, D.C., March 24, 1916, San Carlos Irrigation Project Archives.

6. U.S. Congress, House, Committee on Expenditures in the Interior Department, *Hearings before the Committee on Expenditures in the Interior Department*, 135, 193. U.S. Congress, House, *Conserving the Rights of the Pima Indians*, 11, 17.

7. U.S. Congress, House, Committee on Indian Affairs, *The Pima Indians and the San Carlos Irrigation Project*, 58–59.

8. Charles E. Ellis, Special Agent, to Robert G. Valentine, Commissioner of Indian Affairs, April 10, 1912, RG 75, Letters Received, Indian Division, Office of Indian Affairs. *Superintendents Annual Narrative and Statistical Reports*, 1907–1938, RG 75, M1011, roll 104–105, 1912, 2, 33.

9. "Olberg to Valentine" in U.S. Indian Service, U.S. Indian Irrigation Service, *Annual Report of the United States Indian Irrigation Service, District 4, fiscal year 1913*, 44, RG 75, Records of the United States Indian Irrigation Service, Annual District and Project Records, box 4.

10. Wendell Reed to Cato Sells, Washington, D.C., March 26, 1913, RG 75, Records of the Irrigation Division, General Correspondence, 1901–1931.

11. John F. Truesdell, Department of Justice, to C. R. Olberg, Superintendent of Irrigation, Los Angeles, Calif., Washington, DC, March 6, 1914, Olberg Letterbox, Historical Research, 1913–1914, San Carlos Irrigation Project Archives. F. M. Schanck, Superintendent of Irrigation, United States Indian Service, to C. R. Olberg, Superintendent of Irrigation, Sacaton, Ariz., Los Angeles, Calif., April 28, 1914, ibid.

12. Olberg to Sells, through Wendell Reed, Sacaton, Ariz., February 19, 1914; John S. Layne to C. R. Olberg, Solomonsville, Ariz., May 20, 1914; and Olberg to Reed, Sacaton, Ariz., February 20, 1914. All in Olberg Letterbox, From Central Office to Olberg, San Carlos Irrigation Project Archives. Charles H. Southworth to N. W. Irsfeld, June 22, 1915, Southworth Letterbox, Historical Correspondence, 1914–1916, San Carlos Irrigation Project Archives.

13. U.S. Congress, House, Committee on Indian Affairs, *Indians of the United States*, 1006. Olberg, *Report on Water Rights*, San Carlos Irrigation Project Archives.

14. U.S. Army, *San Carlos Irrigation Project, Arizona*, 54, 65.

15. "Diversion Dam Sure Says Ashurst," *Arizona Blade-Tribune*, May 8, 1915, 1.

16. U.S. Congress, *Diversion Dam on the Gila River*, 14–16.

17. August, "Carl Hayden's Indian Card," 402. Hayden faced opposition from Upper Gila valley water users (Safford, Duncan, and Virden valleys) who were fearful they would be "compelled to abandon their homes" to benefit the Florence–Casa Grande and reservation farmers. "Upper Gila Valley Alarmed over San Carlos Project," *Arizona Blade-Tribune*, April 4, 1914, 1.

18. "An Appeal of the Pimas," *The Casa Grande Bulletin Print*, n.d., Casa Grande, Arizona.

19. "Farmers and Indians Are Unit [*sic*] on San Carlos Matter," *Arizona Blade-Tribune*, March 28, 1914, 1.

20. N. W. Irsfeld to C. H. Southworth, Pima, Arizona, Sacaton, Ariz., February 11, 1915, Southworth Letterbox, Historical Correspondence 1914–1916, San Carlos Irrigation Project Archives.

21. U.S. Indian Service, U.S. Indian Irrigation Service, *Annual Report of the Indian Irrigation Service*, fiscal year 1915, 42, 45, and 46. "Letter of Franklin K. Lane, Secretary of the Interior, to the Honorable Senator Henry Ashurst, Department of the Interior, Washington, D.C., January 28, 1915," in U.S. Congress, *Diversion Dam on the Gila River*, 5. "Extracts from the Hearings before the Senate Committee on Indian Affairs, Thursday, January 28, 1915," ibid., 6, 8.

22. "Reed to Sells," in U.S. Indian Service, U.S. Indian Irrigation Service, *Annual Report of the Indian Irrigation Service*, fiscal year 1915.

23. Reed to Olberg, Washington, D.C., February 10, 1914, Olberg Letterbox, From Central Office to Olberg, San Carlos Irrigation Project Archives.

24. Olberg to Reed, Sacaton, Ariz., February 20, 1914, ibid.

25. August, "Carl Hayden's Indian Card," 402.

26. Off-reservation landowners were "reluctant to give accurate data" to the Indian Service, which was collecting the information. The *Arizona Blade-Tribune* urged readers to cooperate fully since the truth would eventually come out. "Water Rights Data Coming Slowly," *Arizona Blade-Tribune*, June 27, 1914, 1.

27. Schanck to Olberg, Los Angeles, California, April 28, 1914; Merritt to the Director of the Geological Survey, Washington, D.C., March 7, 1914; and Olberg to Reed, Sacaton, Arizona, February 9, 1914, all Olberg Letterbox, Historical Research, 1913–1914, San Carlos Irrigation Project Archives. The Justice Department, believing it was progressing in its protection of Pima water rights, did not intervene on behalf of the Pima. Attorney General James Clark McReynolds errantly believed the *Lobb v. Avenente* case would take into consideration Pima water rights. U.S. Department of Justice, Office of the Attorney General, *Annual Report of the Attorney General 1914*, 38–39. The *Arizona Blade-Tribune* stated on May 30, 1914, 1: "While it is known that the Indian Department has been looking into the matter of water rights in the valley on behalf of the Indians there is nothing to indicate the department will ask to have the case transferred to the federal court."

28. August, "Carl Hayden's Indian Card," 420, note 10. The complaint filed in the case of *Lobb v. Avenente* included more than 250 defendants. The court adjudicated water rights to 11,039 acres in the Florence–Casa Grande area with priority rights between 1868 and 1915.

29. GIS analysis shows 19,067.20 acres, although imperfect edges on the plain table maps precluded precise matching of some fields. The present analysis examines 3,178 fields and is not concerned with discrepancies or total cultivated acres, but rather the disparate proportion of crops (i.e., food and fiber) grown.

30. Charles Olberg, "Report on the San Carlos Irrigation Project and the History of Irrigation along the Gila River," in U.S. Congress, House, Committee on Indian Affairs, *Indians of the United States, Appendixes*, 9–10.

31. Statement of George Pablo, in Southworth, "Statements by Pima Indians," 29, Arizona State Museum Archives. Statement of James Hollen, ibid., 79.

32. Cooperative village was an anomaly, with 49 percent of its fields abandoned.

33. Statement of Juan Enas in Southworth, "Statements by Pima Indians," 14, Arizona State Museum Archives.

34. Southworth, "Statements by Pima Indians," 121, 155, Arizona State Museum Archives. Statement of Samuel Scoffer, ibid., 9. Statement of William Wallace, ibid., 5–6. Statement of Juan Thomas, ibid., 1. In 1926, the Indian Service, in "Gila River Priority Analysis, Water Distribution Chart #3," Florence, Ariz., January 20, 1916, in San Carlos Irrigation Project Archives gave a total of 2,010 acres as having rights to water in the Blackwater Area. Totals from Chart No. 3 will be listed in the notes for each village cluster for comparative purposes only. Each cluster total differs from the Southworth totals in that the 1926 analysis included land not identified by Southworth. GIS analysis for each cluster also differs in acreage. The Southworth numbers are provided for informative purposes only.

35. Statement of Antonito Azul in Southworth, "Statements by Pima Indians," 18, Arizona State Museum Archives.

36. Statement of George Pablo in ibid., 33.

37. Southworth, "Statements by Pima Indians," 122, 133, Arizona State Museum Archives. "Gila River Priority Analysis, Water Distribution Chart #3," San Carlos Irrigation Project Archives, provides a total of 5,215 acres with priority rights in 1914.

38. Statement of Juan Jose in Southworth, "Statements by Pima Indians," 67, Arizona State Museum Archives.

39. Southworth, "Statements by Pima Indians," 133, Arizona State Museum Archives. Statement of Cos-chin in ibid., 61. "Gila River Priority Analysis, Water Distribution Chart #3," San Carlos Irrigation Project Archives, lists 4,539 acres. Statement of Tor White in Southworth, "Statements by Pima Indians," 63. The Santan Indian Canal is often confused with the Santan Floodwater Canal, built between 1908 and 1913 by the U.S. Reclamation Service.

40. Southworth, "Statements by Pima Indians," 125, 127, 137–138, Arizona State Museum Archives. Statement of Joseph Head in ibid., 82.

41. Statement of George Pablo in ibid., 38.

42. Southworth, "Statements by Pima Indians," 126–129, Arizona State Museum Archives. Statement of Benjamin Thomas in ibid., 27. "Gila River Priority Analysis, Water

Distribution Chart #3," San Carlos Irrigation Project Archives, lists 12,527 acres with priority rights to water.

43. Statement of Juan Lagons in Southworth, "Statements by Pima Indians," 76–77, Arizona State Museum Archives. The Simon Webb ditch was also known as the Holden ditch.

44. Southworth, "Statements by Pima Indians," 140, Arizona State Museum Archives. "Gila River Priority Analysis, Water Distribution Chart #3," San Carlos Irrigation Project Archives, lists 993 acres with water rights in 1914.

45. Southworth, "Statements by Pima Indians," 141, Arizona State Museum Archives. Statement of Joseph Head, ibid., 80–81. "Gila River Priority Analysis, Water Distribution Chart #3," San Carlos Irrigation Project Archives, lists 2,102 acres with rights in 1914.

46. Statement of John Rhodes in Southworth, "Statements by Pima Indians," 84, Arizona State Museum Archives. "Gila River Priority Analysis, Water Distribution Chart #3," San Carlos Irrigation Project Archives, lists 2,276 acres.

47. I am indebted to Dr. Wendy Bigler of the Southern Illinois University at Carbondale Geography Department for the GIS data on the adjudication maps. Dr. Bigler and I spent several days in the summer of 2004 examining maps in the San Carlos Irrigation Project archives in Coolidge, Arizona, and preparing to digitize them. U.S. Bureau of the Census, *Sixteenth Census of the United States: Agriculture*, vol. 1: *First and Second Series State Reports*, pt. 6: *Statistics for Counties*, 384–394.

48. Statements of Juan Thomas, 1–2; Havelena, 3; and John Makil, 23, all in Southworth, "Statements by Pima Indians," Arizona State Museum Archives.

49. U.S. Bureau of the Census, *Thirteenth Census of the United States Taken in the Year 1910*, vol. 6: *Agriculture*, 70.

50. "Testimony of Wendell Reed," in *Conditions of Various Tribes, Hearings*, 55.

51. Statements of George Pablo, 31 and Ho-Ke Wilson, 5, in Southworth, "Statements by Pima Indians," Arizona State Museum Archives.

52. U.S. Congress, House, Committee on Indian Affairs, *Indians of the United States*, vol. 1, 1002.

53. U.S. Congress, House, Committee on Indian Affairs, *Indians of the United States*, vol. 2, 1014–15.

54. Statements of Havelena, 3; William Wallace, 6; Samuel Scoffer, 9; Henry Austin, 24; George Pablo, 29–31, 38; Slurn Vanico, 47; Meguel, 52; Harvier, 69; and Joseph Head, 82, all in Southworth, "Statements by Pima Indians, " Arizona State Museum Archives.

55. Lee, *Underground Waters of Gila Valley, Arizona*, 32.

Chapter 9. The Florence–Casa Grande Project

This chapter was adapted from "An Equal Chance? The Pima Indians and the Florence-Casa Grande Project, 1916-1924," *Journal of Arizona History* 45, no. 1 (2004): 63–102.

1. Letter of E. B. Merritt to the Honorable Charles Curtis, United States Senate, Washington, D.C., March 24, 1916, San Carlos Irrigation Project Archives.

2. McCool, *Command of the Waters*, 113.

3. U.S. Bureau of the Census, *Fourteenth Census of the United States Taken in the Year* 1920, vol. 7: *Irrigation and Drainage*, 110.

4. Ibid., 111–112.

5. Lewis Meriam, in *Problem of Indian Administration*, argued the federal government "assumed some magic in individual ownership of property would in itself prove an educational civilizing factor." The result, Meriam opined, tended to "pauperize" the Indians.

6. U.S. Congress, House, Committee on Indian Affairs, *Indians of the United States*, 1004.

7. Charles R. Olberg to Frank Thackery, Superintendent of the Gila River Indian Reservation, Sacaton, September 4, 1913, C. R. Olberg Letterbox, Historical Research, 1913–1914, San Carlos Irrigation Project Archives.

8. Florence landowners formed the new company with the intent of building an entirely new canal. The new diversion was planned 4,000 feet above the existing canal head and surveyed a grade of 2.64 feet per mile for 18.38 miles. J. D. Schuyler, "Water Supply and Proposed Irrigation Works of the Pinal Mutual Irrigation Company of Florence, Arizona, December 5, 1911," in U.S. Army, *San Carlos Irrigation Project, Arizona*, 19–21.

9. U.S. Reclamation Service, *Annual Report of the United States Reclamation Service*, 1902, 289.

10. McCool, *Command of the Waters*, 37.

11. U.S. Congress, *Congressional Record*, 63rd Cong., 2nd sess., vol. 51, June 20, 1914, 10770.

12. Ibid., 10771, 10787.

13. U.S. Bureau of Indian Affairs, *Annual Report of the Commissioner of Indian Affairs*, 1914, 39. Ibid., 1913, 17.

14. U.S. Congress, *Congressional Record*, 63rd Cong., 2nd sess., vol. 51, February 14, 1914, 3661.

15. "Extracts from the Hearings before the Senate Committee on Indian Affairs, Thursday, January 28, 1915," in ibid., 6, 8.

16. Charles Olberg, "Report on the San Carlos Irrigation Project and the History of Irrigation along the Gila River," in U.S. Congress, House, Committee on Indian Affairs, *Indians of the United States*, Appendix A, 87. U.S. Indian Service, U.S. Indian Irrigation Service, *Annual Report of the Indian Irrigation Service*, fiscal year 1915, 40.

17. Bender-Lamb, *Chandler, Arizona*, 80.

18. U.S. Congress, Senate, Committee on Indian Affairs, *Indian Appropriation Bill*, 506.

19. Olberg recommended fifty thousand acres based on the then-current population of the reservation. Ibid., 507.

20. U.S. Congress, Senate, Committee on Indian Affairs, *Indian Appropriation Bill*. The committee agreed and requested Merritt to return at a later date with "an amendment to the amendment" that clearly protected Pima rights to the water, but at the same time gave the secretary authority to make an agreement with non-Indian landowners for the acquisition of the Florence Canal.

21. Ibid., p. 503.

22. "Extracts from the Hearings before the Senate Committee on Indian Affairs, Thursday, January 28, 1915," in U.S. Congress, *Diversion Dam on the Gila River*, 9.

23. U.S. Congress, Senate, *Erosion and Overflow*, 8.

24. U.S. Bureau of Indian Affairs, *Annual Report of the Commissioner of Indian Affairs*, 1911, 17.

25. U.S. Congress, House, Committee on Expenditures in the Interior Department, *Hearings before the Committee on Expenditures in the Interior Department*, pt. 16, 654–656.

26. U.S. Indian Service, U.S. Indian Irrigation Service, *Annual Report of the Indian Irrigation Service*, fiscal year 1915. U.S. Indian Service, U.S. Indian Irrigation Service, *Annual Report: Southern California and Southern Arizona Reservations*, fiscal year 1915, 39–40. *History of the Indians and Irrigation on Indian Reservations*, 81. Olberg to Reed, Sacaton, Arizona, February 23, 1914, Olberg Letterbox, from Central Office to Olberg, 1913–1914, San Carlos Irrigation Project Archives. Of the 6,000 acres, 3,500 acres would be served with ground- and floodwater and 2,500 acres would receive groundwater alone.

27. U.S. Indian Service, U.S. Indian Irrigation Service, *Annual Report of the Indian Irrigation Service*, fiscal year 1914, 5. Allison, *White Man's Friend*, 14.

28. Olberg to Reed, Sacaton, Arizona, February 24, 1914, Olberg Letterbox, Historical Research, 1913–1914, San Carlos Irrigation Project Archives. U.S. Indian Service, U.S. Indian Irrigation Service, *Annual Report: Southern California and Southern Arizona Reservations*, fiscal year 1915, 40.

29. U.S. Indian Service, U.S. Indian Irrigation Service, *Annual Report of the Indian Irrigation Service*, fiscal year 1915. Assistant Engineer Nicholas W. Irsfeld reported that 3,480 acres were under ditch. The remainder of the "approximately 15,000 acres" in the Santan District was "brush land outside the reach of irrigation absent a means of diverting water into the floodwater canal." Work on the north bank was unpopular and resulted in difficulty getting Indian workers. This drove up the costs of the project. Olberg to Reed, Sacaton, Arizona, February 26, 1914, Olberg Letterbox, Historical Research, 1913–1914. The Sacaton Project cost $473,000 to construct. "Statement showing designation of funds and amounts therefrom," San Carlos Irrigation Project Archives.

30. U.S. Indian Service, U.S. Indian Irrigation Service, *Annual Report of the Indian Irrigation Service*, fiscal year 1913, 19. U.S. Congress, House, *Report in the Matter of the Investigation of the Salt and Gila Rivers*, 19.

31. U.S. Indian Service, U.S. Indian Irrigation Service, *Annual Report of the Indian Irrigation Service*, fiscal year 1913, 20.

32. C. H. Southworth, "The History of Irrigation along the Gila River," in U.S. Army, *San Carlos Irrigation Project, Arizona*, 130.

33. U.S. Indian Service, U.S. Indian Irrigation Service, *Annual Report of the Indian Irrigation Service*, fiscal year 1915, 46. "Statement showing designation of funds and amounts therefrom," San Carlos Irrigation Project Archives. It cost $790 to complete the repairs.

34. U.S. Indian Service, U.S. Indian Irrigation Service, *Annual Report of the Indian Irrigation Service*, fiscal year 1914, 8 and ibid 1915, 47.

35. *History of the Indians and Irrigation on Indian Reservations*, 83. The Little Gila Project cost $21,197. "Statement showing designation of funds and amounts therefrom," San Carlos Irrigation Project Archives.

36. U.S. Indian Service, U.S. Indian Irrigation Service, *Annual Report of the Indian Irrigation Service*, fiscal year 1914, 7. The project cost $43,000 to complete. Olberg to Reed, Sacaton, Arizona, February 26, 1914, Olberg Letterbox, Historical Research, 1913–1914, San Carlos Irrigation Project Archives.

37. U.S. Indian Service, U.S. Indian Irrigation Service, *Annual Report of the Indian Irrigation Service*, fiscal year 1914, 9.

38. U.S. Indian Service, U.S. Indian Irrigation Service, *Annual Report of the Indian Irrigation Service*, fiscal year 1914, 98.

39. Ibid., 1917, 64. Olberg to Reed, Sacaton, Arizona, March 6, 1914, Olberg Letterbox, From Central Office to Olberg, 1913–1914, San Carlos Irrigation Project Archives.

40. C. H. Southworth, "The History of Irrigation along the Gila River," in U.S. Army, *San Carlos Irrigation Project, Arizona*, 136–137. The project also included lands in the Old Maricopa, Ancient Sweetwater, Mount Top, and Sranuka districts. An additional 9,984 acres were ready to be allotted within the Casa Blanca Project. "Additional Unallotted Irrigable Lands Gila River Reservation Reserved for Future Allotments as Recommended in Letter of June 29, 1916," Southworth Letterbox, Historical Correspondence, 1914–1916. An additional 2,950 acres were set aside for allotment in the Sacaton Project. Of the 9,984 acres, more than three-fourths was withdrawn from allotment after passage of the Florence–Casa Grande Project bill, with 3,000 additional acres reserved within the Sacaton Project. U.S. Indian Service, U.S. Indian Irrigation Service, *Annual Report of the Indian Irrigation Service*, fiscal year 1916, 55–56.

41. W. A. Walker, Field Cost Accountant, to Commissioner of Indian Affairs C. J. Rhoads, August 8, 1930, Records of the Bureau of Indian Affairs, Irrigation 40378–30, San Carlos Irrigation Project Archives.

42. *Annual Statistical Report*, Pima Agency, Sacaton, Arizona, 1916, RG 75, M1011, 10.

43. U.S. Indian Service, U.S. Indian Irrigation Service, *Annual Report of the Indian Irrigation Service*, fiscal year 1916, 56.

44. "Thackery to Carl Hayden, Sacaton, Arizona, February 3, 1916"; E. W. Coker to Henry Ashurst, Florence, Arizona, February 3, 1916"; and "J. F. Brown to Henry Ashurst, Casa Grande, Arizona, February 3, 1916," all in U.S. Congress, *Diversion Dam on the Gila River*, 25–26. August, "Carl Hayden's Indian Card," 401.

45. "Merritt to Curtis," in U.S. Congress, House, *Hearings on the Indian Appropriation Bill, 1917*, 284.

46. Ibid.

47. U.S. Congress, House, *Hearings on the Indian Appropriation Bill*, 1917, 284.

48. *Indian Appropriation Act for the fiscal year ending June 30, 1917*, 39 Stat. 129.

49. Indian Rights Association, *Annual Report of the Indian Rights Association*, 1916, 42.

50. U.S. Congress, House, *Hearings on the Indian Appropriation Bill*, 1917, 179.

51. "An Agreement of the Landowners to Induce the Secretary of the Interior to Undertake the Florence–Casa Grande Irrigation Project," in U.S. Congress, House,

Committee on Indian Affairs, *Indians of the United States*, 1008–1013. *Indian Appropriation Act for the fiscal year ending June 30, 1917*, 39 Stat. 129.

52. There were 11,039 acres in the Florence area protected by the Lockwood Decree that were included in the project, along with 1,961 acres along McClellan Wash. Some 14,000 off-reservation acres were divided evenly above and below McClellan Wash (or between Florence and Casa Grande).

53. U.S. Indian Service, U.S. Indian Irrigation Service, *Annual Report of the Indian Irrigation Service*, fiscal year 1918, 9. U.S. Bureau of Indian Affairs, *Annual Report of the Commissioner of Indian Affairs*, 1919, 45.

54. U.S. Congress, Senate, Committee on Indian Affairs, *Indian Appropriation Bill*, 501.

55. *Determination and Declaration of Feasibility*, San Carlos Irrigation Project Archives. "Lands Designated under Florence–Casa Grande Project," *Casa Grande Valley Dispatch*, June 11, 1920, 2. The *Dispatch* noted 26,304.5 acres were brought under the project. U.S. Bureau of Indian Affairs, *Annual Report of the Commissioner of Indian Affairs, 1920*, 25. With the passage of the FCGP, the Indian Service surveyed the Florence Canal and purchased it for $50,000 from the Casa Grande Water Users Association on March 16, 1920 (as part of the landowners' agreement). Indian Service construction to extend the canal began in July 1923.

56. "An Agreement of the Landowners to Induce the Secretary of the Interior to Undertake the Florence–Casa Grande Irrigation Project," in U.S. Congress, House, Committee on Indian Affairs, *Indians of the United States*, 1012.

57. See Ibid., 1011.

58. Ibid. "Florence Diversion Dam Assured by Official Act of Secretary," *Casa Grande Valley Dispatch*, May 7, 1920.

59. C. R. Olberg, "Report on the San Carlos Irrigation Project and the History of Irrigation along the Gila River," in U.S. Army, *San Carlos Irrigation Project, Arizona*, 85.

60. "Good News for Land Owners," *The Bulletin*, Casa Grande, Arizona, December 18, 1920. "Florence Diversion Dam Assured by Official Act of Secretary," *Casa Grande Valley Dispatch*, May 7, 1920.

61. "Dedication Ceremony Ashurst-Hayden Dam," *Casa Grande Valley Dispatch*, May 12, 1922. Reed congratulated Olberg on the "completion of the dam [which] is a long step toward the valley's prosperity." Olberg, "History of the Construction of Ashurst-Hayden Dam," 57, San Carlos Irrigation Project Archives.

62. Indian Appropriation Act for the fiscal year ending June 30, 1917, 39 Stat. 129. Another $125,000 was authorized by the Indian Appropriation Act for the fiscal year ending June 30, 1918, 39 Stat. 969 and 974.

63. U.S. Congress, *Diversion Dam on the Gila River*, 13. C. R. Olberg, "Report on the San Carlos Irrigation Project and the History of Irrigation along the Gila River," in U.S. Army, *San Carlos Irrigation Project, Arizona*, 87.

64. U.S. Indian Service, U.S. Indian Irrigation Service, *Annual Report: Southern California and Southern Arizona Reservations*, fiscal year 1915, 43.

65. "C. H. Niemeyer, Clerk, Board of Pinal County Supervisors, to Honorable Carl Hayden, Florence, Arizona, April 16, 1924," in U.S. Congress, House, Committee on Indian Affairs, *Pima Indians and the San Carlos Irrigation Project*, 25–26.

66. It included a fifteen-foot-wide upstream apron, a six-foot-wide main section beneath the weir, and a fifty-two-foot downstream apron. A large expanse of talus protected the downstream side of the bridge from erosion. The concrete was 5' thick under the weir itself (where the water pressure was greatest) and 1.5' thick under the bridge piers.

67. U.S. Congress, House, Committee on Indian Affairs, *Pima Indians and the San Carlos Irrigation Project*, 13.

68. 43 Stat. 33. U.S. Indian Service, U.S. Indian Irrigation Service, *Annual Report: Southern California and Southern Arizona Reservations*, fiscal year 1925, 77.

69. U.S. Congress, House, Committee on Indian Affairs, *Indians of the United States*, 1003, 1006. The 1921 Indian Appropriation Act included an additional $225,000 for construction of the dam. 41. Stat. 408. Fisher, *Report on the San Carlos Project*, 254. Olberg, *Plans for Construction*, 22.

70. *Annual Statistical Report*, 1926, RG 75, M1011, 3. A plaque on the dam simply states the structure was built "with the efficient labor of the Pima and Papago Indians of Southern Arizona." U.S. Bureau of Indian Affairs, *Annual Report of the Commissioner of Indian Affairs*, 1925, 21.

71. U.S. Congress, Senate, *Survey of Conditions of the Indians in the United States*, pt. 6, 2466. The gates and hydraulic machinery to operate the dam were not installed until the winter of 1926, and the dam was not considered operational until that fall. The buildings to house the transformers needed to electrically operate the gates and light the bridge were completed in June 1927. U.S. Indian Service, U.S. Indian Irrigation Service, *Annual Report: Southern California and Southern Arizona Reservations*, fiscal year 1927, 93.

72. Irsfeld to Six, Florence, Arizona, October 9, 1926, San Carlos Irrigation Project Archives. *Annual Statistical Report*, 1925, RG 75, M1011, 16. Data collected from the annual reports of *Distribution of Waters of the Gila River, Gila Water Commissioner*, 1934–1955, San Carlos Irrigation Project Archives.

73. Kneale, *Indian Agent*, 398.

74. Historic American Engineering Record, *San Carlos Irrigation Project*, 134–135.

75. U.S. Indian Service, U.S. Indian Irrigation Service, *Annual Report of the Indian Irrigation Service*, fiscal year 1919, 34–36. This acreage did not include lands west of the Phoenix and Maricopa Railroad (Santa Cruz, Gila Crossing, and Maricopa Colony). *Annual Statistical Report*, 1920, RG 75, M1011, 18. Of this land, 2,500 acres were leased. Ibid., 1923, 25.

76. Indian Rights Association, *Annual Report of the Board of Directors of the Indian Rights Association*, 1922, 36.

77. William Alexander Brown, vice president of the IRA, lamented to H. M. Lord, director of the Bureau of the Budget, that the Pima were "now more helpless" than ever. Brown admonished Lord to consider a $500,000 appropriation to immediately begin building the necessary canals to deliver additional water to the reservation. Not less than

$250,000, Brown reasoned, should be immediately appropriated to begin the construction of a delivery system. Indian Rights Association, *Annual Report of the Board of Directors of the Indian Rights Association*, 1922, 25–26.

78. U.S. Congress, House, Committee on Indian Affairs, *Indians of the United States*, 1003.

79. B. Six, Superintendent of the Pima Reservation, to N. W. Irsfeld, Engineer, United States Indian Service, Pima Agency, Sacaton, Arizona, October 4, 1926, San Carlos Irrigation Project Archives.

80. See 39 Stat. 561, 974; 41 Stat. 3, 408, 552, 1225; 42 Stat. 33, 1141, 1174; 44 Stat. 453; and 45 Stat. 1562.

81. Indian Rights Association, *Annual Report of the Board of Directors of the Indian Rights Association*, 1917, 57. Kneale, *Indian Agent*, 396, 398.

82. U.S. Bureau of the Census, *Fifteenth Census of the United States: 1930, Agriculture*, vol. 2, pt. 3: *The Western States*, 344–345.

83. Preston and Engle, "Report of Advisors," 2465.

84. See Table 6, "Natural flow water diverted from Gila River"; Table 7, "Natural flow and stored water delivered to Indian Reservation and San Carlos Irrigation and Drainage District Canals"; Table 8, "Deliveries of pumped well water"; Table 9, "Deliveries of water to Indian Reservation and San Carlos Irrigation and Drainage District Canal"; and Table 10, "Deliveries of water to Indian and District farms"; all in *San Carlos Irrigation Project*, San Carlos Irrigation Project Archives.

Bibliography

Archives

ARIZONA HISTORICAL SOCIETY/TUCSON

Hayes, Benjamin. "Diary of Judge Benjamin Hayes' Journey Overland from Socorro to Warner's Ranch, from October 31, 1849, to January 14, 1850," MS 341.

ARIZONA STATE MUSEUM ARCHIVES, TUCSON

"Pima Original Allotments (1914–1921)," A–0349.

Southworth, Charles. "Statements by Pima Indians Regarding Irrigation on the Gila River Indian Reservation, June 1914," A–0690.

BRIGHAM YOUNG UNIVERSITY LIBRARY, L. TOM PERRY SPECIAL COLLECTIONS, PROVO, UTAH

Rogers, Samuel Hollister. "Journal of Samuel Hollister Rogers." Provo, Utah: Brigham Young University Library, 1954.

COOK THEOLOGICAL SCHOOL LIBRARY ARCHIVES, TEMPE, ARIZONA

Cook, Dr. Book A, Dr. Cook's First Record Book. Record Group 1, file 13.

NATIONAL ARCHIVES AND RECORDS ADMINISTRATION, WASHINGTON, D.C.

RG 48, M95 Letters Received Relating to the El Paso to Fort Yuma Wagon Road, 1857–1861.

RG 48, M576 Interior Department Appointment Papers, Arizona, 1857–1907.

RG 48, M825 Letters Received by the Indian Division of the Office of the Secretary of the Interior, 1849–1880.

RG 48, M1070 Reports of Inspection of the Field Jurisdictions of the Office of Indian Affairs, 1873–1900.

RG 75, M234 Letters Received by the Office of Indian Affairs, 1824–1881, New Mexico Superintendency, 1858–1859.

RG 75, M234 Letters Received by the Office of Indian Affairs, 1824–1881, Pima Agency 1859–1861.

RG 75, M348 Record Books of the Office of Indian Affairs.

RG 75, M734 Records of the Arizona Superintendency of Indian Affairs, 1863–1873.

RG 75, T21 Records of the New Mexico Superintendency, 1849–1880, Letters Received from the Agencies.

RG 75, T21 Records of the New Mexico Superintendency, 1849–1880, Letters Sent.

RG 75, M1011 Superintendents' Annual Narrative and Statistical Reports from Field Jurisdictions of the Bureau of Indian Affairs, 1907–1938.

RG 75 Office of Indian Affairs, Indian School Service, Office of the Superintendent.

RG 75 Records of the Bureau of Indian Affairs, Central Classified Files, 1907–1939.

RG 75 Records of the Irrigation Division, General Correspondence, 1901–1931.

RG 75 Records of the United States Indian Irrigation Service, Annual District and Project Reports, box 4.

RG 94, M666 Letters Received by the Office of the Adjutant General, 1871–1880.

RG 109, M323 Compiled Service Records of Confederate Soldiers Who Served in Organizations from the State of Texas.

RG 393, M1120 Miscellaneous Records of the Column from California, 1862.

RG 393, M1120 Records of the U.S. Army Continental Commands, Fort Mohave, 1821–1920.

NATIONAL ARCHIVES AND RECORDS ADMINISTRATION, PACIFIC REGION, LAGUNA NIGUEL, CALIFORNIA

United States of America v. Henry A. Wattson and Carrell A. Spicer, in the District Court of the United States in and for the District of Arizona, equity case files, folder E-31, box 3.

PINAL COUNTY HISTORICAL SOCIETY, FLORENCE, ARIZONA

"Irrigation in the Florence District" file folder.

SAN CARLOS IRRIGATION PROJECT ARCHIVES, COOLIDGE, ARIZONA

Determination and Declaration of Feasibility of the Florence–Casa Grande Project, approved by Secretary of the Interior John Barton Payne, April 22, 1920.

"Gila River Priority Analysis, Water Distribution Charts #1, #2, #3," United States Indian Service, Irrigation, January 20, 1926.

"Gila River Priority of Irrigated Acres, Chart #2, United States Indian Service, Irrigation, January 20, 1926."

Olberg, C. R. Letterbox, From Central Office to Olberg.

Olberg, C. R. Letterbox, Historical Research, 1913–1914.

Olberg, Charles R. *Report on Water Rights of Gila River and Feasibility of San Carlos Project*. (Washington, D.C.: U.S. Indian Irrigation Service, 1915).

Olberg, Charles Real. "History of the Construction of Ashurst-Hayden Dam," March 1, 1922, Mimeograph.

San Carlos Irrigation Project: Engineering Studies of Land and Water Resources. [n.p.]: San Carlos Irrigation Project, Bureau of Indian Affairs, 1956.

Southworth, Charles. Letterbox, Historical Correspondence, 1914–1916.

Southworth, C. H. Maps.

"Statement showing designation of funds and amounts therefrom, by years, on the various units comprising the San Carlos Irrigation Project to June 30, 1929."

UNIVERSITY OF ARIZONA LIBRARY, SPECIAL COLLECTIONS, TUCSON

Ezell, Paul Howard. Papers of Paul Howard Ezell, 1939–1987, MS 282, box 15, file 3.

Silas St. John, Pimo Villages, New Mexico, to Sylvester Mowry, November 9, 1859, MS 282, box 15, file 3.

Silas St. John to Sylvester Mowry, October 6, 1859, MS 282, box 15, file 3.

Stout, John H. Letterbook, AZ 119.

UNIVERSITY OF NEW MEXICO CENTER FOR SOUTHWEST RESEARCH, ALBUQUERQUE

Underhill, Ruth. "Pima Government." U.S. Indian Service, 1936. MSS 289 BC, box 18, folder 13.

Government Publications

Abbott, Frederick H. *Briefs on Indian Irrigation and Indian Forests, Letter from Frederick H. Abbott to the Chairman of the Senate Committee on Indian Affairs*. Washington, D.C.: GPO, 1914.

Act of February 15, 1897, 29 Stat. 527.

An Act to Provide for the Sale of Desert Lands in Certain Territories, March 3, 1877. 19 U.S. Stat. 377.

Acts, Resolutions and Memorials of the Ninth Legislative Assembly of the Territory of Arizona. Tucson: Office of the Arizona Citizen, 1877.

Andrews, George W. *Survey of Pima and Maricopa Reservation, George W. Andrews to Ely Parker, August 18, 1870*. 41st Cong., 3rd sess., House Executive Document 139. Washington, D.C.: GPO, 1871.

Arizona. Governor. *Annual Report of the Governor of Arizona to the Secretary of the Interior*. 1893–1896, 1900–1902, 1904. Washington D.C.: GPO, 1893–1896, 1900–1902, 1904.

Board of Indian Commissioners. *Annual Report of the Board of Indian Commissioners*. 1870, 1873, 1879, 1896–1898, 1901, 1902, 1904, 1909, 1911–1912. Washington, D.C.: GPO, 1870, 1873, 1879, 1896–1898, 1901, 1902, 1904, 1909, 1911–1912.

Clothier, Robert W. *Farm Organization in the Irrigated Valleys of Southern Arizona*. Bulletin No. 654. Washington, D.C.: U.S. Department of Agriculture, 1918.

Davis, Arthur P. *Irrigation near Phoenix, Arizona*. United States Geological Survey, Water Supply and Irrigation Papers. Washington, D.C.: GPO, 1897.

———. *Report on the Irrigation Investigation for the Benefit of the Pima and Other Indians on the Gila River Indian Reservation, Arizona*. Washington, D.C.: GPO, 1897.

Emory, William H. *Notes of a Military Reconnaissance from Fort Leavenworth, in Missouri, to San Diego, in California, Including Parts of the Arkansas, del Norte, and Gila Rivers made in 1846–1847*. 30th Cong., 1st sess., House Executive Document 41. Washington, D.C.: Wendell and Van Benthuysen, 1848.

———. *Report on the United States and Mexican Boundary Survey, Made under the Direction of the Secretary of the Interior by William H. Emory*. 2 vols. 34th Cong., 1st sess., House Executive Document 135. Washington, D.C.: A.O.P. Nicholson, printer, 1857.

Fisher, C. C. *Report on the San Carlos Project*. Washington, D.C.: Department of the Interior, United States Reclamation Service, 1920.

Hayden, Carl. *A History of the Pima Indians and the San Carlos Irrigation Project*. 89th Cong., 1st sess., Senate Document 11. Washington, D.C.: GPO, 1965.

Historic American Engineering Record. *San Carlos Irrigation Project*. San Francisco, California: National Park Service, Western Region, Department of the Interior, 1996.

History of the Indians and Irrigation on Indian Reservations. Prepared under the direction of W. M. Reed, Chief Engineer, District No. 4, C.R. Olberg, Superintendent of Irrigation, H. V. Clotts, Acting Superintendent. Washington, D.C.: U.S. Department of the Interior, 1916.

Indian Rights Association. *Annual Report of the Board of Directors of the Indian Rights Association*. 1908, 1910–1913, 1916–1918, 1922. Philadelphia: Office of the Indian Rights Association, 1908, 1910–1913, 1916–1918, 1922.

Jackson, Reverend Sheldon, and Reverend George L. Spinning. *Our Red Reconcentrados—Some Facts Concerning the Pima and Papago Indians of Arizona*. 56th Cong., 2nd sess. *Congressional Record* (January 26, 1901), pt. 2, 1515.

Lee, Willis T. *The Underground Waters of Gila Valley, Arizona*. Water Supply and Irrigation Paper No. 104. 58th Cong., 2nd sess., House Document 742. Washington, D.C.: GPO, 1904.

Nicklason, Fred. "Report for the Gila River Pima and Maricopa Tribes," in *Indian Water Rights of the Five Central Arizona Tribes of Arizona, Hearings Before the Committee on Interior and Insular Affairs, United States Senate*. 94th Cong., 1st sess. Washington, D.C.: GPO, 1975.

Olberg, Charles Real. *Plans for Construction, Sacaton Dam and Bridge*. [n.p.]: U.S. Department of the Interior, Indian Irrigation Service, 1922.

Powell, John Wesley. *Report on the Lands of the Arid West, with a More Detailed Account of the Lands of Utah*. Washington, D.C.: GPO, 1879.

Preston, Porter J., and Charles A. Engle, "Report of Advisors on Irrigation on Indian Reservations," June 28, 1928. Reprinted in U.S. Congress. Senate. Committee on Indian Affairs. Subcommittee on SR 79. *Hearings, Survey of Conditions of Indians in the United States*. 71st Cong., 2nd sess., part 6. Washington, D.C.: GPO, January 21, 1930.

Southworth, C. H. "History of Gila River Reservation." In *History of the Indians and Irrigation on Indian Reservations*. Prepared under the direction of W. M. Reed, Chief Engineer, District No. 4, C.R. Olberg, Superintendent of Irrigation, H. V. Clotts, Acting Superintendent, Washington, D.C.: U.S. Department of the Interior, 1916.

Spinning, George L., and W. A. Jones. *Report of Findings and Recommendations of Committee on Investigation of Conditions and Needs of Pima Indians on Gila River Reservation, Arizona*. Washington, D.C.: GPO, 1904.

University of Arizona Agricultural Experiment Station. *Timely Hints to Farmers*. Pamphlet No. 30. Tucson: University of Arizona Agricultural Experiment Station, 1910.

U.S. Army. *San Carlos Irrigation Project, Arizona: Report to the Secretary of War of a Board of Engineer Officers, United States Army, under Indian Appropriation Act of August 24, 1912, on San Carlos Irrigation Project, Arizona.* 63rd Cong., 2nd sess., House Document 791. Washington, D.C.: GPO, 1914.

U.S. Bureau of Indian Affairs. *Annual Report of the Commissioner of Indian Affairs.* 1857–1859, 1864, 1866–1867, 1869–1878, 1880, 1883, 1887–1889, 1890, 1894–1900, 1904–1905, 1911, 1913–1914, 1919–1921, 1925. Washington, D.C.: William A. Harris, 1857–1859; Washington, D.C.: GPO, 1864, 1866–1867, 1869–1878, 1880, 1883, 1887–1889, 1890, 1894–1900, 1904–1905, 1911, 1913–1914, 1919–1921, 1925.

U.S. Bureau of the Census. *Census of the United States, 1870, 1910, 1920, 1930.* Washington, D.C.: GPO, 1872, 1912, 1922, 1932.

U.S. Bureau of the Census. *Sixteenth Census of the United States: Agriculture*, vol. 1: *First and Second Series State Reports*, pt. 6: *Statistics for Counties.* Washington, D.C.: GPO, 1942.

U.S. Congress. *Congressional Globe.* Washington, D.C.: John C. Rives, 1856, 1859.

U.S. Congress. *Congressional Record.* 1878, 1896, 1901, 1914. Washington, D.C.: GPO, 1878, 1896, 1901, 1914.

U.S. Congress. *Diversion Dam on the Gila River at a Site above Florence, Arizona, Excerpts to Be Used by the Committee on Indian Affairs.* 64th Cong., 2nd sess. Washington, D.C.: GPO, 1917.

U.S. Congress. House. Committee on Expenditures in the Interior Department. *Hearings before the Committee on Expenditures in the Interior Department of the House of Representatives on House Resolution No. 103 to Investigate the Expenditures in the Interior Department*, pts. 4, 5, 15, 16, and 17. Washington, D.C.: GPO, 1911.

U.S. Congress. House. Committee on Indian Affairs. *Hearings before the Committee on Indian Affairs, House of Representatives on H. Res. 330. Authorizing Suspension of Work in Construction of the Irrigation System, Pima Indian Reservation, Arizona*, no. 1. Washington, D.C.: GPO, 1911.

U.S. Congress. House. Committee on Indian Affairs. *Indians of the United States, Hearings before the Committee on Indian Affairs, House of Representatives, on the Conditions of Various Tribes of Indians.* 66th Cong., 1st sess. Washington, D.C.: GPO, 1919.

U.S. Congress. House. Committee on Indian Affairs. *Memorials in RE Investigations of Pima Indians, Arizona.* 62–1–11 H38. Committee Print, 41.

U.S. Congress. House. Committee on Indian Affairs. *The Pima Indians and the San Carlos Irrigation Project: Information Presented to the Committee on Indian Affairs, House of Representatives in Connection with S. 966 An Act for the Continuance of Construction Work on the San Carlos Federal Irrigation Project in Arizona and for other Purposes.* Washington, D.C.: GPO, 1924.

U.S. Congress. House. *Conditions of Reservation Indians, Letter from the Secretary of the Interior, February 21, 1902.* 57th Cong., 1st sess., House Document 406. Washington, D.C.: GPO, 1902.

U.S. Congress. House. *Conserving the Rights of the Pima Indians, Arizona, Letters and Petitions with Reference to Conserving the Rights of the Pima Indians of Arizona to the*

Lands of their Reservation and the Necessary Water Supply for Irrigation. 62nd Cong., 2nd sess., House Document 521. Washington, D.C.: GPO, 1912.

U.S. Congress. House. *Hearings on the Indian Appropriation Bill, 1917*. 64th Cong., 1st sess. Washington, D.C.: GPO, 1916.

U.S. Congress. House. *House Debate on Removal of Southwest Indians*. 45th Cong., 3rd sess. *Congressional Record*, December 19, 1878.

U.S. Congress. House. *Hudson Reservoir and Canal Company*. 54th Cong., 1st sess., May 28, 1896, House Report 2049. Washington, D.C.: GPO, 1896.

U.S. Congress. House. *Report in the Matter of the Investigation of the Salt and Gila Rivers–Reservations and Reclamation Service*. 62nd Cong., 3d sess., House Report 1506. Washington, D.C.: GPO, 1913.

U.S. Congress. House. *Survey and Allotment Work, Letter from The Secretary of the Interior Transmitting Statement of Cost of Survey and Allotment Work, Indian Service, for the Fiscal Year Ended June 30, 1914*. House Document 1287, 63–3. Washington, D.C.: GPO, 1914.

U.S. Congress. House. *Survey and Allotment Work, Letter from The Secretary of the Interior Transmitting Statement of Cost of Survey and Allotment Work, Indian Service, for the Fiscal Year Ended June 30, 1915*. House Document 143, 64–1. Washington, D.C.: GPO, 1915.

U.S. Congress. House. *Survey and Allotment Work, Letter from The Secretary of the Interior Transmitting Statement of Cost of Survey and Allotment Work, Indian Service, for the Fiscal Year Ended June 30, 1916*. House Document 1455, 64–2. Washington, D.C.: GPO, 1916.

U.S. Congress. House. *Survey and Allotment Work, Letter from The Secretary of the Interior Transmitting Statement of Cost of Survey and Allotment Work, Indian Service, for the Fiscal Year Ended June 30, 1918*. House Document 1508, 65–3. Washington, D.C.: GPO, 1917.

U.S. Congress. Senate. [Senate Miscellaneous Document 32.] 49th Cong., 1st sess. Washington, D.C.: GPO, 1886.

U.S. Congress. Senate. *Erosion and Overflow, Gila River, Arizona*. 64th Cong., 1st sess., Senate Report 262. Washington, DC: GPO, 1916.

U.S. Congress. Senate. *Hearings on HR 11353, A Bill Making Appropriations for the Department of the Interior for the Fiscal Year ending June 30, 1903*. 57th Congress, 1st sess., Senate Report 951, 1 April 1902. Washington, D.C.: GPO, 1902.

U.S. Congress. Senate. *Irrigation for the Pima Indians: Letter from the Secretary of the Interior Transmitting Copy of that Part of the Report of Indian Inspector Walter H. Graves Relating to Irrigation for the Pima Indians*. 56th Cong., 2nd sess., Senate Document 88. Washington D.C.: GPO, 1901.

U.S. Congress. Senate. *Report of Explorations and Surveys, to Ascertain the Most Practicable and Economical Route for a Railroad from the Mississippi River to the Pacific Ocean*, vol. VII. 33rd Cong., 2nd sess. Senate Executive Document 78. Washington, D.C.: Beverly Tucker, printer, 1855.

U.S. Congress. Senate. *Survey of Conditions of the Indians in the United States*, pts. 6, 17, Washington, D.C.: GPO, 1930, 1931.

U.S. Congress. Senate. Committee on Indian Affairs. *Indian Appropriation Bill: Hearings before the Committee on Indian Affairs, United States Senate on H.R. 20150*. 63rd Cong., 3rd sess. Washington, D.C.: GPO, 1915.

U.S. Congress. Senate. Committee on Indian Affairs. *Indian Appropriation Bill, 1906, Hearings before the Subcommittee of the Committee on Indian Affairs*. 58th Cong., 3rd sess., January 20, 1905, Senate Report 4240. Washington, D.C.: GPO, 1905.

U.S. Congress. Senate. Committee on Indian Affairs. "Petition of the Indians of the Pima Tribe of the Gila River, November 21, 1911," in *Pima Indian Reservation: Hearing before the Committee on Indian Affairs United States Senate on H.R. 18244*. Washington, D.C.: GPO, 1912.

U.S. Department of Justice. Office of the Attorney General. *Annual Report of the Attorney General 1914*. Washington, D.C.: GPO, 1915.

U.S. Department of the Interior. *Annual Report of the Secretary of the Interior*. 1863, 1869–1871, 1880, 1905. Washington, D.C.: GPO, 1863, 1869–1871, 1880, 1905.

U.S. Department of the Interior. Indian Affairs. *Annual Report of the Department of the Interior, Indian Affairs*, pt. I. 1899, 1900. Washington, D.C.: GPO, 1899, 1900.

U.S. Department of the Interior. Inspector General. *Records of the Inspector General*. Washington, D.C.: GPO, 1870.

U.S. Department of War. *Report from the Secretary of War, Communicating a Copy of the Official Journal of Lieutenant Colonel Philip St. George Cooke, from Santa Fe to San Diego, etc.* 30th Cong., 1st sess., Senate Report 2. Washington, D.C.: Wendell and Van Benthuysen, 1849.

U.S. Geological Survey. *Annual Report of the United States Geological Survey*, Part 4: Hydrology. 1901. Washington, D.C.: GPO, 1901.

U.S. Geological Survey. *Storage of Water on Gila River, Arizona*. Water Supply and Irrigation Papers of the US Geologic Survey. Washington, D.C.: GPO, 1900.

U.S. Indian Service. U.S. Indian Irrigation Service. *Annual Report of the Irrigation Service*, fiscal years 1913–1919. Washington, D.C.: U.S. Indian Irrigation Service, 1913–1919.

U.S. Indian Service. U.S. Indian Irrigation Service. *Annual Report: Southern California and Southern Arizona Reservations*, fiscal years 1915, 1925, 1927. Washington, D.C.: United States Indian Irrigation Service, U.S. Indian Service, 1915, 1925, 1927.

U.S. Indian Service. U.S. Indian Irrigation Service. District 4. *Annual Report of the United States Indian Irrigation Service, District 4*, fiscal year 1913. Washington, D.C.: United States Indian Irrigation Service, U.S. Indian Service, 1913.

U.S. Reclamation Service. *Annual Report of the United States Reclamation Service*. 1902, 1905, 1907–1908, 1911. Washington, D.C.: GPO, 1902, 1905, 1907–1908, 1911.

U.S. Reclamation Service. *Reclamation Record*. Washington, D.C.: Secretary of the Interior, United States Reclamation Service (4:7), July 1913.

United States Statutes at Large, volumes 19, 35, 39, 41, 42, 44, 45. Washington, D.C.: GPO.

Legal Cases

Arizona v. California 373 *U.S. Reporter* 546 (1963).

Kelsey v. McAteer. Third Judicial District Court, Prescott, Arizona (1883).

Lobb v. Avenente (No. 2329) April 6, 1916 (supplemental decree of October 23, 1917), Pinal County Courthouse, Florence, Arizona.

Lone Wolf v. Hitchcock 187 *U.S. Reporter* 553 (1903).

United States v. N. W. *Haggard*, No. 19. District of Arizona, 3rd Judicial District (1903).

United States v. Rio Grande Dam and Irrigation Company, 174 *U.S. Reporter*, 690 (1899)

United States v. Wightman, 230 *Federal Reporter* 277 (1916).

United States v. Winans 198 *U.S. Reporter* 371 (1905).

Winters v. United States 207 *U.S. Reporter* 564 (1908).

Secondary Sources

Aldrich, Lorenzo D. A *Journal of the Overland Route to California and the Gold Mines*. Los Angeles, California: Dawson's Book Shop, 1950.

Alexander, Evaline Martin. *Ladies Union Mission School Association, among the Pimas, or the Mission to the Pima and Maricopa Indians*. Albany, New York: Ladies Union Mission School Association, 1893.

Allison, Lloyd. *The White Man's Friend*. Arizona: [s.n.], 1974?.

Allyn, Joseph Pratt. *The Arizona of Joseph Pratt Allyn*. Edited by John Nicholson. Tucson: University of Arizona Press, 1974.

Altshuler, Constance Wynn. "Military Administration in Arizona, 1854–1865." *Journal of Arizona History* 10, no. 4 (1969): 215–238.

——. "Poston and the Pimas: The 'Father of Arizona' as Indian Superintendent." *Journal of Arizona History* 18, no. 1 (1977): 23–42.

——. "Men and Brothers." *Journal of Arizona History* 19, no. 3 (1978): 315–322.

——. *Cavalry Yellow and Infantry Blue: Army Officers in Arizona between 1851–1886*. Tucson: Arizona Historical Society, 1991.

Ames, George Walcott, Jr. "A Doctor Comes to California: The Diary of John S. Griffin, Assistant Surgeon with Kearny's Dragoons, 1846–47." *California Historical Society Quarterly* 21, no. 3 (1942): 193–224.

Audubon, Maria R. *Audubon's Western Journal 1849–1850, Being the Manuscript Record of a Trip from New York to Texas, and an Overland Journey through New Mexico and Arizona to the Gold-Fields of California*. Tucson: University of Arizona Press, 1984.

August, Jack L., Jr. "Carl Hayden's Indian Card: Environmental Politics and the San Carlos Reclamation Project." *Journal of Arizona History* 33, no. 4 (1992): 397–422.

——. *Desert Bloom or Doom? Carl Hayden and the Origin of the Central Arizona Project, 1922–1964*. Prescott: Sharlott Hall Museum, 1996.

Bahr, Donald M. "Pima-Papago Social Organization." In *Handbook of North American Indians*, edited by Alfonso Ortiz, vol. 10, 178–192. Washington, D.C.: Smithsonian Institute, 1983.

Bahr, Donald M., Juan Gregorio, David I. Lopez, and Albert Alvarez. *Piman Shamanism and Staying Sickness*. Tucson: University of Arizona Press, 1974.

Barnes, Will C. *Arizona Place Names*. Tucson: University of Arizona Press, 1988.

Bartlett, John Russell. *Personal Narrative of Explorations and Incidents in Texas, New Mexico, California, Sonora, and Chihuahua, Connected with the United States and Mexican Boundary Survey*. Vol. 2. New York: D. Appleton, 1854.

Beadle, J. H. *The Undeveloped West: Or Five Years in the Territories*. Philadelphia: National Publishing Co., 1873.

Bell, William A. *New Tracks in North America*. New York: Scribner, Welford & Co., 1870. Reprint, Albuquerque, New Mexico: Horn and Wallace, 1965.

Bender-Lamb, Sylvia Lee. "Chandler, Arizona: Landscape as a Product of Land Speculation." Master's thesis, Arizona State University, 1983.

Berkhofer, Robert F. *The White Man's Indian: Images of the American Indians from Columbus to the Present*. New York: Knopf, 1978.

Bigler, Henry William. *Bigler's Chronicle of the West: The Conquest of California, Discovery of Gold, and Mormon Settlement as Reflected in Henry William Bigler's Diaries*. Edited by Erwin G. Gudde. Berkeley: University of California Press, 1962.

Bolton, Herbert E. *Spanish Exploration in the Southwest, 1542–1706*. New York: C. Scribner's Sons, 1916.

——. *Opening a Land Route to California*. Vol. 2 of *Anza's California Expeditions*. Berkeley: University of California Press, 1930.

——. *An Outpost of Empire*. Vol. 1 of *Anza's California Expeditions*. Berkeley: University of California Press, 1930.

——. *The San Francisco Colony*. Vol. 3 of *Anza's California Expeditions*. Berkeley: University of California Press, 1930.

——. *Rim of Christendom*. New York: Macmillan, 1936. Reprint, Tucson: University of Arizona Press, 1984.

——, ed. *Font's Complete Diary*. Vol. 4 of *Anza's California Expeditions* Berkeley: University of California Press, 1930.

Bringas de Manzaneda y Encinas, Diego Miguel. *Friar Bringas Reports to the King: Methods of Indoctrination on the Frontier of New Spain, 1796–1797*. Edited and translated by Daniel S. Matson and Bernard L. Fontana. Tucson: University of Arizona Press, 1977.

Browne, Ross J. *Adventures in Apache Country*. Tucson: Arizona Silhouettes, 1950. Reprint, Tucson: University of Arizona Press, 1974.

Brownlee, Robert. *An American Odyssey: The Autobiography of a 19th Century Scotsman, Robert Brownlee, at the Request of His Children, Napa County, California, 1892*. Edited by Patricia A. Etter. Fayetteville: University of Arkansas Press, 1986.

Canby, William C., Jr. *American Indian Law in a Nutshell*. St. Paul, Minnesota: West Publishing Co., 1988.

Cannon, John Q., ed. *The Autobiography of Christopher Layton, with an Account of His Funeral, a Personal Sketch, etc., and Genealogical Appendix*. Salt Lake City, Utah: Deseret News, 1911.

Carlson, Leonard A. *Indians, Bureaucrats, and Land*. Westport, Connecticut: Greenwood Press, 1981.

Castetter, Edward, and Willis H. Bell. *Pima and Papago Indian Agriculture*. Albuquerque: University of New Mexico Press, 1942.

Chamberlain, Samuel E. *My Confession*. New York: Harper and Brothers Publishers, 1956.

Chamberlin, William H. "From Lewisburg to California in 1849: Notes from the Diary of William H. Chamberlin." Edited by Lansing B. Bloom. *New Mexico Historical Quarterly* 20, no. 2 (1945): 144–180.

Clark, Harold G. "The Pima Indians and Western Development." *The Genealogical and Historical Magazine of the Arizona Temple District* 6, no. 4 (1929): 7, 23.

Clarke, A. B. *Travels in Mexico and California Comprising a Journal of a Tour from Brazos Santiago, through Central Mexico, by Way of Monterey, Chihuahua the Country of the Apaches, and the River Gila, to the Mining Districts of California*. Edited by Anne M. Perry. College Station, Texas: Texas A & M Press, 1988.

Colton, Ray C. *The Civil War in the Western Territories*. Norman: University of Oklahoma Press, 1959.

Conard, Howard Louis. *Uncle Dick Wootton: The Pioneer Frontiersman of the Rocky Mountain Region*. Chicago: R. R. Donnelly & Sons Co., 1957.

Conkling, Roscoe P. and Margaret B. Conkling. *The Butterfield Overland Mail, 1857–1869: Its Organization and Operation over the Southern Route to 1861; Subsequently over the Central Route to 1866; and under Wells, Fargo and Company to 1869*. 2 vols. Glendale, California: Arthur H. Clark Co., 1947.

Cooke, Philip St. George. *The Conquest of New Mexico and California: An Historical and Personal Narrative*. Chicago: Rio Grande Press, 1964.

Corle, Edwin. *The Gila River of the Southwest*. Lincoln: University of Nebraska Press, 1964.

Couts, Cave Johnson. *Hepah, California! The Journal of Cave Johnson Couts from Monterey, Nuevo Leon, Mexico, to Los Angeles, California, during the Years 1848–49*. Edited by Henry F. Dobyns. Tucson: Arizona Pioneers' Historical Society, 1961.

Cox, C.C. "From Texas to California in 1850: Diary of C. C. Cox." Edited by Mabelle Eppard Martin. *Southwestern Historical Quarterly* 29, no. 1 (1925): 128–146.

Cozzens, Samuel. *The Marvelous Country or Three Years in Arizona and New Mexico*. London: Sampson, Low, Marston, Searle and Rivington, 1890.

Creuzbaur, Robert. *Guide to California and the Pacific Ocean Illustrated by a General Map and Sectional Maps with Directions to Travelers Compiled by the Best Authorities*. New York: H. Long and Brother, 1849.

Darling, J. Andrew. *S-cuk Kavick, Data Recovery at Two Historic Sites (GR-649 and GR-1104) along P-MIP Canal Reach WS-IC in the Broadacres Management Area, Gila River Indian Community, Pinal County, Arizona (Draft)*. P-MIP Report No. 22. Sacaton, Arizona: Cultural Resource Management Program, Gila River Indian Community, 2007.

DeJong, David H. "Forced to Abandon Their Farms: Water Deprivation and Starvation among the Gila River Pima, 1892–1904." *American Indian Culture and Research Journal* 28, no. 3 (2004): 29–56.

——. "None Excel Them in Virtue and Honesty: Ecclesiastical and Military Descriptions of the Gila River Pima, 1694–1848." *American Indian Quarterly* 29, no. 1 (2005): 24–55.

Dillon, Richard H. *Texas Argonauts: Isaac H. Duval and the California Gold Rush*. San Francisco: Book Club of California, 1987.

Dobyns, Henry F. "Who Killed the Gila?" *Journal of Arizona History* 19, no. 4 (1978): 17–30.

——. *Creation and Expansion of the Gila River Indian Reservation*. n.p.: Prepared for the Gila River Indian Community Office of Water Rights with assistance from Gookin Engineers, Ltd., 2000.

Dunbar, Robert. *Forging New Rights in Western Water*. Lincoln: University of Nebraska Press, 1983.

Durivage, John E. "Letters and Journals of John E. Durivage." In *Southern Trails to California*. Edited by Ralph E. Bieber, 201–226. Glendale, California: Arthur Clark Co., 1937.

Eccleston, Robert. *Overland to California on the Southwestern Trail 1849: The Diary of Robert Eccleston*. Edited by George P. Hammond and Edward D. Howes. Berkeley: University of California Press, 1950.

Espeland, Wendy Nelson. *The Struggle for Water: Politics, Rationality, and Identity in the American Southwest*. Chicago: University of Chicago Press, 1998.

Etter, Patricia A. *To California on the Southern Route 1849: A History and Annotated Bibliography*. Spokane, Washington: Arthur H. Clark Co., 1998.

Evans, George B. *Mexican Gold Trail: The Journal of a Forty-Niner*. Edited by Glen Dumke. San Marino, California: The Huntington Library, 1945.

Ezell, Paul H. "The Hispanic Acculturation of the Gila River Pimas." Memoirs of the American Anthropological Association, 90. *American Anthropologist* 63, no. 5, pt. 2, 1961.

Ezell, Paul H., with Bernard L. Fontana. "Plants without Water: The Pima-Maricopa Experience." *Journal of the Southwest* 36, no. 4 (1994): 311–392.

Finch, Boyd. "Sherod Hunter and the Confederates in Arizona." *Journal of Arizona History* 10, no. 3 (1969): 137–206.

Fontana, Bernard. "Pima-Papago Introduction," in *Handbook of North American Indians*, edited by Alfonso Ortiz, vol. 10, 125–136. Washington, D.C.: Smithsonian Institute, 1983.

Foreman, Grant. *Marcy and the Gold Seekers: The Journal of Captain R. B. Marcy, with an Account of the Gold Rush over the Southern Route*. Norman: University of Oklahoma Press, 1939.

Fradkin, Phillip L. *A River No More*. New York: Alfred A. Knopf, 1981.

Garcés, Francisco Tomas Hermenegildo. *On the Trail of a Spanish Pioneer; The Diary and Itinerary of Francisco Garcés in His Travels through Sonora, Arizona, and California, 1775–1776*. Edited by Elliot Coues. New York: F.P. Harper, 1900.

——. *A Record of Travel in Arizona and California, 1775–1776: A New Translation*. Edited and translated by John Galvin. San Francisco: John Howell, 1965.

Golder, Frank Alfred. *The March of the Mormon Battalion Taken from the Journal of Henry Standage*. New York: Century Co., 1928.

Goulding, William. *Diary, Overland to California, 1849*. New Haven: Yale University Library, 1849.

Gray, Andrew B. *Southern Pacific Railroad: Survey of a Route for the Southern Pacific Railroad on the 32nd Parallel for the Texas Western Railroad Company*. Cincinnati, Ohio: Wrightson and Co., 1856.

Green, Robert B. *On the Arkansas Route to California in 1849: The Journal of Robert B. Green of Lewisburg, Pennsylvania*. Edited by J. Orin Oliphant. Lewisburg, Pennsylvania: Bucknell University Press, 1955.

Guiteras, Esubio, ed. and trans. *Rudo Ensayo*. Records of the American Catholic Historical Society of Philadelphia, vol. 5, no. 2. Reprint, Tucson: Arizona Silhouettes, 1951.

Hackenburg, Robert A. *Pima-Maricopa Indians: Aboriginal Land Use and Occupancy of the Pima-Maricopa Indians*. 2 vols. New York: Garland Publishing Co., 1974.

——. "Pima and Papago Ecological Adaptations," in *Handbook of North American Indians*, edited by Alfonso Ortiz, vol. 10, 161–177. Washington, D.C.: Smithsonian Institute, 1983.

Hall, Sharlot M. "The Story of a Pima Record Rod." *Out West* 26, no. 5 (1907): 413–423.

Harris, Benjamin Butler. *The Gila Trail: The Texas Argonauts and the California Gold Rush*. Edited by Richard H. Dillon. Norman: University of Oklahoma Press, 1960.

Hayes, Benjamin Ignatius. *Pioneer Notes from the Diaries of Judge Benjamin Hayes, 1849–1875*. Edited by Marjorie Tisdale Wolcott. Los Angeles: privately printed, 1929.

Hays, Samuel P. *Conservation and the Gospel of Efficiency: The Progressive Conservation Movement, 1890–1920*. New York: Atheneum, 1980.

Hoover, J. W. "The Indian Country of Southern Arizona." *Geographical Review* 19 (1929): 38–60.

Howe, Octavius Thorndike. *Argonauts of Forty-Nine: History and Adventures of the Emigrant Companies from Massachusetts, 1849–1850*. Cambridge, Massachusetts: Harvard University Press, 1923.

Hoxie, Frederick E. *A Final Promise: The Campaign to Assimilate the Indians, 1880–1920*. Lincoln: University of Nebraska Press, 1984.

Hunter, William H. *Missouri 49er: The Journal of William H. Hunter on the Southern Trail*. Edited by David P. Robrock. Albuquerque: University of New Mexico Press, 1992.

Hurt, Douglas R. *Indian Agriculture in America*. Lawrence: University Press of Kansas, 1987.

Kino, Eusebio Francisco. *Kino's Historical Memoir of Pimeria Alta*. Vol. 1. Translated and edited by Herbert E. Bolton. Cleveland: Arthur H. Clark Co., 1919.

Klein, Kerwin Lee. *Frontiers of Historical Imagination: Narrating the European Conquest of Native America, 1890–1990*. Berkeley: University of California Press, 1997.

Kneale, Albert H. *Indian Agent*. Caldwell, Idaho: Caxton Printers, Ltd., 1950.

Lewis, David Rich. *Neither Wolf nor Dog: American Indians, Environment, and Agrarian Change*. New York: Oxford University Press, 1994.

Limerick, Patricia Nelson. *The Legacy of Conquest: The Unbroken Past of the American West*. New York: W. W. Norton, 1987.

——. *Something in the Soil: Legacies and Reckonings in the New West*. New York: W. W. Norton, 2000.

Lummis, Charles F. "In the Lion's Den." *Out West* XVIII (1903): 754–756.

Manje, Juan Mateo. *Unknown Arizona and Sonora, 1693–1721, from the Francisco Fernandez del Castillo Version of Luz De Tierra Incognita*. Edited by Harry Karns and Associates. Tucson: Arizona Silhouettes, 1954.

McCleave, William. "Recollections of a California Volunteer." In Boyd Finch, "Sherod Hunter and the Confederates in Arizona," *Journal of Arizona History* 10, no. 3 (1929): 137–206.

McCool, Daniel. *Command of the Waters: Iron Triangles, Federal Water Development, and Indian Water*. Tucson: University of Arizona Press, 1994.

——. *Native Waters: Contemporary Indian Water Settlements and the Second Treaty Era*. Tucson: University of Arizona Press, 2002.

McDonnell, Janet. *The Dispossession of the American Indians, 1887–1934*. Bloomington: University of Indiana Press, 1991.

McGuire, Thomas R., William Lord, and Mary G. Wallace. *Indian Water in the New West*. Tucson: University of Arizona Press, 1993.

McNamee, Gregory. *Gila: The Life and Death of an American River*. Albuquerque: University of New Mexico Press, 1988.

Meeks, Eric V. "The Tohono O'odham, Wage Labor, and Resistant Adaptation, 1900–1930." *Western Historical Quarterly* 34, no. 4 (2003): 469–489.

Meriam, Lewis. *The Problem of Indian Administration*. Baltimore: John Hopkins University Press, 1928.

Miles, William. *Journal of the Sufferings and Hardships of Capt. Parker H. French's Overland Expedition to California in 1850*. Fairfield, Washington: Ye Galleon Press, 1970.

Miller, Darlis A. *Soldiers and Settlers: Military Supply in the Southwest, 1861–1885*. Albuquerque: University of New Mexico Press, 1989.

Morgan, Henry Lewis. *Ancient Society: Or Research in the Lines of Human Progress from Savagery through Barbarism to Civilization*. New York: Henry Holt and Co., 1877.

Nash, Gerald D. *The Federal Landscape*. Tucson: University of Arizona Press, 1999.

Nichols, Roger. "A Miniature Venice: Florence, Arizona, 1866–1910." *Journal of Arizona History* 16, no. 4 (1975): 335–355.

Noel, Thomas J. "W. Wilberforce Alexander Ramsey, Esq., of Tennessee." *Journal of the West* 12, no. 4 (1973): 565–591.

Officer, James E. *Hispanic Arizona, 1536–1856*. Tucson: University of Arizona Press, 1987.

Otis, D. *The Dawes Act and the Allotment of Indian Lands*. Edited by Francis Prucha. Norman: University of Oklahoma Press, 1973.

Pancoast, Charles Edward. *The Adventures of Charles Edward Pancoast on the American Frontier: A Quaker Forty-Niner*. Edited by Anna Raschall Hannum. Philadelphia: University of Pennsylvania, 1930.

Pfefferkorn, Ignaz. *Pfefferkorn's Description of the Province of Sonora*. Translated by Theodore E. Treutlein. Albuquerque: University of New Mexico Press, 1949.

Pisani, Donald. *To Reclaim a Divided West: Water, Law and Public Policy, 1848–1902*. Albuquerque: University of New Mexico Press, 1992.

——. *Water and American Government*. Berkeley: University of California Press, 2002.

Poston, Charles. *Speech of Charles D. Poston, of Arizona, on Indian Affairs, House of Representatives, March 2, 1865*. New York: Edmund Jones and Co., 1865.

——. *Building a State in Apache Land*. Tempe, Arizona: Aztec Press, 1963.

Powell, H.M.T. *The Santa Fe Trail to California, 1849–1852: The Journal of H.M.T. Powell*. Edited by Douglas Watson. San Francisco: Book Club of California, 1931.

Prucha, Francis Paul. *American Indian Policy in the Formative Years: The Indian Trade and Intercourse Acts, 1790–1834*. Lincoln: University of Nebraska Press, 1962.

Ravesloot, John. "The Anglo American Acculturation of the Gila River Pima, Arizona: The Mortuary Evidence." Paper presented at the 25th Annual Conference on Historical and Underwater Archaeology, Kingston, Jamaica, 1992.

Rea, Amadeo M. *At the Desert's Green Edge: An Ethnobotany of the Gila River Pima*. Tucson: University of Arizona Press, 1997.

Reed, Bill. *The Last Bugle Call: A History of Fort McDowell, Arizona Territory 1865–1890*. Parsons, West Virginia: McClain Printing Co., 1977.

Reid, John C. *Reid's Tramp, or, a Journal of the Incidents of Ten Months Travel through Texas, New Mexico, Arizona, Sonora, and California, Including Topography, Climate, Soil, Minerals and Inhabitants; With a Notice of the Great Inter-oceanic Rail Road*. Selma, Alabama: John Hardy & Co., 1858. Reprint, Austin, Texas: Steck Co., 1935.

Reisner, Marc. *Cadillac Desert*. New York: Penguin Books, 1986.

Rusling, James F. *Across America: Or the Great West and the Pacific Coast*. New York: Sheldon & Co., 1874.

Russell, Frank. *The Pima Indians*. Tucson: University of Arizona Press. Reprint of *Twenty-sixth Annual Report of the Bureau of American Ethnology, 1904–1905*. Washington, D.C.: GPO, 1975.

Salt River Project. *The Taming of the Salt*. Phoenix, Arizona: Communications and Public Affairs Department of the Salt River Project, 1979.

Sedelmayr, Jacobo. *Jacobo Sedelmayr, 1744–1751: Missionary, Frontiersman, Explorer in Arizona and Sonora; Four Original Manuscripts*. Edited and translated by Peter Masten. Tucson: Arizona Pioneers' Historical Society, 1955.

Smith, Karen L. "The Campaign for Water in Central Arizona, 1890–1903." *Arizona and the West* 23, no. 2 (1981): 127–149.

Smith, Karen L., and Shelly C. Dudley. "The Marriage of Law and Public Policy in the Southwest: Salt River Project, Phoenix, Arizona." *Western Legal History* 2, no. 2 (1989): 231–293.

Southworth, C. H. "A Pima Calendar Stick." *Arizona Historical Review* 4, no. 2 (1931): 44–51.

Spicer, Edward H. *Cycles of Conquest: The Impact of Spain, Mexico, and the United States on the Indians of the Southwest, 1533–1960*. Tucson: University of Arizona Press, 1962.

Spier, Leslie. *Yuman Tribes of the Gila River*. Chicago: University of Chicago, 1933. Reprint, New York: Dover Publications, 1978.

Stegner, Wallace. *Beyond the Hundredth Meridian*. Boston: Houghton Mifflin, 1954. Reprint, New York: Penguin Books, 1992.

Stratton, Royal B. *Captivity of the Oatman Girls*. Lincoln: University of Nebraska Press, 1983.

Strentzel, Louisiana. "A Letter from California." In *Covered Wagon Women: Diaries and Letters from the Western Trails, 1840–1890*, edited by Kenneth L. Holmes, 245–269. Glendale, California: Arthur H. Clark Co., 1983.

Trennert, Robert. *Alternative to Extinction: Federal Indian Policy and the Beginnings of a Reservation System, 1846–1851*. Philadelphia: Temple University Press, 1975.

Turner, Frederick Jackson. *The Frontier in America*. New York: Henry Holt and Co., 1920.

Turner, Henry Smith. *The Original Journals of Henry Smith Turner with Stephen Watts Kearny to New Mexico and California 1846–1847*. Edited by Dwight L. Clarke. Norman: University of Oklahoma Press, 1966.

Tyler, Daniel. *A Concise History of the Mormon Battalion in the Mexican War*. Chicago: Rio Grande Press, 1964.

Underwood, Lonnie E. *The First Arizona Volunteer Infantry, 1865–1866*. Tucson: Roan Horse Press, 1983.

Van Nostrand, Jeanne Skinner. "Audubon's Ill-Fated Western Journal Recalled by the Diary of J. H. Bachman." *California Historical Society Quarterly* 21, no. 4 (1942): 289–311.

Venegas, Miguel. *A Natural and Civil History of California*. Vol. 2. London: J. Rivington and J. Fletcher, 1759.

Von Humboldt, Alexander. *Political Essay on the Kingdom of New Spain*. Translated by John Black. London: Longman, Hurst, Rees, Orme, and Brown, 1811. Reprint, New York: AMS Press, 1966.

Wagoner, Jay J. *Early Arizona: Prehistory to Civil War*. Tucson: University of Arizona Press, 1975.

The War of the Rebellion: A Compilation of the Official Records of the Union and Confederate Armies, ser. 1, vols. 4, 9, 34, and 50 (pts. 1 and 2), Washington, D.C.: GPO, 1883, 1897.

Webb, George. *A Pima Remembers*. Tucson: University of Arizona Press, 1959.

Weber, David J. *The Taos Trappers: The Fur Trade in the Far Southwest, 1540–1846*. Norman: University of Oklahoma Press, 1982.

Williams, Robert A. *The American Indian in Western Legal Thought*. New York: Oxford University Press, 1990.

Wilson, John P. "How the Settlers Farmed: Hispanic Villages and Irrigation Systems in Early Sierra County, 1850–1900." *New Mexico Historical Review* 63, no. 4 (1995): 333–356.

——. *Peoples of the Middle Gila: A Documentary History of the Pimas and Maricopas, 1500s–1945*. Report No. 77. Sacaton, Arizona: Gila River Indian Community, 1997.

Wood, Harvey. *Personal Recollections of Harvey Wood*. Edited by Jake B. Goodwin III. Pasadena, California: privately printed, 1955.

Woods, I. C. *Journal of I. C. Woods on the Establishment of the San Antonio & San Diego Mail Line*. Edited by Noel M. Loomis. Brandbook Number One, The San Diego Corral of the Westerners. San Diego: Corral of the Westerners, 1968.

Worster, Donald. *Rivers of Empire: Water, Aridity and the Growth of the American West*. New York: Oxford University Press, 1985.

Index

About the Author

David H. DeJong holds MA and PhD degrees in American Indian policy studies from the University of Arizona and a BA in American history from Arizona State University. His research specialty is federal Indian law and policy and their impact on tribal nations. He has written dozens of articles and two books dealing with federal Indian policy. He is currently the project manager of the Pima-Maricopa Irrigation Project, a construction project funded by the U.S. Bureau of Reclamation to deliver Central Arizona Project and other settlement water to the Gila River Indian Reservation. The project is constructing an irrigation delivery system for up to 146,330 acres of agricultural land within the reservation. DeJong has five children and has been married to his wife Cindy for twenty-seven years.